D0564165

# The Complete Guide
## to
# Preparing Baby Foods
## at Home

SUE CASTLE

GARDEN CITY, NEW YORK

DOUBLEDAY & COMPANY, INC.

ISBN: 0-385-03009-x
Library of Congress Catalog Card Number 72–70132

*To my mother, Jay, Jennifer, and Bethany*
*for their patience, understanding,*
*and aid—thank you!*

# FOREWORD

IN THE MEDICAL, especially pediatric, journals and textbooks, there are a number of specific articles with proper references that critically evaluate various commercial baby foods, or present research on infant nutrition. These articles, even if they were readily available, may not be helpful to the average mother. However, I feel very strongly that most mothers would like to receive guidance in feeding their babies. Most physicians caring for newborn babies attempt this, but have neither the time nor the inclination to go into any details. This book, used in conjunction with your physician, fills this vacuum.

As director of the Premature Institute at The New York Hospital—Cornell Medical Center for ten years, I taught and directed the education of physicians and nurses from all parts of the United States and the world in the latest techniques in the care and feeding of infants. Nearly all of these professional persons agreed with me that most mothers had little, if any, knowledge of the proper nutritional needs of their babies, and they needed assistance. In my own fifteen years of private practice of pediatrics, I have been aware of this same problem. The author frequently refers to Dr. Samuel Fomon. He is professor of pediatrics at the University of Iowa, and has participated in many conferences relating to nutrition of the child. He has written many scientific articles in the medical literature and is accepted by most pediatricians as an authority on this subject. The author must be complimented on her choice of such a valuable authority.

The first chapter, "Nutrition," contains information about the various ingredients of food as relevant to the specific nutritional needs of the infant. Many lists of nutritionally valuable, but inexpensive, foods are given and I find these extremely helpful. I also feel that the chapter on "Feeding Your Baby" is very important. The author keeps stressing the need of advice of a physician and that the information should not replace the advice of a specific doctor. No two children are alike and one cannot generalize, but it is nearly always true that rigid feeding schedules are mostly for a mother's convenience rather than the baby's needs.

It is also true that very few physicians agree as to when to introduce solid foods; the table in the text therefore is extremely valuable as a guide. All mothers will certainly benefit from the many useful suggestions offered in the section on "How to Introduce Solid Foods." There is no doubt that the mother's facial expression when offering a new food to her baby is extremely important. A mother should not show her own personal dislike of food to her baby.

When a baby is approximately one to three years of age, many mothers are extremely worried about their child's lack of appetite. They cannot understand "how baby survives," not to mention weight gain. The suggestions offered by the author are generally accepted by physicians and will be treasured by nearly all mothers.

As we now are a society which is no longer stationary but travels a great deal, the hints on feeding your baby away from home can simplify all efforts of feeding your baby.

If your baby develops digestive difficulties, you should always contact your doctor as is stated in this book. Do not use medications on your own, but only under proper medical supervision.

I feel that the author's repeated statement that there is no need to add salt or sugar to the baby's food is correct. How true is the statement that "the last thing you want to do is to accustom your baby to the controversial adult preference for salted or sweetened foods."

Sue Castle has written a book based on sound medical knowledge and her own experiences of being a mother of two children. The new mother should use this book as a clear and easy guide in preparing nutritious meals for her own child.

Charles H. Bauer, M.D.
Clinical Associate Professor of Pediatrics at
The New York Hospital—Cornell Medical
Center; Attending Pediatrician,
Roosevelt Hospital.

# Contents

# INTRODUCTION

As a new or expectant mother you have, no doubt, been told by many older women that it's "so easy to feed a baby nowadays. I remember when I had to make everything myself." You become even more impressed and appreciative when you go to the supermarket and see the baby-food sections overflowing with a gourmet array of foods, attractively packaged and stamped with official-looking seals of approval. And, of course, you are more than willing to pay any cost for quality in your baby's diet.

*But, are you really giving your baby the best food for all the money you are spending?*

After hearing many mothers complain that their babies often refused to eat their high-priced meals, I became concerned about feeding my own new baby. When I began looking into this question, I found even more disturbing information.

There is growing criticism of the nutritional value and medical safety of commercial baby foods by Dr. Jean Mayer, Professor of Nutrition at Harvard and the President's consultant on nutrition; Dr. Samuel Fomon and Dr. Norman Kretchmer, pediatricians and authorities on infant nutrition; consumer advocate Ralph Nader; and many qualified and respected research scientists.

The most unsettling and widely known controversy has been over MSG (monosodium glutamate), an additive used to enhance the flavor of baby food. Several scientists reported research results showing MSG capable of causing brain damage to infant mice. The baby-food manufacturers revealed, to a senate committee, that they had never conducted research on MSG effects on any infant animal. As a result of this controversy, MSG is no longer being used in the commercial preparation of baby food.

Some preservatives are also under question. Sodium nitrite, used in commercial meat purées, was strongly criticized by Dr. Samuel Epstein, of the Children's Cancer Research Foundation.[1] BHT, often used in cereals and baked goods, is banned in Britain from use in baby foods because it has produced allergic reactions and is possibly related to cancer.

Also present, in most baby foods, are excess amounts of other ingredients such as sugar, modified starches, salt, and water. Dr. Spock warns that sugar, corn starch, rice starch, and tapioca are nutritionally "empty," that is, they are filling without providing nourishment. In addition, recent research is indicating these starches may actually be harmful. Modified food starch was added to baby food as a filler, to solidify food with a high water content. However, it is not completely broken down by the baby's saliva, which adds to the burden on the rest of the digestive tract.

Sugar and starches also contribute to overweight, which is now considered a major health problem in children and adults. Studies by Dr. Jules Hirsch, at Rockefeller University, have shown that an animal who becomes fat at infancy has an increased number of fat cells and tends to remain fat throughout life. Overweight adults have also been shown to have a high number of fat cells in their bodies. So, the image of a "fat baby as a healthy baby" is one that pediatricians are now trying to discourage.

Many mothers fight a constant battle with their children against eating sweets, for weight and dental reasons. Yet, they may be unaware of the high sugar content of many of the commercial baby foods. It is highly possible that infants who become accustomed to the taste of sugar-laden baby food will crave sweets as they grow older. Dr. Fomon states: "The influence of added sucrose in infant foods could be of significance with respect to dental caries and, possibly, obesity well beyond the period of infancy." Recent studies in England have also suggested that babies who are fed large amounts of sugar, or

[1] Commercial baby food manufacturers have voluntarily excluded sodium nitrite from their products; December 1975.

sucrose, will have a tendency to hardening of the arteries or heart trouble as adults.

Yet, babies are not born with a taste for sweets—just give your baby a slice of lemon and watch him enjoy it!

Salt is another frequent ingredient in baby food that is included to please a mother's taste. However, Dr. Samuel Fomon, of the University of Iowa, has demonstrated in tests on infants up to seven months that there is no taste discrimination between salted and unsalted foods. The desire for salt is an acquired taste, one that is sometimes necessary to unlearn later in life. Dr. Louis K. Dahl, chief of staff at the Medical Research Center, Brookhaven National Laboratory, has shown that the salt content of baby food is extremely high, in meats it is five to six times the amount in fresh meats, and in vegetables six to sixty times the amount in fresh vegetables. He suggests that this high intake of salt might be a contributing factor in the development of hypertension in adult life.

Water is a major ingredient, 70 per cent to 90 per cent, of all strained and junior foods. This may be due to economic and processing requirements; however, the commercial foods often contain as much as 25 per cent *more* water than the same food prepared in the home. The modified food starch is then added to give a more solid appearance or texture to the food. Have you ever fed your baby directly from a jar, then found that the remaining food has become useless liquid? This is caused by the saliva on the spoon which breaks down the food starch added to solidify the food. Besides the money that you are spending, or wasting, on this added water and starch, you should consider the loss of nutrition. Your baby can eat only a limited amount, so why fill him up with water and starches?

A simple reading of the label reveals the extent to which these unnecessary and possibly harmful ingredients are present in commercial baby food.

▶ *Sugar,* often in the form of sucrose or dextrose, is present in all fruits, fruit desserts, puddings, vegetables, cereals, dinners.

►*Salt* is present in many fruits, all vegetables, dinners, cereals, meats, egg yolks.

►*Modified Corn and/or Tapioca Starch* is present in many fruits, all fruit desserts, puddings, and cereals.

►*Water* is present as a major ingredient in all baby foods.

We are all concerned with the *amount* that our babies eat. Now it is time to question the content of the food. You must try to avoid those foods with potentially harmful additives and also add real fortifiers, so that whatever amount your baby eats is as nutritious as possible. It appears that the controversy over the possible hazards in the commercial foods is just beginning. The research may take years to show conclusive results since many effects may not show up until later years. Meanwhile, are you willing to take the chance in these crucial months of your infant's development? The only alternative is for you to prepare your own baby foods.

Now, in view of this disquieting information, let us look at the cost, in dollars, of commercial baby food. After considering the content of this food you may view their prices in a new light. Just compare baby-food prices to the prices of fresh, canned, or frozen foods that you buy for your family dinner table and you will discover you are paying, on the average, twice as much for the jars of baby food. When you further consider the amount of non-nutritious thinners in baby food, the dollar difference is even greater. The following comparisons were made at a local, well-known, supermarket chain. In order to render a fair comparison, the regular store products have been prepared as baby food.

|  | *Home Prepared* |  | *Commercial* |
|---|---|---|---|
| Egg Yolks | 2.8¢ ounce | *vs* | 7.5¢ ounce |
| Liver | 3.4¢ ounce | *vs* | 7.5¢ ounce |
| Squash | 1.7¢ ounce | *vs* | 2.6¢ ounce |
| Apple Juice | .8¢ ounce | *vs* | 2.4¢ ounce |
| Peaches | 1.7¢ ounce | *vs* | 2.6¢ ounce |

Bananas, a staple baby food, are a striking example. A commercial jar contains sugar, modified tapioca starch, salt, citric acid, and water, and costs 2.6¢ an ounce. A fresh, ripe banana, requiring only mashing with a fork, and no thinning, cost 1.1¢ an ounce. How much banana is in the ounce of the baby-food jar?

When you can take advantage of sales and specials, the preparation of your own baby food becomes even more economical. Very ripe fruits and vegetables are often reduced and they are excellent as easily prepared baby foods. Another source of economy is leftovers. Leftovers are nutritious, and the baby is one member of the family who will not mind. For many families, this large saving of money is reason enough to prepare your own baby food.

Women today are intelligent consumers concerned with value and nutrition and do not, as baby-food manufacturers claim, place prime importance on variety and taste. The main appeal of commercial baby food is its convenience. When the subjects of cost and safety are discussed, most mothers agree with and are concerned about the criticisms, and the struggle of getting their babies to eat the food. But, they rationalize their use of the commercial products by saying: "I'm lazy," "It's so easy to open a jar," or "I'm too busy to bother with more cooking." On the other hand women, who do make their own baby food, say that there is nothing difficult involved and what is so special about the idea? It appears that thinking about preparing baby food is much more awesome than actually doing it.

I realized the reason for this attitude when I decided to make my own baby foods for my children. The little information or instruction I found was outdated by at least thirty years and did not take into account the advances in equipment (especially the blender), storage methods, or the variety and availability of new foods which can be readily used in baby-food preparation. I began preparing my own baby foods with the thought in mind that if it involved too much work and time, I would stop and resign myself to using the commercial variety. But, after some trial and error, I found that proper planning and using all the modern advances, together with the attitude that baby foods do not have to have gourmet seasoning, wide variety, or sterilization, made the process convenient, economical, and interesting.

I have written this book as an up-to-date complete guide to planning, preparing, and feeding your baby low-cost, high-nutrition meals until he is old enough to eat family table foods.

► You will find the latest facts on infant nutrition in chapter 1 and specific nutritional information under each food and in the *Nutritive Values of Foods* table.

► The chapter on *How to Read Labels* will help you to shop economically and to get the most nutrition for your money while avoiding additives.

► In chapter 3, *Feeding Your Baby,* I have included suggestions from my experience in feeding my own two children; and the *Menu Planning Guide* and *When to Introduce a Food* chart as advised by several pediatricians.

► There are detailed recipes for almost any food that you may want to serve your baby—you can easily look up how and when to introduce it, and how to prepare it.

► The foods are also divided into chapters according to their main nutrition group, so you can easily plan balanced menus.

► *The Baby Food System,* chapter 6, contains the secrets of easy efficient baby-food preparation and shows you how to use or modify any recipe for *your* own convenience.

► The *Instant Foods* chapter, on the use of foods which require no cooking and little or no preparation, will be especially valuable if you are traveling, visiting, or just too busy.

► When your baby begins to feed himself, you will find the chapter on *Finger Foods* very useful.

► On the *Personal Feeding Chart* you will be able to keep

a complete record of the foods your baby eats and his reactions to them. If your baby shows signs of allergies, this will be valuable for your own quick reference and for use by baby sitters.

Since the basic information on good nutrition, smart shopping, and storing and preparing food really applies to *any* simple meal—that *any* member of your family can enjoy—I'm sure that you will use this book long after your baby has graduated from his baby foods.

Whatever your reasons for desiring to prepare your own baby foods, the important thing is to get started. You will decide for yourself which methods and foods fit most easily into your everyday family cooking. For the small amount of extra time or thought that you may put in, you will receive great satisfaction in knowing that you are not taking chances with your baby's present or future health and that the food he eats is highly nutritious. He will also learn to enjoy the natural flavor of good foods that are simply and easily prepared. Where else can you get so much more while paying less!

# 1

## NUTRITION

T H E R E is a growing awareness that Americans, with a high standard of living and a large selection of food, are in many ways overfed but undernourished. This condition is not simply a result of low family income or the amount spent on food. In 1965, a government study showed that only 63 per cent of families with incomes of $10,000 or more were eating what was considered good diets.

We can only assume that the problem is one of not understanding the basics of nutrition. This subject is usually taught early in high school, when we are least interested or least likely to use this information. By the time we are buying and preparing food for our own familes, we have forgotten the essentials and do not have time to catch up, especially with an infant in the house.

There are also very few sources of specific information on a baby's nutritional needs. Since your baby is eating a limited diet and is growing at a rapid rate, his needs are not the same as those of an adult. Good nutrition is even more important in a baby's first year, as research has shown that the earlier a nutritional deficiency occurs, the more serious and permanent the effect. Also, many deficiencies in infancy do not show up until later years, as in the case of rickets. So, a good understanding of infant nutrition is essential and worth going into in some detail.

The specific advisable daily intake of various nutrients are based on information by Dr. Samuel Fomon and his research group at the University of Iowa, who are considered to be authorities on infant nutrition. I have included these amounts so that you can have some basis for interpreting the *Nutritive Values of Foods* tables and the amounts of nutrients that are often listed on product labels. You might also occasionally look at an average daily menu to see if you are supplying your baby with the advisable daily intakes. However, unless you happen to have a lot of spare time and enjoy arithmetic, you do not have to use these specific amounts in planning your baby's daily meals.

*The easiest way to insure your baby's good nutrition is to understand the general principles of good nutrition and to serve a balanced selection of the foods that supply the essential nutri-*

ents. These nutrients are calories, protein, carbohydrates, fat, vitamins, and minerals.

## CALORIES

Calories are present in all foods, especially in high carbohydrate and fat foods. A calorie is a measure of the energy value of the food. A certain amount of calories is necessary each day to maintain growth, good health, and to give your baby energy. An excess of calories will accumulate as fat in the body tissues. An excess of fat, or overweight, can cause a variety of health problems for infants as well as adults. The recommended daily intake of calories is an average of 55 calories for each pound of the baby's weight. For example,

| POUNDS | DAILY CALORIES |
|--------|----------------|
| 8 | 440 |
| 10 | 550 |
| 12 | 660 |
| 14 | 770 |
| 16 | 880 |
| 18 | 990 |
| 20 | 1100 |

A large portion of these calories will be supplied by *milk*. Even if your baby is drinking the minimum of three 8-ounce bottles a day, he will get 515 calories from reconstituted evaporated milk, 480 calories from whole milk, and 270 calories from skimmed or non-fat dry milk. If he drinks four 8-ounce bottles, the calories increase to 686 for evaporated milk, 640 for whole milk, and 360 for skimmed milk. A mixture of half skim, half whole milk will contain 500 calories. As you can see, if your baby is on skim milk, it is important to supply calories from other high-calorie foods such as *cereal grains*.

## PROTEIN

Protein is the main material for growth and development of many parts of the body—muscles, glands, blood, heart, nerves, brain, and skin. It also forms an important part of the enzymes that aid in the digestion and absorption of food. Protein is especially important in the rapid body-building that your baby will do in his first years. A lack of protein in infancy can cause serious problems such as mental retardation and physical impairment, during childhood and in adult life. Resistance to infection can also be lowered.

Since protein cannot be stored in the body, your baby should eat protein food through the day, including some complete protein foods. The recommended daily intake is at least 14–16 grams. This can be adequately supplied by as little as two 8-ounce bottles of whole or skim milk. Human milk contains only one-third the amount of protein as cow's milk, but if nursing is the main source of food, a baby will still receive adequate amounts of protein. It is important, if your baby breast feeds and also eats a good amount of solid food, that you select those foods which contain high amounts of complete protein.

*Complete Protein.* Some foods contain all the elements, called amino acids, that are contained in protein and are required by the body. The following foods are excellent sources of complete protein:

| | | |
|---|---|---|
| MILK | FISH | YOGURT |
| MEAT | EGGS | NON-FAT DRY MILK |
| POULTRY | CHEESE | SOYBEANS |

*Incomplete Protein.* Other foods supply only some of the protein elements that are essential for nutrition and are considered incomplete protein foods. These foods are still an important source of protein, and since they are usually inexpensive, they are good to use as a supplement:

WHOLE-GRAIN CEREALS, BREAD    WHEAT GERM
DRIED PEAS, BEANS, LENTILS
NUTS, PEANUT BUTTER
ENRICHED PASTAS
BROWN and CONVERTED RICE

These incomplete protein foods should always be eaten at the same meal with the complete protein foods. A healthy way to economize is to plan dishes which combine a small amount of the more expensive complete protein food with an incomplete protein food, such as in *Beef and Rice, Noodle and Cheese Pudding, Cereal and Milk.* This is a Cereal/Protein serving.

*Protein Equivalents.* If you keep in mind the different "completeness" of the proteins, the following amounts of food will supply the same quantity of protein:

1 cup milk (whole or skim)
⅓ cup non-fat dry milk powder
1 ounce Cheddar, American, Swiss cheese
1 ounce lean meat, fish, poultry
1 egg or 2 egg yolks
2 tablespoons wheat germ
2 tablespoons peanut butter
½ cup cooked dried peas, beans, lentils
⅓ cup cooked soybeans

# CARBOHYDRATES

Carbohydrates, in the form of sugar and starch, provide at least one-half the total calories that an active baby needs for heat and energy. They are the main source of immediate energy and the only energy source for the central nervous system. If the daily carbohydrate intake is too low, valuable protein will be converted for energy instead of for growth and other necessary functions. If an excess of carbohydrates is eaten, they will be stored in the body as fat. A moderate amount of carbohydrates is necessary each day for an active, healthy baby.

*Starch Sources.* There are many natural sources of starches among foods that you will serve your baby:

| | | |
|---|---|---|
| BANANAS | POTATOES | DRIED BEANS, PEAS |
| CORN | NOODLES | WINTER SQUASH |
| PEAS | CEREALS | |

*Sugar Sources.* There are also many natural sources of sugar in fruits and vegetables:

| | | |
|---|---|---|
| BANANAS | PEAS | ORANGE JUICE |
| APPLES | BEETS | GRAPE JUICE |
| CARROTS | SWEET POTATOES | GRAPES |

*Empty-Nutrition Sources.* If your baby is eating a balanced daily diet which includes cereals, fruits, and vegetables, he will be receiving an adequate amount of carbohydrates. In view of the natural abundance of sugars and starches, the addition of refined sugar and starches to any food is unnecessary. (However, most commercial baby-food fruits have added sugar and many also contain food starches, tapioca, and flour. Many combination dinners also contain starch, and flour. The "desserts" which many doctors advise against, are almost totally refined sugar, flour, and starches.) Research indicates that infants may not properly digest these food starches.

An overabundance of these "empty-nutrition" carbohydrates can affect your baby in several ways. They can give him a false sense of being full, thus decreasing his appetite for other necessary foods. Since these sugars and starches are nutritionally "empty," your baby may become deficient in many vitamins and minerals while giving the appearance of being "fat" and "healthy." The extra fat will be produced because the baby is consuming more carbohydrates than he requires. Research now indicates that being fat during infancy leads to a tendency to become overweight as an adult. A major concern of many adults today is the problem of losing unnecessary weight because of the various health hazards. If your baby becomes accustomed to sweet food, he may also grow up with a craving for sweets that can result in nutritional deficiencies and tooth decay.

So, while carbohydrates are necessary in your baby's daily diet, you should serve them in moderation and choose those sources with the highest nutritional value.

## FAT

Fat, usually thought of as a nasty word, is also a necessary element in nutrition. The calories in fat provide a concentrated source of energy and prevent the loss of protein being burned as energy. Fat helps in the absorption of the fat-soluble vitamins, A, D, E, and K, into the body. Stored fat protects the body from excessive loss of heat and supports and protects the vital organs. There are both liquid and solid sources of fat.

*Oils* are fats that are liquid at room temperature and are generally made from vegetable sources. These oils contain mostly polyunsaturated fatty acids which produce lower levels of cholesterol in the body. Coconut oil is the exception and is high in saturated fats.

Many of these oils are *hydrogenated* in order to harden them for use as margarine and shortening. Research now suggests that this hydrogenation process can cause a nutritional imbalance in the body, so the hydrogenated or "hardened oils" should be avoided. You should use a brand of shortening that lists *"liquid vegetable oil"* as the main ingredient. Nutritionists also recommend the use of these oils in unrefined form. Some polyunsaturated oils are:

| | |
|---|---|
| CORN OIL | COTTONSEED OIL |
| SOYBEAN OIL | PEANUT OIL |
| SAFFLOWER OIL | WHEAT-GERM OIL |

Mineral oil is totally lacking in nutrients and is non-digestible. It absorbs the fat-soluble vitamins in the body and can cause deficiencies. **You should never give mineral oil to your baby.**

*Solid fats* are generally made from animal sources and have a high amount of saturated fat which raises the level of cholesterol in the blood. Although this may be a concern for some adults, most doctors and nutritionists agree that a *moderate* amount of food cholesterol is necessary in an infant's early development. Unfortunately, the commercial formulas use vegetable oils, and so they are low in saturated fats. If your baby is drinking these formulas, or skim milk, you can serve him foods like the following that are high in saturated fats:

| | |
|---|---|
| BUTTER | EGG YOLK |
| ICE CREAM | NUTS, PEANUT BUTTER |
| MEAT | |

*Essential fatty acids* are also found in fat and are indispensable for your baby's growth and healthy skin. Linoleic acid is one of the most important. Breast milk contains more than cow's milk, but both are good sources. The commercial formulas that use coconut oil may be low. If your baby is drinking skim milk, you should be sure to include foods in his diet that are high in essential fatty acids, such as:

VEGETABLE OIL (SAFFLOWER, CORN, SOY, PEANUT, WHEAT GERM)
CHICKEN

SOYBEANS
WHEAT GERM
NUTS, PEANUT BUTTER

The recommended daily intake of linoleic acid is 5–6 grams, which can be supplied by 1 tablespoon of vegetable oil.

# VITAMINS

Vitamins are small substances found in food and are necessary for growth and all the bodily functions. All the vitamins needed for good health can be found in food, or are synthesized in the body.

*Water-soluble* vitamins cannot be stored in the body and foods containing these vitamins should be eaten every day. They are very perishable and can be lost in water, heat, and exposure to air. They are: vitamin C and vitamin-B complex (thiamine or $B_1$, riboflavin or $B_2$, niacin, pyridoxine or $B_6$, pantothenic acid, folic acid, $B_{12}$, choline, and biotin).

*Fat-soluble* vitamins can be stored in the body. The amounts that occur naturally in food cannot cause a harmful surplus in the body. However, supplemental forms of the vitamins can be taken in harmful amounts and should only be given under a doctor's supervision. They can be destroyed by high heat, drying, exposure to air, and rancidity. These vitamins are A, D, E, and K.

### VITAMIN A

Vitamin A is essential for growth, good vision, and healthy skin, and for keeping the lining of the mouth, nose, throat, and digestive tract healthy and resistant to infection. Babies are unable to store this vitamin before birth, so it is necessary in their diet. The following animal foods supply large amounts of vitamin A:

| LIVER | FISH-LIVER OIL |
|-------|----------------|
| KIDNEYS | FISH |
| EGG YOLK | BUTTER |
| CHEESE | WHOLE MILK, BREAST MILK |

Plant foods contain large amounts of carotene which is converted by the body into vitamin A. The highest sources are dark green and leafy vegetables, and the deep yellow fruits and vegetables:

| BROCCOLI | CARROTS |
|----------|---------|
| CHARD | WINTER SQUASH |
| LEAFY GREENS | SWEET POTATOES |
| ASPARAGUS | APRICOTS |
| GREEN BEANS | CANTALOUPE |
| TOMATOES | MANGOES |

The vitamin, while found in many foods, can be destroyed by exposure to air (wilting), high heat, and rancidity. Skim milk and skim-milk products are very low in the vitamin since it is removed with the fat, and so they are often fortified with vitamin A.

Because the vitamin can be stored in the body, a continual overdose can be harmful to your baby. Dr. Fomon states that for normal infants living in countries with good living standards, "The hazards of vitamin-A overdosage exceed the dangers of deficiency." The amount of the vitamin that naturally occurs in food cannot result in overdose; however, the amounts consumed in supplements can reach high levels. Many foods have been fortified with vitamin A, especially non-fat dry milk, skim and whole milk, margarine, and cereals. Many brands of milk are fortified with up to 2,000 I.U. (international units) per quart. A supplement may be prescribed, and you should never give your baby more than the prescribed amount of the supplement. If a little is good, more is *not* better. Try to keep track of the total vitamin A that your baby is consuming in natural foods, supplements, and fortified foods.

The suggested daily intake of vitamin A for a normal infant is 600 I.U. A daily dosage of 20,000 I.U. for as long as a month may be harmful.

### VITAMIN-B COMPLEX

There are at least fifteen different B vitamins which occur in many of the same foods. The best-known ones are thiamine ($B_1$), riboflavin ($B_2$), niacin, $B_6$, and $B_{12}$. These B vitamins are essential to the growing infant in many ways. They enable body cells to obtain energy from carbohydrates, they promote growth, good appetite, digestion, and healthy skin, and they keep the nervous system in balance. A deficiency in these vitamins can result in loss of appetite, irritability, fatigue, eye and skin problems, and poor growth. The B vitamins are found in high amounts in a variety of foods:

PORK
LIVER and ORGAN MEATS
FISH
POULTRY
MILK (WHOLE, SKIM)
BREAST MILK
EGG YOLK
CHEESE
GREEN LEAFY VEGETABLES

DRIED PEAS, BEANS,
   LENTILS
SOYBEANS
PEANUT BUTTER
BROWN RICE
ENRICHED CEREALS
BANANAS
SWEET POTATOES
WHEAT GERM
BREWER'S YEAST

All the B vitamins are water soluble, so they are easily lost in cooking water. They cannot be stored in the body and should be eaten daily. The vitamins are quite stable to heat, with the exception of $B_6$. Riboflavin is particularly sensitive to light, and foods that are served as main sources, such as milk, should not be stored in clear containers or left out in the light. The B vitamins are also lost when soda is used in the cooking water.

A deficiency in some of the B vitamins is more prevalent today because of the practice of refining flours, cereals, and rice, which results in a large loss of all the B vitamins. The Food and Drug

Administration has approved levels of enrichment for refined flours and cereals; however, only thiamine, riboflavin, and niacin are added. Even a large intake of enriched foods can leave a baby deficient in the other B vitamins. One answer is to serve whole-grain cereals, unbleached or whole-grain flour, converted or brown rice, and other foods that are high in the B vitamins. Wheat germ and brewer's yeast can also be used as added fortifiers in your baby's food.

In general, if your baby drinks an adequate amount of breast or cow's milk, he will be receiving a good amount of the B vitamins, with the exception of niacin, which can be supplied by meats, poultry, and enriched cereals. The commercial formulas should be fortified with $B_6$ and will state so on the label. Advisable daily intakes of some of the B vitamins are:

|  | 1 month | 12 months |
|---|---|---|
| Thiamine | .12 mg. | .21 mg. |
| Riboflavin | .27 mg. | .44 mg. |
| Niacin | 3.7 mg. | 6.2 mg. |

## VITAMIN C

Vitamin C, or ascorbic acid, is needed by all body cells. It is crucial to growth, strong bones, and teeth. Current research indicates that it plays an important role in the body's resistance to infection, which is especially important for infants. Vitamin C cannot be stored in the body and must be supplied daily. A deficiency can result in scurvy, gum problems, and frequent infections. There are many high sources of this vitamin among foods:

| | |
|---|---|
| ORANGES | ORANGE JUICE |
| GRAPEFRUIT | GRAPEFRUIT JUICE |
| LEMON JUICE | STRAWBERRIES |
| BREAST MILK | BROCCOLI |
| CANTALOUPE | GREEN PEPPER |
| GUAVA | PARSLEY |
| PAPAYA | |

There are also many fair sources of vitamin C:

| | |
|---|---|
| WATERCRESS | SPINACH |
| ASPARAGUS | COLLARD GREENS |
| TOMATOES | POTATOES |
| TOMATO JUICE | KOHLRABI |
| KALE | |

In spite of the abundance of vitamin C in foods, the vitamin is highly unstable and can be lost in cooking or soaking water, or by exposure to heat, light, and air. Vitamin C deficiency, or scurvy, still occurs even in countries with high standards of living. Dr. Fomon states, "Failure of infants to receive adequate amounts of ascorbic acid can be traced primarily to faulty nutritional education of parents or to failure of physicians to realize that certain milks and formulas are deficient in content of ascorbic acid."

While the vitamin is usually adequately supplied through breast milk, cow's milk is a poor source, and a bottle-fed baby should receive some supplement from birth. Many commercial formulas are fortified and the labels should be checked as to the amounts. Some doctors recommend orange juice, others prefer to delay orange juice until the fourth or fifth month because of the possibility of an allergic reaction. Other supplements are ascorbic acid tablets and water-soluble vitamin concentrates.

The recommended daily intake of 30 mg. (milligrams) of vitamin C is sufficient to prevent scurvy, however, larger amounts of the vitamin may be useful in preventing infections such as colds.

### VITAMIN D

Vitamin D is one of the most important vitamins for babies. The first formation of bone is cartilage, and this vitamin is necessary for the absorption of calcium and phosphorus which causes the cartilage to harden into bone. When a baby is deficient in vitamin D, he may have rickets which is characterized by soft, curved bones, bowed legs, or knock-knees.

The vitamin can be produced in the body by the action of the sun on the skin, but this is not a reliable or adequate source. The main food sources are:

COD-LIVER OIL     HALIBUT-LIVER OIL

It is also present in fair amounts in *liver* and *egg yolk*. The vitamin is added to many kinds of milk—whole, skim, evaporated, and non-fat dry milk powder. You must read the labels to be sure the milk is fortified with 400 I.U. per quart.

Vitamin D is given to babies from the first or second week, in the form of cod-liver oil, a water-soluble concentrate, fortified milk or formula. You should give it during or just after a feeding to make certain that it is absorbed. Breast-fed babies also require vitamin D since it is not adequately supplied in human milk.

The advisable daily intake of vitamin D is 400 I.U. Some research has indicated that excess amounts may be harmful to infants. As with vitamin A, this vitamin should be prescribed as a supplement by your doctor, and you should be aware of the amounts in fortified foods.

## VITAMIN E

Vitamin E is essential for your baby's development. It plays an important part in cell structure and contributes to growth, good muscles, nerves, and skin. The vitamin can be extracted and is available as alpha-tocopherol. It is also found in some foods:

BREAST MILK
WHEAT GERM, WHEAT GERM OIL
PEANUT, SOY, AND SAFFLOWER OIL
WHOLE-GRAIN CEREALS
NUTS

The vitamin can be destroyed by high heat and exposure to air. The practice of refining flours and cereals has removed much natural vitamin E from our diets, and the enrichment of flour and cereal does not include vitamin E. Since heating and chemical extraction of oils can destroy the vitamin, nutritionists recommend using unrefined oils.

Breast milk contains more vitamin E than cow's milk. The American Academy of Pediatricians in 1969 recommended that vitamin E be used in all infant formulas, but there is little indication that this has been done. The advisable daily intake of vitamin E (alpha-tocopherol) is 1.8 mg.

## VITAMIN K

Vitamin K is a fat-soluble vitamin that is essential in blood clotting and liver function. It is found in several foods:

| | |
|---|---|
| SPINACH | CARROT TOPS |
| TOMATOES | CAULIFLOWER |
| CABBAGE | TURNIP GREENS |
| BREAST MILK | |
| COW'S MILK | |

Yogurt is also a source since the yogurt bacteria will produce vitamin K in the body. The vitamin is adequately supplied for normal babies in breast milk, cow's milk, and formulas.

# MINERALS

Minerals are present in the body fluids as soluble salts and affect many bodily functions. *Calcium* and *phosphorus* are the basic elements of bones and teeth. *Iron* and *copper* are elements in the red blood cells. *Iodine* is essential for proper functioning of the thyroid gland. *Sodium, potassium,* and *magnesium* are other important minerals.

Most minerals are adequately supplied by a balanced selection of food. However, minerals are water soluble and can easily be lost if you soak food or cook with a large amount of water. Refining of flours, cereals, and rice also destroys minerals, so the whole-grain cereals and brown rice are better sources. Both breast milk and cow's milk can supply your baby with adequate amounts of most minerals, with the exception of iron.

## IRON

Iron is a mineral that is essential to your baby's health. It combines with protein in the body to form hemoglobin, the substance which carries oxygen from the lungs to all the parts of the body. The body cells must be supplied with oxygen to sustain life. Iron also forms part of several enzymes that break food down so that it can be digested in the body. It is supplied by several foods:

| | |
|---|---|
| LIVER | ENRICHED BREAD and |
| KIDNEYS | CEREALS |
| EGG YOLK | GREEN LEAFY |
| DRIED PEAS, BEANS, | VEGETABLES |
| LENTILS | DRIED FRUITS |
| MEAT | MOLASSES |

Both human and cow's milk are very low in iron. One government study found that babies under one year were, on the average, 50 per cent deficient in the recommended iron intake.

Most commercial formulas are iron fortified, but regular milk is not. For a baby who is breast fed, or on a homemade formula, the iron-fortified dry baby cereals are an important source of iron. By the time your baby is four months old, you can add egg yolks to his daily diet as a source of iron. If he is allergic to egg yolk, you should include the other iron-rich foods in his diet. Molasses can be added to food or a bottle, but since it is a laxative, it must be used in very small amounts.

Although a baby's daily requirement for iron can vary with the individual needs, an average daily intake of 6 to 8 mg. of iron is advised, from the time your baby is four to six weeks old, until at least eighteen months. If iron supplementation is begun at four months or later, then a larger daily amount of 10–15 mg. is advised. The average daily intake should not exceed 15 mg. According to Dr. Fomon, babies who are most likely to develop iron deficiency are those with low birth weight, those of multiple births (twins, etc.), and those who are born to mothers who have had several closely spaced pregnancies, or possibly who are low in iron during pregnancy.

## CALCIUM

Calcium is the most important mineral in the building of strong bones and teeth. Infants have a particularly high need for calcium in the conversion of cartilage to bone and for their rapid growth. It also plays a large part in the prevention and relief of nervous tension and irritability. A calcium deficiency can result in rickets.

The highest source of calcium is *milk,* both whole and skim, breast and cow's milk. Other foods contain calcium in good amounts:

| | |
|---|---|
| ICE CREAM | KALE |
| CHEESE | COLLARD GREENS |
| NON-FAT DRY MILK POWDER | GREEN BEANS |
| | BROCCOLI |

Although spinach, chard, and beet greens also contain calcium, it is not in a form that is usable by the body and should not be considered a source of calcium. Fat is also important in the absorption of calcium by the body.

By the time your baby is a few months old, he should be drinking one quart of milk a day and continue to do so through childhood. This will adequately supply his need for calcium. The following foods contain the same amount of calcium as one cup of milk and can be used as supplements:

1 ounce hard cheese—Swiss, Cheddar, Meunster, etc.

3 tablespoons non-fat dry milk powder

1 cup custard

The advisable daily intake of calcium is 500 mg., and larger amounts are not harmful.

## SODIUM

Your baby will receive an adequate amount of sodium, or salt, from milk, meat, and vegetables. It is unnecessary to salt your baby's food to your own taste, since babies do not show any preference for salted foods—this is an acquired habit. Research has indicated that a high intake of sodium by infant animals results in high-blood pressure and hypertension in adult life. So the safest course is to avoid adding salt to your baby's food, and avoid those prepared foods that are highly salted. Beware that sodium compounds are also used as preservatives in many foods.

## IODINE

Iodine is an essential mineral for the maintenance of the body processes by its role in the functioning of the thyroid gland. If the activity of the thyroid is too slow, the body will store up energy as fat. If the thyroid is overactive, the body will burn up food and energy reserves too quickly.

Iodine is present in:

| | |
|---|---|
| SHELLFISH | SALT-WATER FISH |
| COD-LIVER OIL | MEATS |
| IODIZED SALT | VEGETABLES |

If you live in an inland area, a small amount of iodized salt can be added to your baby's food as a source of iodine. Be sure and check the label on table salt to make certain that iodine has been added.

## PHOSPHOROUS

Phosphorous is essential for the growth of strong bones and teeth and also many bodily processes. It is especially important to the rapidly growing infant.

This mineral is present in large amounts in these foods:

| | |
|---|---|
| LIVER | WHOLE-GRAIN |
| FISH | CEREALS |
| EGG YOLK | PEANUT |
| DRIED PEAS, BEANS, | BUTTER |
| LENTILS | BROWN RICE |
| SOYBEANS | CORN |
| CHEESE | COW'S MILK |

The advisable intake is 220 mg. daily.


# THE "NUTRITIONAL COST" OF FOOD

Now that you are familiar with your baby's nutritional needs, I would like to explain the idea of nutritional cost. Throughout this book I stress the *least expensive* ways to feed your baby. This economy is not the same thing as skimping. We all want our babies to have the best food possible, and we are ready to pay a high price for quality. However, the expensive foods are not necessarily the most nutritious and may even be harmful for your baby. For example, prime meats contain less protein than lower grades, and highly processed foods contain additives and fillers and have often lost nutrients.

But, you must also keep in mind that some less expensive foods may be poor nutritional buys. For example, unenriched white rice is less expensive than brown rice but also has lost many of the nutrients. Fruit "punches" may be less expensive than a juice, but they contain a much higher amount of water and sugar.

Instead, you should select your baby's food by considering the "nutritional cost"; that is, where can you find the most food value for the least amount of money? If you look back over the lists of foods that are high in specific nutrients, you will see that the same inexpensive foods appear on many of the lists:

SOYBEANS*  LEAFY GREENS—TURNIP,
LIVER* (BEEF, LAMB)  KALE, SPINACH,
KIDNEYS*  COLLARD, ETC.
EGG YOLK*  CARROTS
POULTRY*  DRIED PEAS, BEANS,
NON-FAT DRY MILK*  LENTILS
MILK*  ORANGES

So there is simply no reason for any baby to grow up nutritionally deficient, regardless of family income. It is also unnecessary to deprive the rest of your family by buying expensive foods for your baby. You will be able to save money while giving your baby the best possible start in life. This, I believe, is the best reason for you to prepare your own baby food.

* These foods are all excellent sources of complete protein. If some of these foods do not appeal to you, remember that your baby is not born with specific likes and dislikes.

# 2

## HOW TO READ LABELS

NOW THAT YOU KNOW what foods your baby needs, let's look at how to buy these foods in terms of their "nutritional cost." That is, how you can get the most food value for your money and also avoid foods which may be harmful for your baby.

When you consider the immense variety of foods that are available in a supermarket, shopping becomes a challenging game between you and the food industry. The secret of winning is very easy. Just read and take advantage of all the information that is printed on the labels for the protection of you, the consumer.

The U. S. Department of Agriculture and the Food and Drug Administration enforce several laws that cover all food that is sold in interstate commerce or is imported, and many states and localities also have their own laws. These acts require that the food be pure, wholesome, and honestly labeled. The label must include, when applicable, the grade; inspection shield; brand name; weight, measure, or count; description; dates; and a list of ingredients.

In this chapter I want to help you to understand how you can easily use this information in buying the food that you will prepare for your baby. Of course, you will also be able to use your marketing know-how in shopping for the rest of your family. In the Bibliography I have listed additional sources of marketing information.

## U. S. GRADES

These grades are used to classify foods according to their appearance, such as size, shape, color, or by their tenderness. All the grades are equally wholesome, and the lower grades contain the same amount of nutritional value as the highest grade. In the case of meats, the lower grades contain even more protein. These grades are particularly useful in buying food to prepare as purées, since appearance and tenderness is irrelevant once you have puréed the food for your baby. The higher the grade, the more expensive the item usually is, and it is an unnecessary expense to use the top grade. Because the names of the grade vary according to the food, I have indicated the appropriate grade for the various foods in the *Recipe* chapters. Here are some examples of grade marks:

You should always look for the initials "U.S." before the grade, since they indicate that it is a U. S. Department of Agriculture grade.

## INSPECTION SHIELDS

The shields appear on all meat, poultry products, and also on many other foods. Their presence means that the food was prepared under federal supervision and inspected for wholesomeness. You should always try to buy foods for your baby that carry these seals. Here are some federal seals:

Products that do not come under federal control may still carry state or local inspection seals, and you should become familiar with them.

## BRAND NAMES

The label must contain the brand name or the manufacturer's name. You can easily recognize the well-advertised name; however, many supermarkets and other distributors have goods packaged under their own or a private label. Very often, the food is packaged by the same well-known manufacturer who simply puts on a different label. Usually the private labels are less expensive than the well-known ones, since you do not have to pay for the cost of advertising. Because most of the food that you will buy for your baby comes under government inspection and grading, you can get the same food value and quality from the private-label brands and save money.

For many products, such as mayonnaise, canned fruits, juices, and vegetables, the government has established *standards of identity* which define minimum and maximum amounts of major ingredients. So you are assured of getting "at least" a certain amount of fruit and "not more than" a set amount of water in a can of fruit, regardless of the brand.

## WEIGHTS, MEASURES, OR COUNTS

This information on content must be printed clearly on the label. Always compare different brands according to their weight in order to get the most for your money. Do not be deceived by larger packages. You can also use these weights to compare different sizes of the same brand in order to see if you really are saving money by buying the larger size.

In many areas, *unit pricing* is required by law and it makes economical shopping easy and fast. Under each item is listed the price per weight or count. Take advantage of it, and if it is not required in your area, support your local consumer organization in passing such a law.

## DESCRIPTION OF FOOD

The label must clearly and accurately describe the food, such as SLICED GREEN BEANS, ORANGE JUICE, WHOLE CARROTS. If there are two main ingredients, the food that is present in the largest amount must be listed first in the name; such as "BEANS with PORK" instead of the way we usually refer to it as, "PORK and BEANS." Also, if a food resembles a food for which a standard of identity has been set, but does not contain the required ingredients, it must be labeled "IMITATION." The word "FLAVORED" is also used to identify an imitation food.

Often, descriptions are added to the name of a food, and these are usually a good warning that the basic food has been modified. Cheese is a good example of this type of labeling. The word "FOOD" in the label PASTEURIZED PROCESS CHEESE FOOD shows that the product contains less cheese, but added non-fat dry milk and water. The term "SPREAD" in PASTEURIZED PROCESS CHEESE SPREAD indicates an even higher moisture content than the cheese "FOOD." Instead of ORANGE JUICE, you can find cans labeled "ORANGE DRINK," "PUNCH," or ". . . ADE." These beverages all contain more water than those labeled "JUICE." *In general you will get the most food value for your money and least additives and fillers if you avoid those products whose names show modi-*

*fication of the basic food.* By looking carefully at the name of what you are buying, you may not even have to read the list of ingredients.

There are two words that may be added to the name of a food to indicate added food value. The word "ENRICHED" is added to the name of many cereals, flours, and baked goods. This means that the vitamins *Riboflavin, Niacin,* and *Thiamine* and the mineral *Iron* have been added at least in minimum amounts to replace the loss due to processing. Some brands contain amounts that are higher than the minimum, so it is worth your time to look at the amounts or percentages that are listed on the label. The amount of *Iron* and *Niacin* in cereals is particularly important since they will be one of your baby's main sources during early infancy.

The word "FORTIFIED" means that vitamins and minerals not normally in the food have been added to the product. It may also mean that the amounts of some nutrients have been increased above the normal amount. Since these "FORTIFIED" foods are usually *more expensive,* read the label to see what has been added and consider if it is necessary for your baby. If not, you are spending money needlessly for nutrients that are naturally present in other foods that your baby eats. In the case of vitamins A and D, which may be added to many foods, excess amounts may even be harmful to your baby.

## DATES

Most foods are marked with a code to indicate the packing date. Perishable foods always contain the last date on which the food may be sold. This date is used to help the owner of the store in removing spoiled foods and is often in coded form. However, in many areas, laws have been passed which require open and clear dating of perishable foods such as milk, eggs, and baked goods. Take advantage of these dates to buy the freshest food

possible. Even where the date is coded, you can usually interpret it, since it is a combination of month, day, and, possibly,
year. For example, 9033 usually means September 3, 1973; or
1023 on milk means October 23. Some baked goods use letters
to indicate the day of the week. If your area does not have open
dating, try asking your local grocer for information on interpreting dates of perishable items that you frequently buy.

## "MDR" AND "RDA" NUTRITIONAL INFORMATION

You may have seen the abbreviations "MDR" and "RDA"
on a label and wondered what they meant or the difference between them.

"MDR" stands for Minimum Daily Requirement and applies
to 10 nutrients which are regarded as essential in the daily diet
to *prevent deficiency diseases*. These requirements were established by the Federal Food and Drug Administration and include vitamins A, B₁, B₂, C, D, and Niacin, and the minerals
Iron, Phosphorus, Calcium, and Iodine. The amount of a nutrient in a product is expressed as a percentage of the MDR,
usually per serving.

"RDA" stands for Recommended Dietary Allowance and applies to the daily amount of a nutrient that is necessary to *maintain good nutrition* in the average healthy person. The amounts
are established by the Food and Nutrition Board of the National
Research Council and are *generally greater* than MDRs. They
currently apply to 16 nutrients.

This information on a label can be very helpful in selecting the
product with the lowest "nutritional cost" and to help you plan
a balanced, healthy diet. But keep in mind the specific needs
of your baby and look for actual amounts of nutrients that may
also be listed on a label. You can compare these amounts with
the advisable daily intakes that are described in chapter 1.

## LIST OF INGREDIENTS

This list must be clearly printed on the package and it is your most valuable aid in safe and economical food buying. If you read the list, you will know what is in the product and at least the relative amounts. The ingredients are listed in *descending* order of amount. *Thus, the ingredient that is listed first is present in the largest quantity.* If the label on a can of fruit drink reads "water, sugar, and juice," you will be buying more water and sugar than actual fruit juice. Although the drink may be priced lower than a fruit juice, this product may actually be more expensive in terms of its nutritional cost. Whenever you are in doubt about a product, or the name seems confusing, just read the list of ingredients!

### ADDITIVES

It is even more important for you to read this list of ingredients so that you know what additives are in the food that you will be feeding your baby. There are almost 10,000 officially approved additives and most must be included on the label. However, there is a growing criticism of the adequacy of the testing methods which are used in determining whether or not a particular additive is safe. Some additives, such as MSG, which have been used for years have been found to be harmful when they are tested on infant animals. Your baby's relatively low weight and immature digestive system are two important considerations. The United Nations' FAO/WHO Expert Committee on Food Additives recommended in a 1961 report:

Foods that are specifically prepared for babies require separate considerations from all other foods as regards the use of food additives and toxicological risks. The reason for this is that the detoxicating mechanisms that are effective in the more mature individual may be ineffective in the baby. The committee strongly urges that baby foods should be prepared without food additives, if possible. If the use of a food additive is necessary in a baby food, great caution should be exercised both in the choice of the additive and in the level of use.

In addition, there is potential risk in the combination of two or more harmless additives, and also in the accumulation of some additives which are present in so many foods. The frightening part is that the effects of some additives may not show up until later in life and there is no way of taking back what your baby has eaten.

Obviously, the safest course is to avoid all foods which contain additives and one way is to make at home, from basic foods, everything your baby eats. However, if you'll excuse the old expression, you should not "throw out the baby with the bathwater." You will be very busy with a baby in the house, and this may not be the time to start baking bread, or growing vegetables. It would be nice if you could take advantage of the convenience of some prepared foods, especially canned foods, in feeding your baby. Also, some additives are actual nutrients which are used to improve the value of the food and I have chosen to call these "fortifiers."

The most difficult job for the layman is to interpret or recognize the long technical names of the various additives which are printed in the list of ingredients. I have identified some of the most common ones and indicate why they are used. Some are highly controversial and are the subject of current research; others seem unnecessary and are used to improve appearance, texture, or cover lack of quality. You will find them listed on a label either by their specific name or by their type, such as "preservatives."

*Preservatives* are used to delay deterioration or spoilage, which is an advantage with some perishable foods. However, they are often added to prolong shelf life of a product for unnecessarily long periods to increase its chances of sale. You can use a rule of thumb that if a product is inexpensive or is one that you will buy and use immediately, such as bread, select a brand without preservatives. Some common preservatives are sodium chloride, sodium nitrates, sodium benzoate, calcium propionate, sodium propionate, sulfur dioxide, sodium sulphites, and sodium carbonate. *Sodium nitrite* was strongly criticized in 1970 by Dr. Samuel Epstein, of the Children's Cancer Research Foundation, who has shown in research that it can produce harmful effects.

Some organic preservatives, which are generally accepted as harmless, are acetic acid, tartaric acid, lactic acid, sorbic acid, citric acid, and benzoic acid.

*Antioxidants* are a type of preservative and some commonly used ones are propyl gallate, BHA (Butylated hydroxytoluene), and BHT (Butylated hydroxyanisole). The British Food Standards Committee has banned *BHT* from use in baby food and restricted its use in other foods because it has produced allergic reactions and is possibly related to cancer. Many other countries have also banned its use; however, it is one of the most widely used additives in America.

*Emulsifiers* are added to improve the texture or consistency of foods and include monoglycerides, diglycerides, and disodium phosphate. Lecithin is an organic compound found in egg yolks, soybeans, and corn and is generally accepted as harmless.

*Stabilizers,* or thickeners, are also used to add texture and consistency to food. They make food nutritionally expensive, since you are paying for and filling your baby up with a large percentage of non-nutritious fillers instead of the actual food. Some commonly used fillers are the vegetable gums agar-agar, gum arabic, gum tragacanth, and pectin. Gelatin is a thickener that does contain protein. Some cellulose compounds used are *methyl cellulose* and *carboxymethyl cellulose,* and these are currently under controversy. Food starches, such as tapioca, corn starch, and rice starch, are non-nutritious and are difficult for babies to digest. Flour, when enriched or unbleached, can thicken while adding some nutrients; however, the terms "white," "bleached," or "wheat" flour indicate that the flour is merely a filler.

*Hydrogenated,* or *partially hardened,* is often used to describe oils that have been treated to a hydrogenation process to change them to a more solid state. Research now indicates that this process modifies the fatty acids in a way that might be dangerous to bodily functions, and most doctors and nutritionists advise against using them.

*Artificial Colors* are coal-tar dyes and have long been a subject of criticism. These are completely unnecessary in food you will be serving your baby. Some natural food colors are annato, betain, caramel, carotene, chlorophyll, and saffron. These are just as unnecessary, but are less controversial.

*Artificial Flavors,* or enhancers, are widely used and are also unnecessary in your baby's food. Monosodium glutamate (MSG) is an example of an organic-based additive that has been identified as potentially harmful to infants. Hydrolyzed plant protein is also used, and this is an early step in the production of MSG. Salt is a natural flavoring that can be dangerous when it is overused. Some artificial flavorings are amyl acetate (banana), benzaldehyde (cherry, almond), and citral (lemon). One wonders about the basic quality of the food when such enhancers, or added flavors, are considered necessary.

*Artificial Sweeteners,* such as cyclamates and saccharin, have recently been banned.

There are also many forms of sugar which may be called cane sugar, sucrose, corn syrup, sugar syrup, and dextrose. These are empty-nutrition additives which can depress the appetite and contribute to dental decay. It is not considered harmful to occasionally use prepared foods that contain these sugars, but you must be careful not to serve these foods as a steady diet or select foods which contain them as major ingredients.

FORTIFIERS

Vitamins and minerals are added to many foods, and in a sense, they are additives. However, their purpose is to replace those vitamins and minerals which have been removed through processing or to add nutrients that are not readily available in food. They are an attempt to improve the quality of our diet. Some common fortifiers are iron, thiamine, riboflavin, niacin, iodine, potassium iodide, and vitamins A, C (ascorbic acid), and D.

A recent development in food processing has been the use of low-cost *protein fortifiers* in various foods, especially those with incomplete proteins such as cereals, baked goods, noodles, spaghetti, soups, etc. This is an inexpensive means of improving the protein quality of foods with vegetable and grain proteins. They are either composed of nutrients found in foods or are essential amino acids. They will be listed in the list of ingredients on the label and include:

*From animal protein sources:* non-fat milk solids, cheese whey, egg-white solids, sodium caseinate, fish-protein concentrate, whey solids, and hydrolized-milk protein.

*From vegetable sources:* soybean flour, soybean protein, cottonseed flour, cottonseed protein, brewer's yeast.

*Essential amino acids* are lysine, methionine, threonine, and tryptophan.

When you prepare your own baby food, you also have the opportunity to add your own fortifiers. Molasses, rich in iron, can be used as a mild sweetener. Wheat germ, high in vitamin E and B vitamins, can be used as a thickener. Non-fat dry milk powder can be added to almost any food. Lemon and orange juice supply vitamin C and can be used instead of water.

So, if you read the list of ingredients, you will be able to select foods without *unnecessary* or *potentially harmful additives.* You can keep track of those which are under current controversy through the newspapers, consumer magazines, and the Federation of Homemakers. (See Bibliography.) You don't have to memorize these difficult names, instead copy the ones down that you want to avoid, and take the list shopping. You can even practice at home with labels on foods that you have already bought.

Remember that foods containing any additives should be served only occasionally for the sake of necessary convenience. If you are in doubt about any additive or see a long list of long names, just don't buy the food.

In general, the whole process of label reading is less time-consuming than you might think. Since you tend to use the same foods, once you have identified the best ones in terms of safety and nutritional cost, you can simply keep buying them. This is the best way to convey your preferences and objections to the food industry. It really can be a fun game and a rewarding one!

# 3

## FEEDING YOUR BABY

AS YOU READ BOOKS, consult doctors, and talk with other mothers, you will find that everyone seems to have their own specific ideas on breast feeding versus bottle feeding, the age to start solids, which solids, schedules, sterilization, and so on. If you have other children you will already have your own way of feeding your baby. In spite of wide differences of opinion on the various aspects of feeding, babies seem to thrive. They are really very adaptable!

Most experts do agree that the important factor in successful feeding is a relaxed and confident mother. You will be able to maintain this attitude if you try to follow whatever methods are most convenient and comfortable for you. In this chapter, I have tried to show the various choices that you have among the methods that are generally recommended. Of course, if you regularly consult a doctor, he will give you specific advice. Just don't be afraid to ask questions!

## BREAST FEEDING OR BOTTLE FEEDING

The first choice that you will make is whether to nurse your baby or use a formula. You should decide before you go to the hospital, since soon after your baby is born, you will receive medication to prevent the milk from coming if you will not be nursing. This is not the time that you will feel like making the decision.

*Breast Feeding* is becoming very popular and most doctors encourage it both for physical and psychological reasons. Nutritionally, breast milk is nearly perfect and if you are eating a balanced diet, your baby will be well fed during his first four to five months. Compared to cow's milk, it is higher in vitamins C, E, niacin, and in linoleic acid. It contains carbohydrates in the form of lactose which is less sweet and more easily digested than the sucrose or dextrose usually added to formulas. Breast milk does not contain adequate amounts of vitamin D and iron; however, these can be given as supplements. There is less chance that your baby will have digestive trouble with breast milk, and it also supplies him with antibodies that will make him more resistant to infections. Nursing your baby can be very rewarding psychologically for both you and your baby. This is his first contact with another person, and he cannot help but feel warmth and love when he is cuddled so close to your body.

There are also several advantages for you, personally, in nursing. This is really the most convenient, economical, and easy way to feed your baby. The milk is always available and sterile. You don't have to buy or mix formulas, sterilize bottles, or store them. Some women object that nursing may tie them down, but a daily relief bottle can be given and that gives you up to eight hours between feedings. If you feel that you may be too busy to nurse, remember that it also gives you a good excuse to retreat by yourself for a while and relax.

Then, there is the all-important job of regaining your figure. You will do so faster since nursing naturally causes the uterus to contract. You will be supplying extra calories in the milk you produce, so you can eat great amounts without gaining weight and can even lose any extra pounds easily. Really a pleasure if you have been calorie watching for the past nine months!

The only reason not to nurse is if you have strong feelings against it. If you are unsure, remember that you can wean your baby, or stop nursing, at any time. So it seems a good idea to try it, at least for two or three weeks.

Before your baby is born, try to get some advice from other mothers who have nursed their babies. You should contact La Leche League which distributes information on nursing and often has women on call to talk with about specific problems. There are now branches in most areas, or you can write to their main office. (See Bibliography.) Often, the local YWCA, or a hospital, will have information or courses on breast feeding. The government booklet, *Infant Care,* also contains a good section on breast feeding.

Here are some general suggestions on successful nursing:

► Get as much rest as possible.
► Eat a balanced diet, especially including as much milk as you can.
► Drink a good amount of fruit juices.
► Watch out for allergic reactions in your baby to foods that you are eating, and avoid them. These are also foods that may cause a reaction when he eats them as solids.
► Be careful of drugs you might take that can affect your baby. If you can, avoid using any drug.
► Find a comfortable place to nurse—a rocking chair is excellent. Place a pillow under your arm.
► Don't worry about how much milk your baby is drinking. If he is gaining weight and seems satisfied, the actual ounces aren't important.
► If you have an older child who is suffering from acute jealousy—this is a good time to read him a story, or sing.
► If you do run into problems, call your doctor, or a friend who has nursed.
► If you begin to have pain in one breast, stop nursing on that side and contact your doctor at once.
► Relax!

*Bottle Feeding.* If you decide not to nurse, a bottle is also a very satisfactory way to feed your baby. The hospital will put your baby on a specific formula and you will receive instructions when you go home. A recent development has been the use of commercial formulas, either in concentrated form, or already mixed. Although these are more expensive than preparing your own, they are very convenient. Their composition does vary, but they should be fortified with vitamins D, E, iron, and vitamin C. Dr. Fomon has questioned the use of vegetable oil in these formulas, since the lack of butterfat results in a very low intake of the cholesterol in saturated fat. In any case, their use should always be discussed with a doctor.

HOW TO PREPARE A FORMULA

The classic way of preparing a formula is to dilute evaporated milk with boiled water and add sugar. This results in a composition that is similar to breast milk. Whole homogenized milk can also be mixed with sugar and water. The formula depends upon the individual needs of your baby, so follow the one prescribed by your doctor. Remember that cow's milk is lacking, or low, in vitamins D and E, iron, niacin, and also vitamin C.

If you do not have a doctor to help plan the formula, you can use these sample formulas. You would gradually shift from the first formula to the later formulas over the first two to three months, increasing the amount as your baby's appetite grows. By the time he is three months, if he is gaining weight and eating solids, you would give 24–32 ounces of undiluted whole milk, or evaporated milk that is diluted with equal parts water, and omit the sugar.

|  | *First Formula* | *Later Formulas* | |
|---|---|---|---|
| *Evaporated milk* | 6 ounces | 10 ounces | 13 ounces |
| *Water (boiled)* | 10 ounces | 15 ounces | 19 ounces |
| *Sugar or corn syrup* | 1½ tablespoons | 2½ tablespoons | 3 tablespoons |
| — OR — | | | |
| *Whole milk (boiled)* | 12 ounces | 20 ounces | 26 ounces |
| *Water (boiled)* | 4 ounces | 6 ounces | 6 ounces |
| *Sugar or corn syrup* | 1½ tablespoons | 2½ tablespoons | 3 tablespoons |

You will first divide the formula into six 3-ounce bottles, then six 4-ounce bottles. As your baby starts to drop the extra feedings, you will have five 6-ounce bottles, then four 8-ounce bottles.

Goat's milk and soybean-based formulas are also sold. These are given to babies who are allergic to cow's milk. Since they require specific nutritional supplements, you should never use them without a doctor's instruction.

As with nursing, before your baby is born, find a good source of information on sterilization and bottle feeding. Your doctor can recommend one, or send for one of the government booklets. (See Bibliography.) Remember that even if you are nursing you will occasionally give a bottle.

*Sterilization* of bottles and formulas is important when you are preparing a day's supply of formula that you will be storing in the bottles. The sterilization will slow down the growth of bacteria and spoilage. If you are making each bottle just before a feeding, or using an occasional bottle to supplement nursing, you can prepare the formula in a well-washed bottle. You should, however, use boiled water. Sterilization is usually stopped at around three months, the same time that you switch from formula to regular container milk. The age at which you can make this switch depends upon your baby's individual growth and you should consult a doctor. The *Beverages* chapter covers the various types of milk you can use.

Since bacteria and germs will not grow on clean, dry surfaces, you do not have to sterilize feeding spoons, dishes, or the baby's toys.

*Bottles*. You have a wide choice in the type of bottle that you can use. The clear glass bottles seem to me to be the most inconvenient to use because of the possibility of breaking. The clear glass will also allow light to destroy the riboflavin in the milk. There are plastic bottles in various colors which are opaque and so screen out any light. These can be sterilized as well as the glass bottles.

The most convenient bottles are the disposable, sterilized liners that fit inside an opaque plastic holder. The only part that you boil, and even that isn't always necessary, is the nipple that snaps on top of the holder. The nipple turns inside out and is very easy to clean. Besides their convenience, these disposable bottles have some advantages for your baby. The plastic bag will collapse as he drinks, so there is less chance of swallowing air. Also, the nipple is shaped so that it does not collapse and prevent milk from flowing—very frustrating to a baby. The only disadvantage in using these bottles is their expense. They cost from one cent to two cents apiece and you can use 8 to 10 bottles a day. One way of reducing this expense is to wash the bottles that are used for water and juice and reuse them. Of course, if you are nursing, these bottles are ideal for the occasional relief bottle of water or juice.

The *temperature* of the milk is often a major concern. The standard test is to drop some on the inside of your wrist, and it should feel warm. This test is used to prevent feeding a baby milk that is too hot; it does not mean that the milk must be warmed to this temperature. *Many hospitals do not warm milk for newborn infants.*

There are some clear advantages in feeding your baby milk directly from the refrigerator. The cold milk allows less chance of spoilage and you can save unused portions in the refrigerator for the next feeding. You also save those few minutes of listening to a screaming baby while waiting for the bottle to warm. If you are traveling, it is very convenient to be able to give a cold bottle. The important thing is to accustom your baby gradually to cold milk, then be consistent with this temperature.

So, whether you decide to nurse your baby, or use a formula in a bottle, depends upon your own feelings. Most important is for you to have a confident and relaxed attitude toward the whole process. Your baby will respond to this more than to where his milk is coming from. You also may find that feeding was going well in the hospital, but becomes unsettled when you first come home. Or, the reverse may happen. Your baby may have difficulty feeding in the hospital and then settle down at home. Most feeding problems are usually resolved within the first two weeks, so just try to be patient and relax.

## SCHEDULES

A feeding schedule is more for your convenience than your baby's needs. You will be able to plan your day if you know when your baby is going to eat. This is especially important if you are nursing. When you are feeding solids, you will want to choose mealtimes that best fit in with your family's schedule. The most relaxed time may be after you and your family have eaten.

In the first few weeks you will probably work out some compromise between your baby's demands and the schedule you prefer. The interval between feedings that you should aim for is 4 hours, and most babies naturally settle into this; however a very young or small baby may become hungry in 2½ or 3 hours. You may allow him to cry a few minutes to encourage him to wait a little longer, but it will be painful for both of you to wait out the full 4 hours. Fortunately, the days of strict schedules are over. Even after your baby is on a schedule, don't be surprised if he wakes for a feeding at a strange time!

You will be able to gradually shift your baby to the 4-hour interval that is most convenient for you. The hospital usually starts the day at 7 A.M., which means feedings at 7 A.M., 11 A.M., 3 P.M., 7 P.M., 11 P.M., and 3 A.M. If you like to stay up late and sleep late, you will give the first feeding at 9 A.M. Hopefully, your baby will soon drop the middle-of-the-night feeding. When he does drop a feeding and when you start adding solids, the whole schedule may shift around. So try to stay flexible, and you won't become a frantic clock watcher. If you are a person who dislikes keeping to any schedule, you do not have to follow one. Your baby will then be on "demand" feeding.

When you begin feeding your baby solids you will space them out so that they roughly fall into breakfast, lunch, and dinner. Again, this is for your convenience. We happen to live in a 3-meal-a-day society, but some research has shown that it may be healthier to eat more frequent, smaller meals. So you should not hesitate to give midmorning and midafternoon "snacks," such as juice, fruit, or crackers if your baby is hungry. If he is eating healthy foods, you really can't "spoil his appetite."

One thing to avoid are the "strung-out" meals which last a half hour or more as you try to get down one more bite. You can end up spending much of your day with a spoon in your hand, and your baby will never get the idea of specific meals. He may even come to resent spending so much time eating. Try to remember that if your baby does not eat much at one meal, he will be hungrier for the next one.

## PLANNING A BALANCED MENU

The most important part of feeding your baby is to make sure that you offer him a balanced menu of the foods that he requires. Experiments have even shown that, from a variety of foods, a baby will choose those that contain the necessary nutrients. Since your baby's basic needs are similar to those of the rest of your family, this menu planning will require very little additional time. It really is very simple—just become familiar with the four basic food groups and the number of servings from each group.

This book is designed to help you, with the recipe chapters divided into the three main food groups—*Cereal Grains, Fruits/ Vegetables,* and *Protein Foods.* The other important group, *Dairy,* will be satisfied by your baby's daily intake of formula or milk.

You can then select any food from within the basic group. This allows you considerable room for substitution in order to take advantage of foods that are available and convenient at a particular time, especially those that fit in best with family meals. For example, a serving of cereal grains does not always have to be cereal, you can also use rice or spaghetti. Or, if you don't have meat prepared, you can occasionally give an extra egg. Fruits and vegetables can be interchanged, and you don't have to serve a different one at each meal, or even each day. If your baby becomes tired of one food, he will let you know!

A balance among the food groups will give you the best nutrition, and it is unnecessary and time-consuming to try to offer a wide variety each day. Of course, too much of any one food should also be avoided, no matter how nutritious that food is. For example, one egg serving a day is recommended, but you should limit eggs to 7 to 9 in a week. Organ meats, such as liver, should not be served more than 3 times a week. Even milk should be limited to one quart a day. Just remember that there is no "wonder food!"

The following *Menu Planning Guide* indicates the daily servings of each food group and when they are usually added to make up a complete menu by the age of six months. Although protein and calories are essential each day, many other nutrients can be stored so that you can also balance your baby's menu over a few days. The day is divided into breakfast, lunch, and dinner mainly for convenience, but you can serve these foods at any time during the day.

A "serving" is really whatever your baby will eat. In order to plan, you can count an average serving, for a 6-month baby, as *1–2 food cubes or 3–6 tablespoons*. A *"food cube"* is the amount that can be frozen in the form of an average ice cube, or *about 3 tablespoons*. (See *Food Cube* section in chapter 5.) Do try to give equal amounts of the various foods. If you are serving an "all-in-one" meal such as a stew, increase the amount to 3–6 food cubes.

## MENU PLANNING GUIDE

|            | *Breakfast* | *Lunch*   | *Dinner* |
|------------|-------------|-----------|----------|
| 4 *Weeks*  | Cereal      |           | Cereal   |
| 2 *Months* | Cereal      | Fruit     | Cereal   |
|            | Fruit       |           | Fruit    |
| 3 *Months* | Cereal      | Fruit     | Cereal   |
|            | Fruit       | Vegetable | Fruit    |
| 4 *Months* | Cereal      | Fruit     | Cereal   |
|            | Fruit       | Vegetable | Fruit    |
|            | Egg Yolk    | Protein   |          |

|  | *Breakfast* | *Lunch* | *Dinner* |
|---|---|---|---|
| 5 *Months* | Cereal | Fruit | Cereal |
|  | Fruit | Vegetable | Fruit |
|  | Egg Yolk | Protein | Vegetable |
| 6 *Months* | Cereal | Fruit | Cereal/Protein |
|  | Fruit | Vegetable | Fruit |
|  | Egg | Protein | Vegetable |

Also snack of extra juice, crackers, etc.

So, from six months on, your baby's daily menu will include:

2 Protein Foods (including 1 egg)

2–3 Cereal Grains (including 1 cereal/protein)

5 Fruit/Vegetable (including 1 serving of juice, 1 dark green or yellow)

3–4 cups Milk (24–32 ounces)

This is the balanced diet that your baby should continue eating for several years!

*Supplements:* Your doctor may also prescribe vitamins C and D supplements that you will give your baby from about three weeks through his first year. *Never give more than the amount prescribed.* They will usually be in the form of water-soluble drops that you can put in a bottle or directly in the mouth. If it is an oil-base vitamin, or fish-liver oil, you should give it immediately *after* a feeding by dropping it in the corner of his mouth, to make sure it is fully absorbed. If you are not nursing, do ask your doctor about supplements of vitamin E and linoleic acid, since cow's milk is lower in these nutrients.

If you cannot regularly consult a doctor, or purchase the concentrated drops of vitamins C and D, you should still give these supplements. Vitamin C can be supplied daily with a 3-ounce serving of orange juice or larger servings of other juices. (See chapter 12, *Beverages.*) You can also dissolve a 50-mg. vitamin-C tablet in a little water. This would be useful if your baby is allergic to orange juice. You can supply vitamin D with 1 teaspoon of cod-liver oil each day. (See *Nutrition* chapter for amounts and sources of other vitamins and minerals.)

# WHY, WHEN, AND HOW TO INTRODUCE SOLID FOOD

You will feed your baby solid food in the form of purées to supply him with vitamins and minerals that are lacking in milk, and to satisfy his increasing appetite. He will gradually become accustomed to new tastes and textures, so that he will easily make the switch to regular family food. In the past, solids were often delayed until a baby was eight to ten months old and the result was often weaning and feeding problems. There is still a wide range of opinion among doctors as to the best time to introduce solids. Some recommend that breast-fed babies, who are gaining well, wait until four to five months. One doctor has shown that babies will eat the full range of solid food, including meats, as early as two to three weeks; however, this really creates unnecessary work for you.

The *When to Introduce Foods* table was created from the recommendations of several pediatricians and from personal experience, as a practical *order* for introducing the different foods. The *earliest* advisable ages are given, but you can begin at any later time. After your baby is four to five months old, you have leeway of a month or so for any specific food, so don't consider this list as the last word. Many foods are included that you may not have considered as "baby food"; however they are nutritious and often economical. Also, don't feel that you have to feed your baby every food that is listed here, and don't be afraid to try foods that may have been left out.

## WHEN TO INTRODUCE A FOOD

| Age | Cereals | Fruit | Vegetables | Proteins |
|---|---|---|---|---|
| 4 Weeks | Rice (dry infant cereal) | Orange Juice | | Yogurt (plain) |
| 6 Weeks | Other infant cereals— Oatmeal Barley High-Protein } *or* | Banana (raw) Applesauce | | |
| 2 Months | Enriched— Farina, Cream of Wheat Cream of Rice Pearl Barley Wheat Germ | Cooked— Pears Apricots Peaches Prunes Plums Nectarines | | Yogurt (with any introduced fruit) |
| 3 Months | | Cooked— Pineapple Guavas Mangoes Papayas | Cooked— Carrots Green Beans Winter Squash Peas Tomatoes | |
| 4 Months | Whole-Grains— Oatmeal Whole Wheat Brown Rice Wheatena Ralston | Cooked— Cherries Grapes Raw—Pears | Cooked— Spinach Asparagus Broccoli Green Leafy Summer Squash Celery Corn | Egg Yolk Egg-Yolk Custard Cottage Cheese Grated Cheese |
| 5 Months | | Raw— Apple Plums Apricot Nectarines Citrus Fruit Grapes | Raw— Tomatoes Carrots Cooked— Beets Rutabaga Turnips Parsnips Okra | Chicken Veal Liver Kidneys Beef Lamb Turkey |

| Age | Cereals | Fruit | Vegetables | Proteins |
|---|---|---|---|---|
| 6 Months | Crackers Hard Toast | Any Cooked Fruit Raw— Pineapple Tropical Cantaloupe Avocado | Cooked— Potatoes, Sweet White Lima Beans Cauliflower Kohlrabi | Ham Pork Lean Fish |
| 7 Months | Enriched— Noodles Spaghetti Macaroni | | Peanut Butter Lentils Dry Peas, Beans Raw—Greens, Cucumber | Soybeans Duck Whole Egg |
| 8 Months | | Any raw fruit | Cooked— Brussels Sprouts Eggplant Cabbage Onions Mushrooms | |
| 9 Months | All Table Foods | | | |

## HOW TO INTRODUCE NEW FOODS

The way that you introduce a food is really more important than the taste or texture. Always offer a new food with a smile and some encouraging words. Your baby soon becomes an expert at interpreting your expression and can acquire your own likes and dislikes of specific foods. Here are some other suggestions:

► Give a new food in the morning or at lunch. If you give it at dinner and he has a reaction, you may be in for a sleepless night.

► Always start with a small amount—about one teaspoon for the first time, then increase daily.

► Introduce one food at a time and wait four days before giving another new food. Then, if he has an allergic reaction, you will know which food caused it.

► A reaction to a food may show up as a rash, hives, gas pains, vomiting, or diarrhea. Allergies are not very common, but they often occur in the same family, and with similar types of food.

► Some foods that may cause a reaction are orange juice, egg white, chocolate, nuts, berries, seafood, green beans, and green leafy vegetables; so watch out for these.

► If your baby does show an allergy to a specific food, wait one to two months, then try again. If allergic reactions occur frequently, you should consult your doctor.

► Your baby is most likely to accept a new food if you offer it at the beginning of a meal when he is most hungry. You can also mix it slightly with a favorite food such as a fruit. This is especially good for introducing meats and foods with coarser textures.

► When your baby first begins to taste solid food, his natural sucking response will cause most of the food to spill out. Do not feel that he is spitting out the food because he dislikes it; he will soon learn how to swallow. Some babies find it easier to manage a fairly thick purée, so you can try different consistencies of food.

► There is always the question of whether you offer solid food before or after the bottle. Obviously, if he has just finished a full bottle, he will not be interested in solid food. But, if he is starving, he will not be in the mood to experiment. The best time to offer solids, at least in the early months, is after he has finished about half a bottle, or to wait an hour after a full milk feeding.

► If your baby shows an obvious dislike of a specific food after you have offered it at several meals, forget it for a month or find a substitute. Other than milk, no one food is really essential.

► If you will be using a reclining infant seat, get your baby accustomed to sitting in the seat before you offer food for the first time.

► If your baby starts coughing or decides to sneeze just as you have given him a mouthful of food, hold your hand an inch or so away from his mouth. A wet hand is easier to clean than a shower of puréed food all over you!

It is to your own advantage and your baby's that he begins eating regular family foods as soon as he can. You will save preparation time and your baby will be getting the most nourishment from foods that have not been thinned. Also, when he is eating food that he can pick up and feed himself, he will have a feeling of independence and you will have the freedom from feeding him every bite. Since you can control the consistency of baby food that you prepare yourself, your baby will make the switch easily at an early age. An extra bonus from making your own baby food!

When your baby is six months old, you can begin to gradually accustom him to coarser purées, then finely chopped food, then finger foods. Don't worry about how many teeth he has or doesn't have, he will be able to manage most foods very nicely with his gums.

Here are some general suggestions that I have found practical.

► Introduce your baby to each new consistency or texture very gradually—one food a day. Do not force them.
► Start with foods that are particular favorites—fruits and vegetables are good ones.
► If you have a blender, you can make a coarser texture by using a slower speed for a shorter blending time. It is very easy to make gradual changes with a blender.
► You can also begin mashing many foods with a fork.
► If you are thinning a food, start using less liquid.
► When you are giving a coarser food such as ground meat, mix it with a little smooth fruit or vegetable purée.
► Most important—do not look anxious—SERVE WITH A SMILE!

## FEEDING EQUIPMENT

You will not need any special or expensive equipment to feed your baby. The important thing is to use whatever is most practical for you.

*Feeding dishes* can range from any small dish to an electric three-compartment feeding dish. The latter is the most expensive and is designed to keep the food at a constantly warm temperature. This may be a disadvantage if you leave the food in the dish for any period, since it is an ideal temperature for bacteria to grow. It will also accustom your baby to eating food that is always the same temperature and this can be a problem if you find yourself without this dish. There is no medical reason for your baby to eat food at a constant warm temperature.

The big advantage in using any warming dish is that you can quickly heat your baby's food without creating an extra pot to wash. You can use the inexpensive plastic dishes that can be filled with hot water; or a small heatproof dish that can be put in the oven or in a pan of hot water (a custard cup, heavy dish, or the Mini-Blend jar can be used). You can also wrap any food in aluminum foil and heat it in the oven. This is a fast way to heat a frozen "food cube." Of course, there is no reason why the food has to be warmed at all. Your baby will adapt to any temperature and you just have to learn to ignore the cries of outrage from other mothers and grandmothers!

*A spoon* should be small, narrow, and shallow—it does not have to be silver! A demitasse spoon is perfect if you have one and the small plastic picnic spoons are also a good size. When you first offer solid foods, try using a wooden tongue depressor, a dull butter knife, or a well-washed popsicle stick. These flat sticks are also good for your baby's early attempts at feeding himself.

*A bib* is a feeding necessity. Use a big plastic bib, with a catch-all pocket (see chapter 14 for instructions on making one), and a slide or snap fastener. Since a young baby does not have much of a neck and can't lift up his head, it can be a real problem to tie a bib on. The plastic bibs can be easily wiped off, dry quickly, and are more practical than the terry-cloth or cotton bibs.

*A feeding chair* is not a necessity, but it is a great convenience. You won't have to juggle a wriggling baby and a spoon. The first chair to use is a plastic recliner that sells for as low as $5.00. It sits on the table and you can put your baby in it as young as three to four weeks. You can even improvise one from a sturdy rectangular box by cutting the sides on one short end, folding the end under, and securing it with tape.

When your baby is five to six months old, he will become very restless in a recliner, and it will be time to switch him to a high chair. Select one that is easy to clean, has a removable tray with a raised edge to catch spills, and a wide base so it won't tip over when your baby starts leaning over. I would have preferred a decorative antique cane high chair, which would have tipped easily and been impossible to clean. Luckily, I was talked out of it! If you do not have the room for a high chair, there are several seats available that either fasten to a chair or on to the edge of the table. Your baby then sits right at the table. These seats are less expensive than a high chair and are very practical for traveling.

## WHEN YOUR BABY WON'T EAT

After you have planned balanced menus, carefully bought the food, and prepared nutritious dishes, you still have to get the food into your baby. This is probably the subject of greatest concern among mothers, yet you will have the most success if you can just relax and not worry about it. Again, serve with a smile!

Feeding is your baby's earliest contact with another person and just as food is essential for his physical growth, happy mealtimes will help him get the idea that people are really very nice. At one time, the thought was that a baby should consider eating as serious work, so playing was discouraged. The result was often a problem eater. There is no reason why you can't sing, make faces, or give your baby a toy to play with while you are feeding him. Most important is for your baby to look forward to mealtimes with pleasure.

You must not allow feedings to become a battleground over the choice of foods or the amount. If your baby dislikes one food, there is always another from the same food group that you can substitute. Your baby's appetite will also vary with each meal or each day. Since the baby food that you prepare will be inexpensive, you should not mind throwing out any uneaten portions.

It will also be easier for you to maintain this casual attitude if you can forget the idea that a baby must be fat to be healthy, and that it is a sign of success as a mother to have a fat baby, or stuff in as much food as you can.

Your baby is not a turkey and there is even a limit to how many nutrients he can use. Also, since your own baby food will not be laden with sugar and starches, you are less likely to have a fat baby. So be ready to resist advice from grandmothers and even total strangers on how to "fatten up" your baby.

There are some subtle ways that you can encourage your baby if he starts to show a lack of interest in eating.

▶ You can offer him some different foods or prepare foods with a coarser texture.
▶ Or, he may be ready for finger foods as an attempt at feeding himself.
▶ If he seems restless in a reclining seat, change the position so he has something else to look at; or move him to a high chair if he can sit up.
▶ You can even try feeding him at the same time the rest of the family is eating, although this may take some organization on your part.

You may encounter real stubbornness, and your baby may decide to give up eating completely for a day or so. Remember that a baby has very few ways that he can assert himself and not eating is one of them. If you show that it bothers you and you make a feeding a major battle, you can have a problem eater. Your baby will probably still continue to drink milk and this will supply him with enough nutrients for a while. You can fortify his bottle (see Homemade Fortified Milk), but be careful not to give him more than one quart of milk a day or he may not become hungry enough to begin eating again. You may also not even attempt to feed him for a meal or two, and the chances are that he will forget why he stopped eating in the first place. This may be hard to do, but remember that babies do not want to be hungry and there has never been a case of a baby choosing starvation. Sooner or later he will begin eating again.

## SELF-FEEDING

There will come the day when your baby begins to grab for the spoon, try to hit it out of your hand, or put his hands in the food. This means that he has the idea of feeding himself. If you discourage him and don't allow him to try, you may be feeding him for the next year. So, try to cheerfully accept the mess that is about to begin and consider that it is a step toward the day when he will be neatly feeding himself. There are some ways that you can at least control the mess.

► At first, you can give your baby a spoon to hold and play with while you are feeding him. This may satisfy him for a week or so.
► At the end of a meal give him a spoon or popsicle stick and let him practice with a thick purée such as bananas. If he tries to feed himself when he is hungry, he may become very frustrated and discouraged.
► If he begins fingerpainting on the tray with food, allow it

for a few meals so that the novelty will wear off, then gently
discourage it by removing the tray and ending the meal.

▶ If your baby feeds himself with his fingers, it is a step in
learning, but keep offering a spoon.

▶ Put newspaper under the high chair.

▶ If he refuses to allow you to feed him altogether, but cannot
manage a spoon well enough to eat an adequate amount,
start serving finger foods. (See chapter 9 on *Finger Foods.*)

▶ When he seems ready to try a cup, buy a training cup with
a cover, and give only a small amount at a time. Juices
are most readily accepted from a cup.

▶ Unless you have a real aversion to a bottle, there is no reason
to push him to drink from a cup. It is really more trouble
for you.

▶ In general, do not discourage self-feeding, but do not force
your baby into it.

## DIGESTIVE DIFFICULTIES

Since your baby's digestive system might take a while to start
working properly, he is likely to react to feeding with digestive
problems. Here are some common ones to look out for, and some
suggestions. Of course, you should always contact your doctor
when one occurs.

*Colic,* or gas pain, may be very common during your baby's
first three months. It is a result of food not being completely
digested by the baby's immature digestive system, and your baby
will show his pain by loud, constant crying and sharply draw-
ing his legs up. It is very similar to hunger crying, but although
the baby is calmed by eating, he soon begins crying again. Often
the crying will follow a schedule, an hour or two at specific
times during the day or night.

Your doctor may feel that it is an allergic reaction to a kind of
milk and prescribe a special milk or formula. If it only occurs
after eating certain foods, you can avoid them for a month

or so. Most likely, the colic will be a painful stage for both you and the baby and you will just have to wait it out—with earplugs if necessary!

*Rashes or hives* are usually an allergic reaction to a specific food, and you can eliminate that food for a month or so. A light dusting with corn starch will relieve the itching, but be careful not to get it in the baby's eyes or nose.

Often a baby of one to two months will develop a pimply rash that looks like adolescent acne. This is usually not related to a food allergy, but is caused by clogged pores. You should keep the baby's face well washed, and powder with corn starch to dry up the excess oil.

*Diarrhea,* or very loose, watery bowel movements, can be a sign of teething, an oncoming illness, a reaction to a specific food, or to a spoiled food. If it continues for more than a day, your baby may become dehydrated, so you should definitely contact your doctor. The recommendation for mild cases is to increase the amount of liquid that the baby drinks. Diluted skim milk (or formula) may be given. Do not give boiled skim milk, or add dry milk powder. Other foods that may help are carrot soup, carrot/rice soup, rice cereal, eggs, and bananas.

*Celiac disease* is a form of diarrhea in which the bowel movements are frothy, foul smelling, and contain undigested food. It is usually a result of an inability to digest and absorb food properly. You should contact your doctor who will plan a special diet for your baby.

*Constipation* is usually not a serious problem. It is not necessary for your baby to have a bowel movement every day. You should watch out for hard dry movements that are painful. They may be softened by feeding him barley cereal, prune juice, stewed dried fruits, or adding dark brown sugar or molasses to his bottle. *Do not give your baby an enema, laxative, or mineral oil.*

*Vomiting* is a forceful throwing up of a large amount of food. It may be caused by oncoming illness, a reaction to a specific food, or eating spoiled food. If it occurs frequently, it may be a sign of a more serious problem. In any case, contact your doctor.

A less serious but very annoying problem is when your baby "cheeses" or spits up a small amount of food as he burps. It may be caused by a difficulty in digesting fat or by just overeating. A switch to skim, or half-skim milk may help, but ask your doctor first. Most babies outgrow it in several months, so be patient and always have a towel handy.

## FEEDING YOUR BABY AWAY FROM HOME

We all travel around with our babies, and we are likely to be away from home at a mealtime. Here are some suggestions that may be helpful.

- ▶ If your baby is on formula, you can carry the individual bottles of commercial formulas that do not require refrigeration until they are opened. You just screw on a clean nipple. These formulas are also available in small cans, which are less expensive.

- ▶ If you are using bottles with the canned formula, or for water and juice, use the plastic disposable bottles that fit inside a holder. You won't have to worry about washing or sterilizing bottles.

- ▶ If you are using your own formula and you will need several bottles, you can save room in your thermos bag in the following way. Mix as much water and sugar as you need in a jar. Carry a can of evaporated milk, or place it in a thermos. Then you can mix each disposable bottle as you need it. Only the concentrated milk needs to be kept cold after opening.

- ▶ If your baby is off formula and drinking regular milk, just carry the non-fat dry milk powder. It does not need to be refrigerated and you can mix each disposable bottle as you need it, right in the bottle. Use 2 ounces of dry milk for an 8-ounce bottle. Even if your baby is regularly drinking whole milk, the non-fat milk will not disagree with him. (See chapter 12 on *Beverages* for specific information.)

► Solid food is not really necessary in the early months, and your baby probably won't mind missing a meal. If you do want to feed him solid food when you are away from home, you can look for an "instant" food. (See *Instant Foods* chapter.) *Do not introduce new foods when you are away from home*.

► You can also carry the frozen "food cubes" with you. Place enough cubes for a meal in a plastic bag, and they will defrost in time without any need for special storage. Some cooked fruits will keep for several hours. You can then feed your baby out of the plastic bag and throw it away. If you are carrying milk, the cubes will also help keep the milk cold.

► Be sure to accustom your baby to eating cold food and milk, when necessary. This will be most convenient when you are traveling.

# 4

# EQUIPMENT FOR EASY COOKING
# AND PURÉEING

I HAVE BEEN SAYING, throughout this book, that it is easy as well as nutritious to prepare your own baby food. Your mother and grandmother might doubt this, but they did not live in our gadget-conscious modern world. You have a wide choice of equipment for easy cooking and puréeing of baby food. Some of these things you may already own. If not, they may be acquired at modest cost, and remember, this equipment is not limited to baby food. Your entire family will benefit from the many uses of your new equipment long after you have stopped preparing baby food.

## COOKING WITH STEAM

You probably have your own favorite cooking methods and utensils but keep in mind that many of the vitamins and minerals are water soluble and thus are lost in the cooking liquid. Many nutrients are also destroyed by high heat, long cooking time, and the cutting of food into small pieces before cooking.

There is unanimous agreement among nutritionists that the *steam method* of cooking best preserves the vitamins and minerals in food. One study showed that, in steam cooking, only 6 per cent of the vitamins were lost while pressure cooking resulted in a 12 per cent loss. Boiling in water caused a loss of 29–39 per cent. Vegetables are most often the victims of the water-boiling method and yet they are eaten as a major source of nutrients.

In the *steam method,* the food is held above rapidly boiling water and cooks in the rising steam. While it is especially important that the food your baby eats is as nutritious as possible, this method also produces food that retains its natural flavor and color. Your entire family will appreciate these steamed fruits and vegetables that are both nutritious and flavorful. This method is also the easiest and simplest way of cooking. You can choose from a variety of low-cost utensils or improvise one of your own.

*A Steamer/Blancher* is the best utensil for the steam method. It consists of a deep pot, with a tight-fitting cover, and another pot that is completely perforated and fits inside the first pot to within one inch from the bottom. It is similar in appearance to a double boiler. The water in the bottom will boil and the food will cook in the rising steam without being immersed in the water. This utensil is sometimes called a blancher because it is used to quickly immerse fruits and vegetables in boiling water before freezing. It is also a useful pot for cooking spaghetti and noodles, and is also called a *spaghetti cooker.*

I have found a low-cost, practical 6-quart steamer in the catalogue of a major stamp-redemption company. It sells for the equivalent of $6.00. This utensil is also available in other stores, especially those that carry home-canning and freezing equipment such as a hardware store. An imported, more expensive heavyweight steamer is sold in some stores that carry gourmet and professional cooking equipment. Since you may use the steamer daily, the extra cost may be justified; however, the inexpensive steamer is quite adequate.

*Steam Baskets* are also sold for use in steam cooking. There are several types available for $3.00–$8.00. Most are adjustable to fit inside any pot you already own to convert it into a steamer by raising the food out of the cooking water. You must be sure that the steam basket fits well inside the pot so that the cover will fit tightly. One disadvantage of the steam basket is in removing it from the pot. Since all parts are inside the pot, it is not difficult to burn yourself. Also, if you have a full pot, the basket may tip while removing it.

Since the main principle in the steam method is to keep the food supported about one inch above the bottom of the pot, just out of the water, you can improvise in creating your own steam basket. A small colander might fit inside a large pot or you may have a round wire rack of the kind used in baking. If you are in the country, you may use well-washed stones in the bottom of the pot, probably the oldest means of steam cooking. Remember, whatever you use as a platform, it must have holes in it to allow the steam to come through.

*A Double Boiler* is a common utensil that will give almost the same results as a steamer for some foods, and is also useful for making custards and cooked cereals. Since the food cooks at a temperature below boiling, some of the bacteria that cause spoilage may not be destroyed. You should be especially careful in storing foods cooked this way. A double boiler can be purchased for as low as $5.00.

If you already own and are familiar with the use of a *Pressure Cooker,* you may wish to use it to prepare your baby's food. This method of cooking with steam under high pressure has the advantage of reducing the cooking time; however, you must be careful not to overcook the food. The cost of a non-electric pressure cooker is around $15 and an electric one can be bought for $25–$30. If you buy one, look for the Underwriters Laboratory Seal as a check on quality and follow the manufacturer's instructions. An improperly used or malfunctioning pressure cooker can be dangerous.

*Electric Crocks or Bean Pots* are quite new on the market. This is a heavyweight, tightly sealed utensil which maintains a low heat. The food simmers slowly, steaming in its own juices for 10 to 12 hours. This slow cooking retains the vitamins and minerals and tenderizes the food. Thus, it is especially good for meats and poultry. Several foods may be combined and it is suitable for making large quantities. The main drawback to this

utensil is its price—$20–$30. A heavy stone or earthenware casserole used in a very slow oven would produce the same result;
however, you might find it impractical to have the oven in use
for the necessary length of time.

*Aluminum Foil* and the clear roasting wraps offer simple
means of nutritious cooking of almost any food. The food is
tightly sealed in a double layer of foil and bakes in a slow (325°)
oven. The cooking time for most food is slightly longer than with
the steamer. This is a very good way to cook meats, since the
slow moist heat will soften the tough fibers for easier puréeing.
The cooking time for meat is about the same as with potting or
braising. There is no need to add any water since the food will
steam in its own juices. The tight seal will prevent the loss of
those vitamins that are destroyed by air.

The cleanup is effortless—just throw the foil away. But this
can also be a disadvantage if you are concerned with cost. The
roasting bags are convenient for cooking large amounts, combining different foods, or for foods which contain a large amount
of juice. If your oven is already in use in preparing the family
meal, it is very convenient to use foil to cook baby food at the
same time.

Instead of foil, you can also use a heavy baking dish with a
tight-fitting cover. Unless the food is very juicy, it will be necessary to add a little water when you begin cooking.

In general, here are the points that you should remember
when selecting and using any steaming equipment.

> ► Buy a large utensil so that you can cook a large amount
> of food, or combine different foods, at the same time. This
> will save you clean-up and preparation time.
> ► Make certain that the lid is tight fitting and heavy enough
> so that the steam cannot lift it. You can add curtain weights
> if necessary.
> ► Steam food whole and in the skin whenever possible. It is
> most nutritious and saves you cutting and peeling time. It is
> even easier to remove skin or pits after cooking.

► Be careful not to let the water in the bottom of a steamer boil away during a long cooking time.
► Rinse the pot immediately after use for easy cleaning.

# THE ELECTRIC BLENDER

In the past, food had to be scraped and strained in small quantities. No wonder we heard that making our own baby food would be difficult and time-consuming!

Now, *electric blenders* have revolutionized the processing of baby food. The modern high-speed blenders can quickly and easily purée almost any food, even meats and poultry, into the finest consistency for the youngest infant. The blenders range in type from 4 speed to 16 speed, and some have specialty features or solid-state controls. The prices will vary accordingly, from $13 for a basic blender to $70 for one that cooks and stirs. You can find many blenders in the $13–$30 range that have the necessary speed for processing baby food.

## SELECTING A BLENDER

Here are some features that should be considered:
► Solid-state controls, which assure even processing at the lower speeds regardless of the load factor, are not a necessity in processing baby food where you will usually use the higher speeds. This feature does cost more.
► A blender with a *wide base* and larger blades is convenient because you do not have to cut the food into small pieces before blending. This blender is also excellent for processing *large* loads quickly and evenly. However, the wide base is a disadvantage in puréeing a small amount, since the food will disperse along the sides away from the blades. This problem will be helped somewhat if you leave the lid slightly ajar.

► Blenders with *narrow* bases are more suitable for making *small* amounts.

► Do not use the small drink blenders or coffee mills to process baby food.

► It will be neccessary with most blenders, when puréeing a heavy consistency, or a small amount, to carefully move the food from the sides of the container into the blade area with a rubber spatula.

► The *Mini-Blend jar,* an Oster blender attachment, is an innovation that offers the ideal solution for processing a small amount (1 cup or less) of food. The Mini-Blend jar is a heavy 8-ounce jar that screws onto the blade assembly, replacing the large container. After the food is puréed, a cap can be screwed on the jar and the jar can be used for storage. You will save your time and effort by blending, feeding, and storing in the same jar. You will find it most practical for puréeing leftovers, or food from the current family meal, into baby food. It is also very convenient to reblend food, in the container, to add more food, or to change the consistency.

► The Oster blender is sold with one jar, but additional jars may be purchased for $.69. Other jars, such as home-canning jars, with a 2½-inch neck and the proper screw thread, may be used, but may be less efficient in blending. Be careful not to use a light jar since the action of the food and the blades may cause it to break. In using any jar, do not fill it more than ¾ full to allow for expansion of the food during processing.

► If at all possible, look for and buy this type of blender and jars. You will have a head start on preparing your baby food easily and economically.

► Some other blenders can also accommodate the Mini-Blend and similar jars, although they are not advertised with this feature. You may check for this on your own blender by unscrewing the container from the base (if possible), and attempting to screw on a Mini-Blend jar.

► The *Cycle* or *Pulse* feature on some blenders is useful in chopping foods evenly. The blender will stop at intervals during processing. This is an advantage in controlling the coarseness of purées that you are preparing for an older baby. However, it is not a necessity and may add to the cost of the blender.

► Another advantageous feature of a blender is the ability to add ingredients through the top of the blender while it is operating, without removing the entire lid.

USING YOUR BLENDER

Your blender will easily process baby food if you use it properly and care for it. If you are not satisfied with the blender you already own, you may not be following the manufacturer's instructions. In general, these are the important things to remember in using any blender:

► Read the instruction book carefully. If you do not have one, you can write to the manufacturer, giving the model number.

► Set the blender on a clean, dry, solid surface.

► Be sure the cover is firmly in place before starting, and add ingredients through the top if possible.

► Do not place or remove the container from the base while the motor is running. Never leave the blender while processing.

► When using an older or less powerful blender, start the motor on a slower speed before adding ingredients, then switch to a faster speed.

► If liquids are used, pour them in before adding the dry ingredients.

► If the blender has a small base, cut the food, especially meats, poultry and cheese, into one-inch cubes.

► Allow boiling or steaming foods to cool slightly before blending.

► If you are puréeing a small quantity and it disperses along the sides, stop the motor, push the food down with a rubber spatula, and restart. It may be necessary to repeat this several times.

► Do not allow the motor to labor when processing a heavy or thick load. Either stir to introduce air, add liquid, or switch to a higher speed. If the mixture is very thick, make only a small amount at a time.

► If there is any burning smell, shut the motor off immediately, clean the blades and check the repair directions.

► Clean your blender immediately after use by adding some detergent and water and running the blender on a medium speed for a few seconds. Finely puréed foods can stick like glue if they are allowed to harden. Eventually the turning ability of the blades will be slowed.

► Do not put the blade assembly in the dishwasher because the lubricating oils will wash away and the blades will not turn easily, thereby putting strain on the motor.

► Remember that most blenders will not mash potatoes, grind raw meat or poultry, or extract juices from fruits and vegetables.

The way that you use your blender for preparing your baby's food depends upon the speed selectors and the general condition of your particular blender. In general, you will be using the highest speeds (*Blend, Frappé, Purée*) to process food for the youngest infant. These speeds will produce the finest consistency. As you prepare various types of food, you will soon find the proper speeds.

As your baby grows and after a food has been introduced, you can begin reducing the blender speed, processing time or using the cycle feature for a coarser consistency. If the baby has difficulty swallowing or digesting a particular consistency, it is easy to thin or reblend the food. However, your aim should be to accustom your baby to eating increasingly coarser food until he can chew and swallow small bits of regular table food at family meals. An electric blender will give you the most control and ease in regulating the consistency of your baby's food.

## REPAIRING YOUR BLENDER

When you are regularly using your blender to process your baby food, any breakdown is a major inconvenience. There are several faults that you can test for and repair yourself before you surrender your blender to the repair shop.

1. If the blender will not start and makes no sound: Plug another appliance into the outlet. If that does not start, then the outlet is at fault, not the blender.

    If the other appliance does start, then check the electric cord and the plug on the blender. If these are disconnected, you can buy a replacement plug at any hardware, or five-and-ten store.

2. If the blender hums and tries to start: *Stop* the blender. Remove the blender container from the motor base, start the blender to see if the mechanism that turns the blade assembly now turns. If it does not, then the fault is in the motor itself, and you will probably require professional repair. If you have access into the blender base, you can try to clean any encrusted food, then oil.

    If the motor is turning, then your problem may be the common one of a frozen blade assembly. Food has probably become lodged around the blades or under the turning axle. Soak the blade assembly in detergent or a penetrating oil, then clean with a brush and thin thread or dental floss, then lubricate. If the problem persists, you may be trying to process too heavy a load.

3. If the motor overheats or smokes: *Stop* the blender. Clean out any dust and food to allow for better cooling. Lubricate any parts of the motor you can reach. Clean the blade assembly as in the preceding section.

4. If the blender is very noisy or vibrates: *Stop the blender*. Check the blades for accidental bending and straighten

them. Lubricate the blade assembly and gearbox. If the problem persists, you will need professional repair.

Used carefully, the electric blender is a valuable aid in processing your baby food. It is fast, effortless, allows you to make large or small quantities, and gives you control over the consistency of the food. A blender is also the only way you will be able to prepare many raw foods, such as citrus purées, that are highly nutritious. If you do not already own one, try to purchase even a low-cost or used blender. It's a good investment. Aside from substantial savings in making your own baby food, the blender offers many uses and savings for the entire family.

## OTHER WAYS TO PURÉE

As handy as the blender is, there are alternative methods of processing food, which are still adequate, although slower. Some of these utensils are even more practical than some blenders for processing smaller amounts. Also, they are easy to carry or are readily available if you go away from home.

*Food Mills* can be purchased in small or large sizes for $3.00–$6.00. The food is placed in the basket, and, as you turn the rotary handle, the blade presses food through holes in the bottom of the basket. It is actually a more automatic version of the spoon and strainer method. It is, however, considerably faster and requires less effort. The food mill strains *most cooked foods*, with the exception of meat, to a smooth consistency acceptable to even the youngest infant. It also works well with *soft, raw fruits* such as bananas, pears, and plums. Meat and poultry will require more effort and will be processed more coarsely. The mill will purée liver or organ meats to a strained consistency that is fine enough to serve as a first meat food. *You may also prefer to use a mill to remove seeds, skin, and fibers from fruits or vegetables after cooking.* If you cannot use an electric blender, you will find the food mill is a very adequate utensil for processing your baby food, either in large or small batches.

*Graters* come in a wide range of types, sizes, and prices. Most will process food suitable for an *older baby,* with similar consistency to the junior foods. If you own one, experiment with various foods to see if you can achieve the right consistency for your baby. You may even use it for grating some raw fruits and vegetables. A grater is particularly useful in processing small amounts, so if you have an electric blender which does not work well with small loads, you may also want to use a grater.

A rotary grater, such as a Mouli, is especially efficient for making small amounts. The food is placed in the small magazine and is grated as you rotate the handle of the drum. By varying the pressure on the cover of the magazine, you can grate a fine or coarser consistency. It is safe, easy to clean, and small enough to carry when traveling.

*Strainers* are probably the oldest means of processing baby food, but they require time and effort for most foods. The food is strained by pushing it through holes in the strainer with the back of a spoon. This is impractical for making large quantities. Strainers vary in size and in the fineness of the holes. A fine strainer will purée fruits and vegetables comparable to the strained foods for the youngest infant. They are not usable for any meat or poultry.

The one strainer that you should keep handy, even if you are using a blender for other foods, is a *small, very fine strainer* to strain juices for your baby's bottle. You can carry it when traveling to prepare small servings of soft fruit and vegetables.

*Forks and Spoons* are the most available and least expensive means of preparing baby food. You will find them adequate for mashing some soft foods to a coarse texture. Some foods, such as bananas, egg yolks, or canned pears, can be mashed finely enough for the youngest infant. If a fork or spoon is the only means available at a particular mealtime, don't be afraid to experiment. A hungry baby can become very adept at swallowing!

## MISCELLANEOUS UTENSILS

There are also several ordinary household utensils that you should use in preparing baby food. You probably already own them.

- ▶ A stiff brush for cleaning fruits and vegetables. The most nutritious method of cooking produce is in the skin, but it must be free of dirt and chemicals.
- ▶ A good sharp paring knife with the slot in the middle of the blade. If it is necessary to remove the skin on produce, this knife will take the thinnest layer.
- ▶ A juicer for preparing fresh citrus juices. A manual juicer can be bought for around $3.00, while an electric juicer costs $20 and up. A juice extractor, sold through health food stores, can be used for any fruit and vegetable juice. They are very expensive, starting at $60, and not necessary.
- ▶ An egg beater, if you do not have a blender, for preparing fruit or egg beverages.

As you can see, the type of equipment that you will use in preparing your baby's food depends upon the amount of money, time, and effort you want to spend. You may already own many of these utensils or suitable substitutes. If you can co-ordinate preparation of your baby's food with that of the rest of the family, using the same equipment, you will save both money and effort. Just look at any piece of equipment and ask how you can use it. Discovering new uses for common utensils can be fun!

# RECOMMENDED EQUIPMENT LIST

Paring Knife
Vegetable Brush
Rubber Spatula
Hand Juicer
Six-quart Steamer/Blancher
Aluminum Foil
Electric Blender—varying speeds, good quality, with Mini-
  Blend jars
Food Mill
Small, fine Strainer

# 5

## THE SAFE AND HEALTHY WAY
## TO STORE FOODS

NUTRITIOUS, well-balanced meals may be planned for your baby, and the freshest and best quality foods purchased. However, you may still end up with food that is lower in vitamins. Storage is very important in the preservation of vitamins that can be destroyed by exposure to air and light. Improper handling and storage can also be dangerous to your baby's health, since bacteria, which is present in all food, can grow to harmful levels in just hours.

## HOW SPOILED FOOD CAN AFFECT
## YOUR BABY

Babies are particularly susceptible to digestive upsets and when you notice "something" did not agree with your baby, what may really have happened is that bacteria in poorly kept foods are causing the upset. The discomfort usually takes the form of gas or diarrhea. Other forms of bacteria can produce toxins which can be more harmful and even fatal. You should be aware of the dangers of improper handling and storage. The U. S. Department of Agriculture has published the following information on these bacterial illnesses:

*Salmonellosis* is caused by bacteria which are widespread in nature and live and grow in the intestinal tracts of human beings and animals. The bacteria grow and multiply at temperatures between 44° and 115° F. The symptoms are severe headache, followed by vomiting, diarrhea, abdominal cramps, and fever. Infants are particularly susceptible, and, of course, cannot tell you some of their symptoms. These bacteria in food can be destroyed by heating the food to a temperature of 140° and holding for 10 minutes, or to a temperature even higher for less time. Refrigeration at 45° or below inhibits the increase of these bacteria, but they remain alive in the refrigerator, freezer, and even in dried foods.

*Perfringens poisoning* is caused by bacteria that grows in the absence of oxygen, particularly in cooked meats, gravies, and meat dishes that are held without the proper refrigeration. The symptoms are nausea without vomiting, acute inflammation of the stomach and the intestines. To control the growth of surviving bacteria on cooked meats that are to be eaten later, you must cool the meats rapidly and refrigerate them immediately at 40° F. or below.

*Staph poisoning* produces mild symptoms of vomiting, diarrhea, and abdominal cramps that are often attributed to other causes. The growth of bacteria that produce the toxin is inhibited by keeping hot foods above 140° F. and cold foods at or below 40° F. The toxin is very difficult to destroy by heating.

*Botulism* is caused by a toxin that is produced in cans or sealed containers where there has been an absence of oxygen. The toxin produces severe symptoms of double vision, inability to swallow, speech difficulty, and progressive respiratory paralysis, with possible fatality. The bacteria can be destroyed by the high temperatures obtained only in a pressure canner. This form of posioning can occur through improper home-canning methods, especially with meats and vegetables. If you suspect a food, throw it away without tasting.

You should always contact a doctor if anyone in your family shows signs of the above-listed symptoms.

SIGNS OF SPOILAGE

While it is not always possible to detect—by taste, smell, or appearance—when food has become spoiled, some common signs are:

▶ Off odors
▶ Mold (green or white fuzzy spots)
▶ Fermented odor of fruit juices
▶ Rancid odor or flavor
▶ Slime on meats or poultry
▶ Sour tastes in bland foods
▶ Cans which are bulging, leaking, or spurting liquid when opened. *These conditions may be caused by botulism and the contents should be thrown away without tasting.*

# GENERAL RULES OF HANDLING AND STORING FOODS

If this introduction to the various types of food poisoning frightens you a little, that's good! If you are familiar with the possibilities of food poisoning, it need never occur with your baby or the rest of your family so long as you follow the basic rules of proper preparation and handling. Time and temperature are the important factors and the danger lies in holding foods for any length of time at temperatures above refrigerator temperature and below serving temperature of hot food. Remember:

▶ Work with clean hands when preparing food.
▶ Work with clean utensils, especially grinders, blenders, can openers, cutting boards. The bacteria in these surfaces can be destroyed by rinsing the utensil with chlorine laundry bleach in the proportion recommended on the package or bottle.

▶ Cook or prepare a food immediately after removing it from refrigeration. If you use the new automatic ovens, remember not to hold the food in the oven more than three hours before cooking.

▶ Cooked food, if not served immediately, should be cooled as quickly as possible. Put the dish in cold water if it cannot be put immediately in the refrigerator. Keeping the food cold will inhibit the growth of food-poisoning bacteria.

▶ The temperature range of 60°–120° is the most dangerous zone; one in which bacteria multiply quickly.

▶ When you are using leftovers as baby food, purée and use the recommended storage time from when they were first prepared.

## PURÉES NEED SPECIAL CARE

Prepared baby food is particularly susceptible to spoilage, since the food is usually creamed, puréed, or ground. More important, you probably serve your baby food that is warm, instead of hot or cold, and this is the temperature at which bacteria grows rapidly. The electric warming dishes are designed to hold food at this dangerous temperature. How often have you warmed food in preparation for a feeding, and then spent half an hour or more preparing your baby? Many babies are also notoriously slow eaters and a feeding may last another half hour. If he does not eat, you may feel the baby is not hungry just now, and put the food aside for a while. *Remember, that from the time the food is taken from the refrigerator, or out of the fresh jar, bacteria can be growing.* If there is leftover food, you may put it back to use at the next feeding, but the new refrigeration will only slow the bacterial growth which has occurred while the food has been out. Instead, follow these basic habits:

▶ If you prefer to warm your baby's food, do it immediately before his feeding.

▶ Only warm as much food as he usually eats, then throw

away the leftovers if it has been out for more than a half hour. (Since your homemade food was not as expensive as the commercial, you won't feel so guilty if you waste some.)
► Serve cold foods that adults usually eat cold, such as fruits, custards, and puddings. Even the youngest infant will eat cold food, if he is accustomed to it from birth. In addition to the lessened danger of food poisoning, you will find it very convenient when traveling or in a hurry.

Now, let's go into some detail on the various ways you can store your baby's food, both before and after you prepare it.

## PANTRY STORAGE

While most of the foods that you will use in preparing your baby food will require at least refrigeration, some foods can be stored in the pantry. The pantry or area used for storage should be in the coldest part of the kitchen, and away from the oven and refrigerator exhaust. A basement, where the temperature is 60°–68° F., is a good place for storage of certain vegetables and for long-term storage of canned goods. While most of the pantry foods will not spoil to a harmful degree, they will lose quality and texture. In general, keep most pantry foods, other than vegetables, covered, preferably in airtight containers, and dry. The following list gives suggested storage times for those foods you are most likely to use in preparing your baby's food.

| FOOD | TIME |
|------|------|
| Cereals, ready-to-eat | 4 months |
| dry | 6 months |
| | |
| Evaporated milk | 1 year |
| Non-fat dry milk | 6 months |
| Flour | 1 year |

| FOOD | TIME |
|------|------|
| Honey, Molasses | 1 year |
| Rice | 2 years |
| Pastas | 2 years |
| Bread | 1 week |
| Crackers | 3 months |
| Sugar, brown | 4 months |
| granulated | 2 years |
| Fruits, dried | 6 months |
| Vegetables, dried | 1 year |
| Soups, dried | 1 year |
| Bananas | Until yellow with brown spots |
| Oranges, Grapefruit, other citrus fruits | 1 week |
| Melons | 1 week |
| White Potatoes, Sweet Potatoes Onions, Hard Squash, Eggplant, Rutabagas | 1 week at room temperature 5 months at 60° F. |
| Peanut butter, unopened | 9 months |

Note: Canned foods are included in the section on Canned Storage.

## REFRIGERATOR STORAGE

Most fresh and perishable foods and all cooked foods require proper refrigeration. The low temperatures will retard spoilage by slowing the growth of bacteria and will also prevent the loss of essential nutrients. When storing food in your refrigerator, you should be aware that different areas can vary in their temperatures.

►The temperature range in the middle of the refrigerator should be 38°–42° F.

▶ The chill tray or meatkeeper, which is usually located next to the freezer compartment, should be the coldest area, about 32°–35° F.

▶ Milk, cheese, and other dairy products should also be kept in the coldest area.

▶ The temperatures at the bottom of the refrigerator and in the door are the highest.

▶ Heavy frost on the freezer unit and warm weather can cause temperatures to rise several degrees. At those times it may be necessary to use a colder temperature setting.

▶ The newer frost-free refrigerators and freezer combinations usually have more uniform temperatures, but different makes can vary.

The only way that you can be sure of setting your refrigerator controls to the proper setting is to check the temperature with a refrigerator thermometer or a common outdoor thermometer. At night, place the thermometer in the area of the refrigerator that you want to test, so that it does not touch any metal surface or grill. In the morning, read the thermometer when you open the door for the first time. If the temperature in the center of the refrigerator is 42° or above, change your control to a lower setting, and check again in a day or so.

Your refrigerator should be kept clean and any spoiled food should be removed immediately, since bacterial decay can be passed to other foods. The movement of air in the refrigerator will cause drying and loss of vitamin C, so tightly wrap, or cover, all foods, using plastic wrap, plastic bags, airtight containers, or foil. Beware of the practice of using aluminum foil to wrap small amounts of leftovers. Since you can't see the contents, it's easy to forget about these little packages until they have spoiled. Raw meat, poultry, and fish should be loosely covered to retard the growth of bacteria. (The only exceptions to covering are fruits and tomatoes, which keep longer uncovered.)

The following storage times are maximum and since you often

do not know how fresh the food is when you purchase it, use it as soon as possible and look for signs of spoilage before using. These storage times are based on the proper degree of refrigeration.

| FOOD | TIME |
|---|---|
| DAIRY | |
| Butter, margarine | 1–2 weeks |
| Yogurt | 5 days to 2 weeks |
| Cheese—cottage, ricotta | 5 days |
| cream, Neufchatel | 2 weeks |
| American, Cheddar, Swiss, etc. | 2 weeks, if sliced, 3–4 weeks, whole |
| Milk—liquid, reconstituted | 4–5 days |
| Evaporated, in open can | 4–5 days |
| Eggs—in shell, raw, cooked | 2 weeks |
| yolk and/or whites | 2 days |
| Custards, puddings, etc. | 3 days |
| FRUIT | |
| Apples | 1 week |
| Apricots, avocados, grapes, nectarines, pears, peaches, plums, and rhubarb | 3–5 days |
| Berries, cherries | 1–2 days |
| Pineapples, ripe | 2 days |
| Raw purées | 1 day |
| Cooked purées | 1 week |
| VEGETABLES | |
| Asparagus, broccoli, Brussels sprouts | 2 days |
| Cabbage | 1–2 weeks |
| Cauliflower | 3–5 days |
| Carrots, beets, radishes | 1–2 weeks |
| Green peas, limas, corn | 1–2 days |
| Lettuce and green, leafy | 1–2 days |
| Other vegetables | 3–5 days |
| Cooked purées | 2–3 days |

| FOOD | TIME |
|------|------|
| MEATS, FISH, POULTRY | |
| Uncooked meat | |
|   chops, roasts, steak | 3–5 days |
|   stew, ground | 1–2 days |
|   liver, kidneys, etc. | 1–2 days |
| Cooked meats and meat dishes | 2–3 days |
| Gravy, broth, or stuffing | 1–2 days |
| Fish—fresh or cooked | 1–2 days |
| Poultry—uncooked | 1–2 days |
| Frankfurters | 4–5 days |
| Ham—whole, halves, steaks | 5–7 days |
|   canned, unopened | 6 months |
| Cold cuts, cured meats | |
|   sealed | 3–5 days |
|   vacuum packages | 2 weeks |
| OTHER FOODS (opened) | |
| Wheat germ | 2 months |
| Cooking and Salad oils | 3 months |
| Honey, molasses | 1 year |
| Peanut butter | 6 months |

## FREEZER STORAGE

The freezer gives you the best opportunity to conveniently feed your baby with home-prepared foods. One of the most common reasons that women give for using commercial foods is that "it is too much trouble and time to make and purée food for each meal." Now, the freezer enables you to prepare and store several months' supply of food at one time . . . baby food that is fresh and ready to feed to your baby at a minute's notice.

Freezing preserves the nutritive value of food better than canning, and the value is nearly equal to that of fresh foods. The protein, fat, and carbohydrate content of food is not affected by freezing. There is little loss of vitamin C in frozen fruits and other vitamins and minerals are well retained.

Freezing foods will also prevent the growth of bacteria when the food is stored around 0° F. and used within the recommended time. The organism that produces the botulism toxin in canned non-acid and protein foods does not grow in frozen foods.

## HOW TO CHECK YOUR FREEZER TEMPERATURE

While we usually think of freezing temperatures as anywhere below 32° F., the long-term storage of high-quality foods requires a temperature of 0° F. or below. Storage temperatures above 10° F. will result in a rapid loss of nutritional value and quality. You can check your freezer temperature with an outdoor thermometer in the same way that you check the temperature of your refrigerator. Do not rest the thermometer on the freezer coils; instead place it on a frozen package in the middle of the freezer. Leave it in overnight and take a reading in the morning. If your freezer temperature is above 5° F., and you cannot set it lower, plan to store the frozen baby food for only two to three weeks. In the side-by-side refrigerator/freezers, there are often areas in the freezer that are above 10° F. These shelves should not be used for long-term storage.

## WHAT AND HOW TO FREEZE

You can freeze almost any raw or cooked food that you have prepared as baby food. You can save time and money by buying seasonal or sale foods and preparing large quantities of baby food. Or, you can also save time and money by puréeing and freezing small quantities of food that are left over from family meals. Here are some basic principles of proper freezing which will give you a ready supply of safe and nutritious foods for your baby.

► Cook or prepare food as soon after buying as possible, to prevent loss of nutrients and spoilage.

► After cooking, chill the food quickly in the refrigerator and freeze immediately.

► If you are using leftovers, don't allow them to sit at room temperature for too long. If possible, *purée* and freeze the leftover food immediately after the meal.

► It is important not to stir air into the puréed mixtures before freezing, so purée the food then allow it to settle. Watch out for this if you are using a blender.

► It is safe to freeze *cooked* baby food that has been prepared from frozen *raw* meats, fish, poultry, fruits, or vegetables.

► *Do not freeze* any baby food that has been prepared from food *already cooked, frozen,* and *thawed.* (See the section in this chapter on refreezing.)

► Freeze the food as quickly as possible to preserve the quality. Place the food directly on the freezing coils for fast freezing. If possible, lower the freezer temperatures below 0° F. when freezing large amounts.

► Wrapping materials are very important in terms of preservation and time-saving. Since the dry air of the freezer can produce a loss of moisture and nutrients, you must use a wrap that is moisture resistant and as airtight as possible. Rigid containers of aluminum or plastic and flexible freezer wraps, such as aluminum, plastic bags, or plastic wraps, can be used. The flexible wrapping requires that the ends be sealed with tape, and bags should be closed. A new type of storage bag even allows you to freeze food, then heat it by placing the entire bag in boiling water. Ordinary paper, waxed paper, and thin plastic wraps are not suitable.

► Thaw foods covered or in freezer packages.

These storage times are based on a freezer temperature of 0° F. The food may not spoil when kept longer or at higher temperatures, but it will lose nutritional value and quality. The following USDA times are given for fresh food that you may freeze before preparing and for raw and cooked baby food.

| FOOD | TIME |
|---|---|
| **FRESH** | |
| Ground pork | 3 months |
| Ground beef, lamb, veal | 4 months |
| Roasts, steaks | |
|   beef | 1 year |
|   lamb, veal | 9 months |
|   pork | 6 months |
| Fish, lean | 6 months |
| Chicken | 1 year |
| Turkey, duck | 6 months |
| Liver, kidneys, etc. | 3 months |
| | |
| Citrus-juice concentrates | 1 year |
| Fruit | 1 year |
| | |
| Vegetables | 8 months |
| | |
| Butter, margarine | 9 months |
| Cottage cheese | 3 months |
| Cream cheese | 1 month |
| Other cheese | 3 months |
| Milk | 3 months |
| Ice cream, ice milk, sherbet | 1 month |
| Eggs, whites, and/or yolks | 1 year |
| **COOKED OR PREPARED** | |
| Baked goods | 1–2 months |
| Ground beef, lamb, veal | 4 months |
| Ground pork | 2 months |
| Ground ham | 1 month |
| Liver, kidneys, etc. | 1 month |
| Frankfurters | 1 month |
| Bacon | 1 month |

| FOOD | TIME |
|------|------|
| Luncheon meats, cold cuts | 1 month |
| Fish | 2 months |
| Poultry | 3 months |
| | |
| Fruit purées | 1 year |
| Vegetable purées | 1 month |
| | |
| Combination dishes with gravy, sauces, etc. | 1 month |
| Soup—bean, split pea, lentil | 2 months |
| | |
| Steamed pudding | 6 months |
| Frozen desserts | 1 month |

### REFREEZING FOOD

You may want to refreeze food that has become accidentally thawed because of power failure. If the power fails, most freezers will maintain temperature below freezing for at least two days if the door is not opened. Or, you may begin to thaw food and then decide not to use it. It would be wasteful to have to throw the food away and you should be aware of when you can safely refreeze food.

► If there is any off-odor to the food, throw it away.
► Any food that is partially thawed and still contains ice crystals may be refrozen.
► Uncooked foods that are completely thawed, but are held at refrigerator temperature for no longer than one day may be refrozen. If the food has warmed above refrigerator temperature, do not refreeze.
► Cooked foods which are completely thawed cannot be refrozen. This applies to many baby foods.
► Commercially frozen fruits, vegetables, and red meats can legally be thawed and refrozen if they have been held at

refrigerator temperature for a day. Try to avoid buying any frozen foods that have been refrozen since there may be a loss of nutrients, texture, and flavor. Signs to look for are frost inside the package, boxes which are solid on the bottom with space at the top, and sweating or battered packages.

## FOOD CUBES

Since puréed and frozen baby food will spoil quickly after thawing, it is most efficient to freeze baby food in individual portions that can be taken out for a day's meals or, even better, before each feeding. I strongly recommend the following method of freezing your baby food as both convenient and safe.

1. Cool the puréed food quickly.
2. Pour it into ice-cube trays. The individual plastic cubes are ideal if you can find them. Cover with wrap.
3. Freeze the food cubes quickly.
4. For long-term storage, transfer the frozen food cubes to plastic freezer bags, cover and seal.
5. Date and label the containers. Frozen baby-food purées all look the same. In general, keep the protein foods, cereals, vegetables, and fruit in separate containers. It's easier to select a meal.
6. Before a meal, take out the food you want to serve. Allow half an hour to thaw at room temperature, or you can thaw and heat the cubes quickly in the oven or warming dish.

You will find this method is really the key to feeding your baby easily and conveniently with food you have prepared yourself. You can always keep an adequate supply on hand and you will never need to rush to prepare food for a hungry baby.

## CANNED FOODS

Canning is a widely used form of preserving food. Commercially canned foods are usually safe from food poisoning and retain a large amount of vitamins and minerals, although less than frozen foods. Many of the foods that you will feed your baby can be prepared directly from cans, so it is important to know how to buy and store canned goods.

► Do not buy or use cans that are leaking, have bulging ends, or spurt liquid when opened. These may be signs of botulism and the food should be thrown out without tasting.
► When buying vacuum-packed jars, be sure the lid has not been opened.
► The ideal temperature for storing canned goods for more than one month is 65° F. At this temperature vitamins are well retained for as long as a year.
► In general, the longer the storage period and the higher the storage temperature, the greater the loss of nutrients.
► Read the labels carefully to select brands of canned goods which have the fewest additives and are without unnecessary sugar or salt.
► Where possible, buy food that is packed in its own juices. *About one-third of the water-soluble vitamins and minerals in canned food and vegetables will be in the liquid.* To get the full nutritive value, use this liquid or juice as a thinner when preparing your baby's food. Or, strain it and serve it as a beverage.
► Wash the top of a can before opening. If you are opening a vacuum-packed jar with a turn-off lid, rinse under the edge of the lid. The air rushing in when you open the jar will pull in any dirt under the lid. When you open a vacuum-packed jar, listen for the "pop" sound. If you do

not hear it, the jar may have been previously opened and the food spoiled.

▶ Opened canned food can be covered tightly and stored in the refrigerator in the original jar for the recommended time. I prefer not to store food in opened metal cans.

The maximum storage times for opened canned food that is stored in the refrigerator at 35°–40° F. are as follows:

| | |
|---|---|
| Meats | 2 Days |
| Fish | 1 Day |
| Poultry | 1 Day |
| Fruit | 1 Week |
| Vegetables | 3 Days |
| Soups | 2 Days |
| Tomato-based Sauces | 5 Days |
| Citrus Juices | 3 Days |
| Evaporated Milk | 4–5 Days |

## HOME CANNING

Canning your own baby food is an alternative to the frozen "food cube" method, especially if you do not have adequate freezer space. If you are already an experienced home canner and you own the necessary equipment, canning your prepared baby food is convenient and safe. You may do your baby-food purées at the same time you are canning food for the family. You can use the smallest size canning jars.

Unless you are already doing your own canning, it will not be worth the time and expense to start for the few months that you will be preparing baby food. Fruit is the one food that might be worth experimenting with, since it is inexpensive and nutritious in season. For fruit and tomatoes that contain acid, the safe method of canning is quite simple. The method used is called the "boiling-water-bath canner."

▶ Use a metal pot with a tight-fitting cover and a rack on the bottom on which to rest the jars. The steamer/blancher described in the *Equipment* chapter can be used.

▶ Prepare the fruit or tomato purée as for baby food.

▶ Pour the hot purée in the clean jars. The jars and lids should be freshly washed, but do not need sterilization.

▶ Pack within ¼ inch of the top and close the lids.

▶ Immerse the jars in the boiling water. Make sure that the tops of the jars are covered with an inch of water.

▶ Cover and boil for 10–15 minutes.

▶ Store as for commercially canned fruits.

Other vegetables, meats, poultry, and fish can only be safely canned with a pressure canner, following specific times for each of the various foods. Improperly canned vegetables and protein foods can allow the growth of the toxin that causes botulism—the most harmful of food poisoning. If you are interested in learning how to can all types of food, send for the booklets published by the Department of Agriculture that are listed in the Bibliography or buy a good canning cookbook.

# 6

## THE BABY-FOOD SYSTEM

SINCE YOU probably want to spend as little time as possible preparing your own baby food, in the following recipe chapters you will find everything you may want to know about any food you choose to prepare for your baby. You should not have to refer to any other cookbook. But first, here are the essentials of the easy baby-food system, and it really is easy if you know how.

## HOW TO PLAN

The most important fact to remember in preparing your own baby food is that you must *plan ahead*. The last thing that you want to do is to cook and purée your baby's meal while he is shrieking with hunger. Just as you would buy a supply of the commercial baby foods, you should plan to keep on hand a supply of frozen food cubes (see *Food Cubes* in chapter 5); or fresh, canned, or frozen "instant foods." (See *Instant Baby Food,* chapter 13.) This supply is particularly important when your baby is young and eating only a limited variety of foods. Even when your baby is older and is eating more family foods, this planning is very convenient.

You can also save money by preparing large amounts of foods that are in season or are on sale. You don't have to worry about a large variety, just make a balanced selection of a few highly nutritious foods (see *Nutrition* chapter) and use the simplest recipes. Or, prepare a large supply of all-in-one meals, such as stews.

Just remember not to make more food than your baby will eat in the recommended safe freezing or storage time. Also, do not make a large amount of a food until you have successfully introduced it to your baby. This is especially important with the foods that tend to cause allergies.

You can plan to feed your baby entirely from this store of home-prepared or *instant* foods as conveniently as if you were buying baby food. Of course, if a family dish is ready and suitable, you can always purée it and serve it to your baby.

## HOW TO SAVE TIME

The most convenient and easiest time for you to prepare baby food is when you are already in the kitchen making your family's food. You will also save time and effort by making large amounts of various foods at the same time. To save preparation and cooking time:

► Prepare the *same kind of food* for your baby that you are making for your family. The recipe section is designed so you can easily look up any food. For example, if you are cooking fried chicken, put a few pieces in the steamer for Chicken Purée. This will also save you time marketing.
► Use the *cooking method* that fits in with the way you are already cooking. (But never fry foods for your baby.) If you are using your oven for roasting, then use a recipe for baking or aluminum-foil steaming.
► Whenever possible, use leftovers from family meals.

To save clean-up time:

► Cook your baby's food in the same pots or steamer that you have used for your family's vegetables.
► Cook several fruits, vegetables, meats, etc., in the same pot, baking dish, or steamer. You can then purée them separately or in any combination.
► Remember that you can cook almost any food by wrapping

it in aluminum foil and steaming it in a 325° F. oven. There is no cleanup, just throw the foil away.

► Purée different foods, one after another. You will only need to quickly rinse your blender or food mill in between each food. It is always easier to use this equipment when it is already out.

## • HOW TO USE LEFTOVERS

One of the easiest and most economical ways to prepare baby food is to combine leftovers from family meals. The cooking is already done. You can use any food that you have already introduced, as long as it is not highly seasoned or fried. Just be sure that the food, especially the meat, poultry, or fish, has not been kept for more than a day. *Use "fresh" leftovers!*

You can even plan to have leftovers from the family dishes that your baby can eat. If you make a large batch, you can freeze enough for a month or two and always have a nutritious meal on hand. Or, you can purée just a small amount to serve your baby the next day. It's even easier if you have a blender with the Mini-Blend jar—you can blend, store, warm, and serve the meal and only wash one jar.

## MEAL-IN-ONE LEFTOVER PURÉE

Here is a well-balanced, all-in-one meal that you can prepare from any leftovers. The recipe will help you use the right amounts and types of food, but you can use your imagination and the *Food-Combination Guide* in combining other foods.

1 cup cubed cooked poultry, meat, organ meat, fish
⅔ cup vegetables or fruit (raw or cooked)
½ cup cooked rice, noodles, or cereal
1 cup (or less) liquid (cooking juice, vegetable, or fruit juice)

1. Place liquid in blender. Add other ingredients.
2. *Purée* to desired consistency.
3. Freeze in food cubes at once. Can be kept frozen for 1–4 months depending on the type of food that is used. (See chapter 5.)

YIELD: 3 cups or 15 food cubes or 4 to 5 meals.

## HOW TO PURÉE

The type of equipment that you use to prepare purées depends upon what is available, as well as the consistency that your baby will swallow. In general, you should gradually increase the coarseness of the food so that your baby easily makes the transition to finger and family foods at an early age. This is one of the advantages in making your own baby food. If you make a food too coarse and your baby rejects it, you can just go back to a smoother texture.

Under the specific foods, I have suggested the best equipment to use in preparing purées of different textures. Here are some general guidelines.

► Use an *electric blender* for almost any food. You can vary the speed and blending time for a smooth or coarse purée. The only foods that should not be puréed in a blender are those with skins (if your baby is not eating skins), fibers, such as raw celery, or seeds.

► Use a *food mill* for most foods except meats and poultry. Organ meats can be puréed, but it is a very slow process. The food mill is an excellent way to purée while removing skins, fibers, and seeds of either raw or cooked foods. (You will find it is easy to cook a food unpeeled or cored, such as apples, and then strain with the food mill after it has been cooked.) The mill also produces a very smooth purée.

► A *hand grater* can be used to grate small amounts of

raw vegetables such as carrots or beets. These foods will not be as smooth as those made with a blender. Chilled meats and poultry can also be grated very fine. A rotary grater is the easiest to use.

▶ A *strainer* is a slow version of a food mill. It will make a very fine purée of most foods but is not suitable for meats and poultry.

▶ A *fork or spoon* is adequate for preparing coarser purées or for mashing smooth foods such as egg yolks or bananas. You can also use a spoon to scrape smooth purées from some raw fruits or cooked meats.

See *Equipment* chapter for more specific instructions on purées.

### THINNING—THICKENING

Many of the purées that you will make will need some kind of thinning, a few will require thickening. I have found that the terms "a little" or "enough" liquid are not satisfactory. If you make a mistake in preparing a large amount of baby food, you will end up with either soup or glue. So, in all the recipes I have given specific amounts for thinning and thickening your purées. Depending on your own baby's preferences, you can change the amounts. Remember that the thicker a purée is, the more original nutrients the specific food serving will contain.

One of the advantages of making your own purées is that you can thin purées with more nutritious liquids than plain water, and thicken them without using refined flour or food starch. This is where you can make every bite count!

| NUTRITIOUS THINNERS | NUTRITIOUS THICKENERS |
|---|---|
| Fruit juice | Egg yolk (hard-boiled) |
| Vegetable juice | Wheat germ (whole or ground) |
| Cooking or canning water (boiled down, without salt) | Soybean purée |
| Evaporated milk (undiluted) | Whole wheat or soy flour (in cooked purées) |
| Milk (whole or skim) | Cooked whole-grain cereal —oatmeal, rice |
| | Non-fat dry milk powder |

You can improve the consistency or "swallowability" of some foods by adding a little mayonnaise, white sauce, yogurt, or butter or oil.

A specific thinning liquid or thickener may be mentioned in a recipe. If you do not have it on hand, you can pick a substitute from the above list.

## FOOD-COMBINATION GUIDE

Here is another way to change the consistency and flavor of your baby-food dishes without using liquid thinners or sweeteners. You can combine foods according to their tastes and juiciness, either when cooking or during a feeding. The following guide is useful as a quick reference, and you can have some fun in making up some unusual, but nutritious combinations. Your baby may love peanut butter and bananas, or peaches and lima beans, or fish and oranges.

|  | THIN | MEDIUM | THICK |
|---|---|---|---|
| SWEET | apple, sweet, cooked<br>apricots<br>beets, cooked<br>cherries, sweet<br>grapes, sweet<br>guava<br>mango<br>melon<br>nectarine<br>papaya<br>peaches<br>pears<br>banana | beets, raw<br>carrots<br>banana<br>corn<br>peas<br>apple, sweet, raw | parsnips |
| BLAND | asparagus<br>cucumber<br>mushrooms<br>squash, summer | avocado<br>beans, green<br>beans, wax<br>cauliflower<br>squash, winter | cereal<br>cooked dried<br>   peas, beans,<br>   lentils<br>potatoes<br>rice<br>egg yolk<br>chicken<br>fish<br>meat |
| SOUR<br>or<br>STRONG | apple, sour, cooked<br>berries<br>eggplant<br>grapefruit<br>lemon<br>orange<br>onions<br>okra<br>pepper<br>rhubarb<br>cherries, sour<br>tomatoes | apple, sour, raw<br>Brussels sprouts<br>broccoli<br>leafy greens<br>pineapple<br>turnips<br>rutabagas | peanut butter<br>wheat germ<br>ham |

# HOW TO USE AND MODIFY THE RECIPES

The recipes in the following chapters contain specific detail and you can "go by the book." I have also shown how you can modify any recipe to *your* convenience. This is more important than using the exact ingredients or cooking methods and is really the key to the easy preparation of baby foods. Please feel free to substitute as shown in the previous section on *How to Purée*. Just keep in mind the general principles of healthy simple cooking.

Most of the recipes are also simplified in the use of seasonings and flavorings. The last thing you want to do is to accustom your baby to the controversial adult preferences for salted or sweetened foods. So resist the temptation to taste and season the baby foods that you are preparing. You do want to teach your baby to enjoy the natural flavors of foods that can be simply and easily prepared.

### COOKING METHODS AND TIMES

One thing to avoid is *overcooking*. Just because you will *purée* a food does not mean that you have to cook it to a pulp. Many foods even become tough and stringy when they are overcooked. I have also found that the longer you cook a food, the more likely you are to forget and leave it on the fire. Burned liver has a powerful smell and it is almost impossible to clean the pot! In general, cook your baby food to a minimum, just until it can be easily puréed and digested.

Fortunately, *the most nutritious cooking is the simplest*. Many vitamins and minerals can be lost in water, air, or high heat. So, try to steam your baby food in a tightly covered container, with little or no water, and over a low heat. The cooking times given in the recipes, especially for fruits and vegetables, are minimum times for whole food to be puréed in a blender. You can decrease cooking time by cutting food into smaller pieces, but you will lose nutrients. You may have to increase the time if you are using equipment other than a blender.

SALT

Dr. Lewis K. Dahl, head of the Research Medical Service of Brookhaven National Laboratory, has stated that "a baby's needs for salt are amply satisfied by the salt it gets from either mother's or cow's milk." Your baby will also obtain natural salt from many foods he eats, especially meats. So, there is no need to add salt in food that you prepare especially for your baby, and research has shown that high intake of salt in infancy might be related to high blood pressure in later life. Very few of the recipes in this book contain salt. If you are preparing food for the rest of your family and want to use salt, try to add it after you have separated your baby's portion. But, for the sake of convenience, you may occasionally feed your baby a family dish that contains some salt. Remember, it is the use of *large* amounts of salt that may be harmful. If you live in an inland area, your baby may even benefit by the use of small amounts of iodized salt as a source of iodine.

FATS AND OILS

Whether or not you use saturated fats (butter) or un-saturated fats (vegetable oils) in cooking food, or preparing purées, depends upon your doctor's advice. (See section on *Fat* in chapter 1.) *Linoleic Acid* is an essential fatty acid that is best supplied by corn, soy, peanut, and safflower oils and in mayonnaise. Butter contains almost no linoleic acid. The one type of fat that most doctors and nutritionists feel should be *avoided* is the hydrogenated or hardened vegetable oils, which are used in solid shortenings or margarine. If you use margarine, read the labels and select the ones that list *"liquid (vegetable) oil"* as the first and major ingredient.

SWEETENERS

There are very few foods that will require sweetening for your baby to eat them. Although children and adults put a value on "sweets" and dislike very sour foods, it is unlikely that your baby has been born with these preferences. Research has shown that babies cannot tell the difference between sweet and sour tastes. You can test this out on your baby. Just give him a slice of lemon, and the chances are he will suck it with relish. So there is no need to load his food with sugar and train him in a habit that can contribute to tooth decay and overweight in later years. Your baby will get enough natural sugar from fruits, vegetables, and milk. You may also combine naturally sweet fruits and vegetables with sour ones. However, if you want to use sugar, as when you are preparing a dessert for the whole family, you may choose sweeteners other than refined white sugar; sweeteners that do have food value other than carbohydrates.

*Molasses* is the brown syrup that remains when most of the sugar has crystallized. It contains more vitamins, and minerals (especially high in iron) than any other form of sweetening. The darkest molasses (blackstrap) contains the most nutrients and is often used as a fortifier. It can have a laxative effect.

*Brown sugar* is usually processed sugar that has molasses added; however this does add some vitamins and minerals, especially in the dark brown type.

Raw sugar, often called turbinado sugar, is not refined. You can find it in "health food" stores and some supermarkets, but it is fairly expensive in spite of the lower processing cost.

*Honey* contains the same amount of vitamins as brown sugar, but is lower in minerals. The type of sugar in honey is fructose, which is easily digested since it is already in a form that can be absorbed by the body. The lighter colored honey usually has the mildest flavor. Some honey is graded by the government and the Grade B or Choice is adequate for use in cooking.

The honey should be added, if possible, after the food is cooked to prevent change in flavor.

Store molasses, brown sugar, and honey in tightly covered containers in a dry place for several months. If honey crystallizes, you can place it in a pan of warm water until the crystals disappear.

If you do use sweeteners:

► In most recipes you can substitute brown sugar or honey in place of white sugar. Use the same amounts.

► Do not use honey in making teething cookies, since the honey will keep the baked goods moist. Use brown sugar.

► Molasses can be substituted for half of the amount of sugar that the recipe calls for.

► You can add very small amounts of dark molasses (¼–½ teaspoon) to your baby's bottle once a day as a fortifier, but remember that blackstrap molasses can act as a laxative.

## MEASUREMENTS

Since you may want to change any recipe to make either a single serving or a month's supply, these equivalent measures are useful.

| | | |
|---|---|---|
| 3 teaspoons | = | 1 tablespoon |
| ⅛ cup | = | 2 tablespoons |
| ¼ cup | = | 4 tablespoons |
| ⅓ cup | = | 5 tablespoons + 1 teaspoon |
| ½ cup | = | 8 tablespoons |
| ⅔ cup | = | 10 tablespoons + 2 teaspoons |
| ¾ cup | = | 12 tablespoons |
| 1 cup* | = | 16 tablespoons |
| 2 cups | = | 1 pint |
| 4 cups | = | 1 quart |

*1 cup makes about 5 food cubes. 1 food cube equals about 3 tablespoons or 1½ ounces. (See *Food Cubes*, chapter 5.)

SUBSTITUTIONS

Here is a handy list to use with any recipe, showing how to substitute a more nutritious ingredient or what to use if you do not have a certain food on hand.

1 whole egg = 2 egg yolks

1 cup buttermilk = 1 cup milk + 1 tablespoon vinegar or lemon juice.

1 cup whole milk = ½ cup evaporated milk + ½ cup water = 1 cup skim milk + 2½ teaspoons vegetable oil

1 cup skim milk = ⅓ cup non-fat dry milk powder + 1 cup water

1 part corn starch = 2 parts flour = 4 parts dry infant cereal

1 cup white flour = ¾ cup whole-wheat flour + 20 % more moisture

1 cup white or whole-grain flour: replace 3 tablespoons with soy flour

1 cup dry cereal: add up to ½ cup wheat germ

1 cup white sugar = 1 cup brown sugar = 1 cup honey = ½ cup molasses + ½ cup white sugar.

The following recipes are divided into chapters according to their main nutritional food group—**Cereal Grains, Fruits, Vegetables, and Protein Foods.** I have arranged the recipes in this way so that you can easily select a balanced diet for your baby. (See *Planning a Balanced Menu* in chapter 3.) Some recipes, such as desserts, stews, leftovers, custards, etc., are combinations of different food groups.

You will see there is a very wide variety of foods, including some you may not have thought of as baby food. You may easily look up any food that you have on hand, or are preparing for your family, to see if and how you can serve it to your baby. Please do not feel that you have to try every food or recipe.

Most of the recipes give very basic and easy instructions on how to prepare a food in the most nutritious way, and, short of puréeing, *they can be used to prepare plain food that anyone can enjoy.* There are also some recipes that are often *family favorites* and that only require puréeing for your baby to enjoy them.

In selecting and using any of these recipes, remember to always keep in mind what is most convenient for *you!*

# 7

## CEREAL GRAINS

THE VARIOUS CEREAL GRAINS are highly economical sources of protein (incomplete), carbohydrates, minerals, the B vitamins and vitamin E. They also contain trace elements that are essential in a balanced diet. You should include 2–3 servings in your baby's daily menu. The grains are processed into many products that your baby can eat—cereals, flour, pastas, baked goods, rice, etc. The different grains are:

Oats (highest in protein, iron, and fat),

Wheat (used mainly for flours and cereal, possible source of allergy),

Barley (slightly laxative),

Rice (lowest in protein, good for treatment of diarrhea),

Corn (corn meal and grits),

Rye and Buckwheat.

The amount of nutritional value in any cereal grain depends in large part on the way it was processed or refined. All cereal grains start out as *whole-grain*. If they are processed, the *bran*, which is the outer covering, is removed and a large amount of the B vitamins and minerals are lost. Often the *germ*, or heart of the grain, is removed. This is the most nutritious part of the grain and contains the highest amounts of protein, minerals, vitamin E, and the essential fatty acids. If the bran and germ are removed, the resulting grain is mostly starch, highly refined, and should *not* be counted as a *cereal* serving, since it lacks the iron, protein, and other nutrients that are essential to your baby.

The federal government, in order to prevent deficiencies, has set minimum levels of voluntary enrichment for four of the nutrients lost in the refining process—thiamine, riboflavin, niacin, and iron. The other B vitamins, vitamin E, and many minerals are still missing in refined, enriched cereal grains. Do read the label for the term "enriched" and read the list of ingredients to identify those products that may be enriched such as breakfast cereals, baked goods, pastas, and rice. You can also compare the levels of enrichment, since some brands use higher amounts than the minimum levels. In general, the "enriched" products are more expensive than the original whole-grain products, since you are paying for the cost of refining, and also enrichment.

In the wide variety of cereal products, it is confusing and difficult to identify those products that are *whole-grain*. Often the label will proudly state "whole-grain" or "stone ground." Some other products are whole-wheat flour, unbleached flour, rye flour, cracked wheat, barley, oatmeal, oat flour, brown rice, whole-wheat cereals, kasha, and whole-grain corn meal. It is worth your time and money to read labels in order to buy whole-grain products or at least enriched ones. Remember that these cereal grains are your baby's main sources of many of the essential nutrients.

If you understand and keep in mind the differences between the various grains and ways of processing, you will be able to select the most nutritious products which include *cereals; rice; pasta, flours* and *baked goods;* and *wheat germ.*

## • CEREALS

**Nutrition:** Cereals are high in incomplete protein, iron, and B vitamins, and contain fair amounts of vitamin E and minerals. The cereals are particularly important in your baby's early months to supply the iron and niacin that are low in milk.

**Introduce:** In general, the dry infant cereals can be started as early as four weeks, enriched refined cereals at two months, and whole-grain cereals at four to five months.

**Buy:** As you have seen, the amounts of the nutrients vary due to the type of processing and enrichment. So, it is important to look at the different types of cereals that you can feed your baby.

*Precooked dry infant cereals* are produced by the major commercial baby-food companies. They include oatmeal, barley, mixed cereals, rice, and high protein. They have been refined, then enriched with high levels of niacin, riboflavin, thiamine, and particularly iron. The amount of enrichment is the same for each cereal made by the same company; however, the amount of enrichment varies among the different companies. The *high-protein* cereals provide 2–5 times more protein at the same cost.

It is important to read the nutritional information on the packages since the manufacturers may change the levels of enrichment and you should select those with the highest amounts. Remember that the nutritional information or percentages are based on one ounce of dry cereal, which will make a serving of ⅓ cup. This may be more than most babies, especially in the early months, can eat at one meal. It may be more realistic to consider that one ounce as two cereal servings.

You should also remember that the other B vitamins and minerals that were lost in processing may not have been replaced. *But, most important, these cereals do offer the highest source of iron, especially for the first four months, and are the most convenient to prepare and the smoothest in texture.* So you should serve them to your baby.

*Do not use* the sweetened variety of these cereals, since they often contain additives. The sweetening is unneccessary and only accustoms your baby to sugar at the earliest possible age. You should *avoid the wet-pack* jars of cereal, or cereal-fruit, cereal-egg combinations. As of this writing, their iron enrichment is far below that of the dry cereals. You are also paying a very high price for a jar that is more than 80 per cent liquid. Since you are feeding your baby cereals to give him specific nutrients, you should be sure that he is getting them by selecting and diluting the cereal yourself, always with milk or formula.

*Whole-grain cereals* are more difficult for very young babies to digest, but they can be introduced by four or five months. They should not be given to a baby who has diarrhea. These cereals supply all the B vitamins, especially $B_6$, $B_{12}$, and folic acid, plus the other minerals that are in the original cereal grains. Their iron level is not as high as the dry infant cereals, but by this time your baby will be getting iron from meat, egg yolk, and other foods.

You can conveniently use the same types of whole-grain cereals that you serve your family, such as oatmeal, Ralston, Wheatena, kasha, and barley. There is a Swiss cereal, "Baby Familia," that is often available in supermarkets or can be ordered. This is a highly nutritious and convenient whole-grain cereal that is precooked and only requires thinning with milk.

*The refined enriched cereals* include enriched farina (wheat), enriched cream of wheat, and enriched cream of rice. Again, read the labels and select the brand with the highest level of enrichment. Some may be fortified with vitamins A and D, and calcium; however they are usually more expensive and these vitamins are supplied in other foods that your baby is eating. The level of their iron enrichment varies and often is lower than that of the dry infant cereals. Read the label to make certain that $\frac{1}{2}$ ounce of the uncooked cereal or $3\frac{1}{2}$ ounces of the cooked cereal supplies at least 6 mg. of iron. These cereals can be used if no other cereal is available, but you may as well serve the dry infant cereals until your baby can eat the whole-grain cereals.

Store all cereals in tightly covered containers at cool room temperature and they may be kept for several months. Cooked cereals can be covered and stored in the refrigerator for 1–2 days. If your family does not regularly eat cooked whole-grain cereals, and you want to feed them to your baby, you will find it convenient to cook a quantity and freeze the cereal in food cubes for up to one month. *Two cups of cooked cereal will make about 10 cubes or servings.*

PREPARING CEREAL

In general, when preparing a specific cereal, you should follow the instructions that are printed on the box. To increase the nutritional value, or save time, you can also:

▶ Dilute all instant cereals with milk or formula, usually 1 part cereal to 6 parts liquid. You should gradually decrease the amount of dilution so that the cereal is as thick as your baby will eat. *It is the cereal that is important here, not the milk.*

▶ You can fortify the dry infant cereals by mixing in grated or regular wheat germ. (See *Wheat Germ*, this chapter.) Use about ½ teaspoon wheat germ for each 1 teaspoon of dry cereal.

▶ If you have a blender, you can grind regular oatmeal very finely so that it is more easily digested. One part of the ground oatmeal can be mixed with 3 parts hot milk. This ground oatmeal can also be used as a nutritious thickener.

▶ If you want to serve your baby cooked whole-grain cereals at an early age, you can also strain or purée them in a blender after cooking. However, the amount of iron will still be less than in the dry infant cereals.

▶ Pearl barley can be cooked, then mashed with a small amount of milk. It is one of the more digestible whole-grain cereals.

▶ You can always use milk instead of water when you are cooking any cereal. The milk is important in supplementing the incomplete cereal protein. Reconstituted non-fat dry milk is an inexpensive milk to use in cooking.

▶ Cooked cereals will be creamier and smoother if you put the cereal into the cold water, or milk, and then bring them to a boil together.

▶ You can use any instant cereal as a nutritious thickener for juicy fruits and vegetables. Add ¼–½ teaspoon dry cereal to each ¼ cup of purée (or 1–2 teaspoons per cup).

► You can also save any cooked cereal that is left over from the family breakfast, or even make some extra, to use as a thickener.

## • FLOUR, PASTA, BAKED GOODS

**Nutrition:** Flour and products made from flour—breads, noodles, spaghetti, crackers, etc.—have the same nutritional value as the grains that they are made from. They can be substituted for a cereal serving; for example, *1 slice whole-wheat bread=½ cup oatmeal=2 tablespoons whole-wheat flour.* As with any cereal grain, the nutritional value depends on the amount of processing and enrichment. Durum flour, often used in pastas, contains the most protein.

**Introduce** baked goods like hard crackers and toast around six months as a teething food, but your baby will not eat enough at first for this to count as a cereal serving. Spaghetti and noodles can be added around seven months. Unbleached or whole-wheat flour can be used as a thickener at any time.

**Buy:** It is very important for you to read labels on flour and flour products in order to buy those that are whole grain or enriched. *Do not buy* or use any refined flour or product that lists as the main ingredient: "flour," "wheat flour," "white flour," "rice flour," or "bleached flour." These cannot be counted as a *cereal* serving. Remember that if it is enriched, it will read "enriched flour."

Whole-grain flours are often listed as "whole-wheat flour," "unbleached flour," "rye flour." You should avoid the whole-grain breads which contain entire pieces of grains, since these will be difficult for a young baby to digest. They can be served from eight months on. Soy flour contains the largest amounts of many nutrients and the protein is also complete. It can be substituted for one-eighth of the flour in any recipe. Unbleached and whole-wheat flours can be substituted in most recipes calling for "flour," with the exception of cake flour. Other whole-grain flours are available in special stores, but these require the use of recipes that are designed for them.

**Starches:** You should not confuse starches with flours. Starches are extracted from cereal grains and they are almost completely carbohydrate. They do not contain protein, vitamins, or minerals that are present in flours. Starches are widely used as thickeners in prepared foods, especially in the commercial baby foods. They are also difficult for your baby to digest.

You can recognize these starches in the list of ingredients by the names "corn starch," "rice starch," "tapioca," and "modified food starch." *Do not buy* any prepared food that contains these as major ingredients. *Do not use* these to thicken any of your home-prepared baby foods. If a recipe calls for starch, you can substitute twice that amount of flour.

**Store** flours in tightly covered containers in the refrigerator for long periods or in hot weather. Breads and pastas should be placed in plastic bags and stored at room temperature.


USING FLOUR

Beside the common use of flour in recipes for baked goods, there are other ways that you can use enriched, whole-wheat, and soy flour.

► You can use a small amount of flour to thicken cooked fruits and vegetables.
► You can substitute flour for corn starch (non-nutritive) in most recipes if you use twice the amount.
► Supplement the protein in flour by adding non-fat dry milk powder to any recipe. You can add at least 2 table-spoons of non-fat dry milk powder for each cup of liquid that is used. Mix the powder in with the dry ingredients.
► Substitute 2 tablespoons of soy flour in each cup of flour called for in a recipe.

## USING BAKED GOODS

► You can use whole-wheat bread crumbs, finely ground in a blender, as a thickener for fruit and vegetable purées.

► You can soften graham crackers, arrowroot cookies, and other enriched baked goods that will absorb milk, into a soft mush. These are a change from the regular cereals and are a good instant food. Do read the labels on these products to avoid those with additives, especially the controversial preservative BHT.

► Whole-grain or enriched breads and cakes can be sliced and baked in a very slow oven (250° F.) until they are very hard. The slices make excellent teething foods and snacks.

## USING PASTA

► When pastas are combined with small amounts of *Protein foods,* such as in spaghetti and meat balls, they make economical *cereal/protein* dishes that are filling dinner dishes. (See *Noodle* and *Cheese Pudding.*)

► Do not wash noodles or spaghetti before cooking. After cooking, drain the noodles of most excess water but do not rinse them. You can use a small amount of the cooking water as a thinner and add some non-fat dry milk powder as a protein supplement.

► You can also easily purée any pasta dish that you have cooked for your family as long as it is not highly seasoned or contains foods that you have not already introduced.

► You can even plan to cook an extra amount and take out your baby's food before adding seasonings or foods that he is not accustomed to.

► Pasta dishes can easily be mashed and puréed, using a strainer, food mill, or blender. You may have to add a little more milk or juice to thin, about 3 tablespoons for each cup of pasta.

▶ These puréed foods may be frozen in food cubes for up to one month.

▶ You can use any of the canned pasta dishes and you will save preparation time. They are almost instant foods since they require only a blender or food mill for smooth puréeing. Read the label carefully to avoid those with additives and fillers.

## NOODLE AND CHEESE PUDDING

This is a good family dessert that you can serve your baby as a *cereal/protein* dish at any meal, especially for a light, nourishing supper.

> 1 box broad noodles
> 2 eggs, beaten (egg yolks alone may also be used)
> 2 cups cottage cheese
> ¼ cup raisins
> ½ cup brown sugar or honey
> ½ pint sour cream
> 2 tablespoons melted butter
> 2 tablespoons lemon juice (optional)
> 1 teaspoon cinnamon (optional)

1. Preheat oven to 350° F. Lightly butter casserole.
2. Cook noodles in boiling salted water.
3. Drain and cool slightly.
4. Mix noodles and other ingredients together in casserole.
5. Bake for 50 minutes.
6. *Purée* with any equipment, adding a small amount of milk to thin, if necessary.
7. You may freeze the casserole, or purée, for up to one month.
YIELD: 6–8 servings (adult).

## MACARONI AND CHEESE

This is a good family dish that you can serve your baby as a purée or a finger food.

    1 8-ounce package macaroni (shells, twists, etc.)
    ¼ pound mild American cheese, thinly sliced or grated
    2 tablespoons butter
    ¼ cup non-fat dry milk powder (optional)
    2 cups milk (whole or skim)

1. Preheat oven to 350° F.
2. Lightly grease a casserole. Or, use several small individual baking dishes or cups.
3. Cook macaroni according to package instructions for use in baking.
4. Drain the macaroni, do not rinse.
5. Arrange macaroni in casserole in layers with the cheese and bits of butter.
6. Mix the non-fat dry milk powder with the milk. Pour over the casserole.
7. Bake for 45 minutes.
8. Prepare as a purée in strainer, blender, or food mill. You can also mash a small amount with a fork for a coarser purée. You should not need any additional thinning. Or, serve whole pieces as a finger food.
9. Store in refrigerator for 3–4 days. Or, freeze for one month.

YIELD: 3 cups or 15 food cubes.

## • WHEAT GERM

**Nutrition:** Wheat germ is the most valuable part of the wheat cereal grain, yet it is often removed during the refining of wheat in cereal and flour. It contains the greatest amount of protein, minerals, all the B vitamins, and linoleic acid (an essential fatty acid). Wheat germ is also one of the few good sources of vitamin E, which many doctors feel is very valuable in an infant's diet and is found in lower quantities in cow's milk than breast milk.

**Introduce** wheat germ around two or three months after you have introduced wheat as a cereal. Since wheat is a possible source of allergies, you should begin with a very small amount. If your baby has no reaction, it can be an important addition to his diet.

**Buy:** You may think of wheat germ as a "health" food and difficult to find. However, a popular brand is available in most supermarkets either plain or sweetened with honey. You should avoid using the latter.

**Store** wheat germ in a tightly covered container in the refrigerator for 2–3 months. Since it contains oils, it is likely to become rancid if left at room temperature.

### USING WHEAT GERM

The texture is fairly hard and mixed with milk it may be a difficult consistency for a young baby to swallow. You will get the smoothest texture by grinding it in a blender and cooking it with milk for 5 minutes, or allowing it to soak until soft.

► The best way to introduce and use wheat germ is to grind it, then mix it with a food that has a smooth consistency, such as bananas.

► When you mix wheat germ with another food, always add extra liquid, about twice the amount of wheat germ. Allow the purée to stand a few minutes to soften the wheat germ.

► You can add wheat germ, either ground or whole, to juicy fruits and vegetables as a thickener. Use about 1 tablespoon for each cup of purée.

► You can also mix 1 part wheat germ to 2 parts dry infant

cereal and you will have almost the nutritional value of a whole-grain cereal.

As you can see, you will be able to use your imagination in finding ways to use wheat germ in your baby's food. You may find nutritious and tasty combinations that your entire family will also enjoy.

## ● RICE

**Nutrition:** Rice is a cereal grain that can be used as a cereal or in many main dishes and desserts. It can also be used as a nutritious thickener. It contains less protein than the other cereal grains, but it is a good source of the B vitamins, especially niacin. The amount of nutrition depends upon the type of processing.

*Brown or natural rice* contains all of the nutrients in the rice— it is a whole grain. You can find this in most supermarkets and should use it whenever possible.

*Converted or parboiled* has been processed so that some of the B vitamins are carried into the grain before the bran or outer part is removed. It is a white rice, easily digestible, and is the next best rice nutritionally. If the converted rice is also enriched, it may be even higher than brown rice in iron and thiamin.

*Enriched polished rice* has had many of the vitamins and minerals removed during processing. Thiamine, riboflavin, niacin, and iron have been added according to government standards. It is lower in protein than coverted or brown rice. I can see no reason to use this instead of the converted rice. The instant or quick-cooking rice may also be enriched.

*Polished white rice* that has not been enriched should not be used since it has a very low nutritional value. Rice flour is made from this highly processed rice and is usually unenriched.

**Introduce** converted or enriched rice as a cereal as early as two months. Because of the bran, you should not introduce brown rice until your baby is around four or five months old.

**Store** rice in tightly covered container at cool room temperature for up to two years. Cooked rice may be covered and kept in the refrigerator for 2–3 days. You may also freeze it as a purée for one month. This is convenient for rice that requires longer cooking times.

COOKING RICE:

▶ To retain the nutrients, especially thiamine, do not wash the rice before cooking and do not drain or rinse the rice after it is cooked.

▶ Use only as much liquid in cooking that can be absorbed by the time the rice is soft, usually 2 to 3 times the amount of rice.

▶ You may use milk as the cooking liquid to supplement the quality of the rice protein. When you use milk, do not cover the pot or else the milk will boil over.

▶ If you cook rice in a double boiler, you can cover the pot and it will require very little watching or stirring.

▶ The cooking times given here are for brown or converted rice. If you are using precooked or instant enriched rice, use the cooking times on the package.

▶ A nutritious time-saving way to cook rice is to use the same pot and cooking water in which you have just prepared a vegetable, or stewed chicken, etc. Just measure the desired amount of liquid, bring to a boil, and add the rice.

## BASIC RICE PURÉE

This makes a good substitute for a serving of cereal.

1 cup brown or converted rice
3 cups water, vegetable juice, or milk
¼ cup non-fat dry milk powder (optional)
¼ cup milk

1. Place rice and liquid in pot and bring to a boil.

2. Reduce heat and simmer uncovered for 30–45 minutes or until the rice is soft. Add more liquid if necessary.

3. Cool and *purée* with any equipment, adding ¼ cup milk, and optional non-fat dry milk.

YIELD: 2 cups purée or 10 food cubes.

**VARIATION:**

**Rice and Wheat-Germ Purée.** Add ¼ cup of wheat germ during the last 10 minutes of cooking.

**Leftover Rice Purée.** Use any rice that is left from a family meal and thin with 2 tablespoons of milk for each cup of rice.

**Rice Cheese.** *Purée* with ¼ cup grated cheese or ½ cup cottage cheese.

## SOYBEAN/RICE PURÉE

This dish is high in protein and can be used as an economical substitute for a serving of meat. Double the amount for a cereal/protein serving.

½ cup soybeans
1½ cups water
½ cup brown or converted rice
1 cup skim milk (or water)
½ cup skim milk

1. Soak beans overnight in water; or bring to a boil, cover, and allow to sit for 2 hours.

2. Boil rapidly for 1 hour, uncovered. Reduce heat to simmer.

3. Add 1 cup of skim milk, and rice.

4. Simmer uncovered for 45 minutes. Stir occasionally and add more water or milk if necessary.

5. Cool and *purée*, adding about ½ cup of milk to thin.

YIELD: 2½ cups or 12 food cubes.

# RICE PUDDING

This is a nutritious dessert that counts as a cereal and is also high in protein. The rest of your family can enjoy it as a dessert or an unusual breakfast food.

    1 cup rice, brown or converted
    4 cups milk (whole or skim)
    2 eggs beaten (You may also use only the yolks)
    2 tablespoons non-fat dry milk powder (optional)
    ½ cup sweetener (brown sugar or honey) (optional)
    1 teaspoon vanilla (optional)

OVEN METHOD:

1. Butter casserole. Preheat oven to 325° F.

2. Mix rice and milk in casserole and bake uncovered for 1 hour or until rice is soft. Stir every 15 minutes.

3. Mix a little of the rice mixture with the beaten eggs, then mix the eggs and any optional ingredients into the casserole.

4. Bake for 15 minutes.

DOUBLE-BOILER METHOD:

This will require less watching.

1. Bring the milk and rice to a boil in the top of a double boiler. Place on the bottom part, cover, and steam for 45 minutes.

2. Remove from heat. Stir some rice or milk into the beaten eggs, then mix the eggs into the rice and milk. Add any optional ingredients.

3. Return to heat and stir until the spoon becomes coated. Cool pudding and *purée* with any equipment. No additional thinning should be necessary.

VARIATION:

**Rice/Fruit Pudding.** Add ½ cup of fruit purée (apricot, peach, plum, berry, or banana are good) after the rice is cooked and before mixing in the eggs.

## RICE AND MEAT DISHES

If you prepare main dishes with rice for your family, you can easily use them as baby food as long as they are not highly seasoned and your baby has already been introduced to all the main ingredients. The protein of the meat will improve the quality of the rice protein and you will have an economical and nutritious dish for your baby.

▶ For each cup of the rice and meat dish, *purée* with about ⅓ cup of milk or tomato juice as a thinner.

▶ These are good dishes for introducing your baby to a coarser texture in preparation for eating regular family meals.

▶ If you *purée* these dishes the same day they are made, you can freeze the purée in food cubes for up to one month.

## SAUTÉED RICE

This is a nutritious, easy, and economical all-in-one dish that can be made from leftovers. You can use it as a main dish for your family and purée some for your baby's dinner.

½ cup chopped onions (optional)
½ cup chopped leafy greens (optional)
2 tablespoons butter
1 egg, beaten
2 cups cooked brown or converted rice
½ cup cooked diced chicken, liver, beef, or pork
2 tablespoons soy sauce

1. Sauté onions and leafy greens in butter.
2. Add egg and scramble lightly.
3. Stir in rice, meat, and soy sauce.
4. Cook over low heat for 5 minutes.
5. *Purée* with a blender (Mini-Blend jar is good) or food mill, adding about ¼ cup milk to thin.
6. You may freeze the purée for up to one month.

YIELD: 4 cups.

# 8

## FRUITS

FRUITS are among the first solid foods that you will feed your baby. They are high in natural sugar, an easily digested source of carbohydrates, and they contain good amounts of minerals, especially phosphorous and iron. Some fruits are major sources of vitamins A and C. By the time your baby is several months old, he should be eating daily one serving of citrus fruit and at least two servings of other fruits.

Fruits are also the easiest and most economical baby foods that you can make yourself. Many fruits can even be served raw and mashed only with a spoon. Most do not require any thinning or added sweetening, so every bite will contain the most nourishment. You can choose from among the wide variety of fresh, frozen, canned, and dried fruits.

**Fresh Fruit** is inexpensive, flavorful, and highly nutritious when it is selected and stored properly. Many fruits are given grades based on appearance and size, such as U. S. Extra Fancy, U. S. Fancy, and U. S. Extra ⚹1. You can save money by buying the lower, but equally nutritious, grades for use as baby food. You should select those fruits that are in season, since they are inexpensive and the best quality. You should also take advantage of specials on very ripe fruit that you will use immediately or freeze.

*Ripe Fruit* contains the most sugar and vitamins and is easiest for your baby to digest. You can buy unripe fruit and ripen it at home if it was mature when picked. Fruit is *mature* when it was fully grown when picked. If fruit is *immature* when picked, it will not ripen properly and will be lacking in flavor and nutrients. (The signs for recognizing mature fruit are given under the specific fruit.) Fruit will ripen at room temperature and should not be placed in the refrigerator or in the sun.

Before storing fruit, sort out any brushed or decayed pieces, since they will cause the other fruit to spoil more quickly. Whether or not you should wash a fruit before storing depends on the specific fruit. You should always wash fruit before using to remove any pesticides.

*Raw Fruit* has the highest nutritional value and will require the least preparation—it is one of your best "instant foods." Most babies can eat raw fruit at quite an early age and really enjoy the taste.

▶ The skin of raw fruit is more difficult to digest and should not be included in the purée until your baby is about eight months old and the fruit has been introduced.

▶ You can remove the skin with a sharp knife, by blanching, or by using a food mill or strainer to purée. For an individual serving of some fruits, such as peaches, you need only to cut the fruit in half and scrape out the pulp.

▶ Always try to cut or peel the fruit just before using to prevent the loss of vitamins.

▶ Most raw fruit can be frozen either whole or puréed in food cubes for as long as one year and this is very practical for seasonal fruits.

▶ Raw-fruit purées spoil quickly so you should plan to use them within two days.

*Cooked Fruit*. The main purposes of cooking fresh or frozen fruit are to soften the texture or improve the digestibility of less than ripe fruit. Most fruit only needs to be cooked for the young baby or when first introducing a fruit. The main cooking methods are BAKE (in the skin, or aluminum foil); STEW in a little water or in a double boiler (good for very juicy fruits; or STEAM in a steamer (ideal for any fruit with a fairly thick skin which will retain the juice).

You should choose the cooking method which fits in best with your daily family cooking. For example, if you are roasting, wrap some fruit in foil and bake it at the same time. In general, fruit should be cooked over low heat for as short a time as possible. If only a fork or spoon is available for mashing, it may be necessary to cook the fruit until it is very tender. If water must be used in cooking, or juice is produced from cooking, use it in the purée or save it as a thinner or beverage. In these recipes, little or no liquid is used in cooking.

Fruit should always be cooked in the skin in order to save the most vitamins and minerals. Cooked skins can usually be puréed with the fruit unless the skin is very thick or sour or there is a large amount of skin, such as with grapes. The skin should be removed when you are introducing purées to a very young baby.

Cooked purées can be frozen in food cubes for as long as 1 year and some are also easily canned at home. They can be stored in the refrigerator up to one week. (See *Storage*.)

**Frozen Fruit** has the same nutritional value as fresh fruit if it has been frozen and stored properly. Select packages that are solidly frozen and not stained. In the case of fruits that are out of season, the frozen fruit may be better quality and less expensive. You will prepare frozen fruit in the same ways as fresh fruit and it can be substituted in any of the recipes. Since it is usually cleaned, you will even save some preparation time. The cooked purées can be frozen in food cubes.

**Canned Fruit** retains a very high amount of vitamins and minerals, although less than fresh or frozen fruit. It should be stored at cool room temperature and used within a year. This is a very convenient form of fruit, since it is already prepared, cooked, and often mashed. They are some of your best "instant foods," with some soft enough to purée with a fork or spoon.

The "U. S. Grade B" canned fruits are economical for use as baby food. Be careful not to buy cans that are leaking, bulging, or badly dented. If the fruit is packed in a vacuum glass jar, listen for the "popping" sound when you open it to make sure that the jar was not already opened and the fruit spoiled.

*Before opening, always wash the top of a can or the underneath edge of the lid of a glass jar in order to remove any dirt.*

Try to buy fruits that are packed in their *own juice,* or in water, instead of syrup. The juice or water should be used in thinning the fruit or other purées, or served as a beverage, since this liquid can contain as much as *one-third of the vitamins and minerals.* If you can only buy fruit that is packed in syrup, the light syrup will contain less sugar than the heavy syrup. Always drain this fruit and *do not give the syrup to your baby.* This fruit should not be served too often because of its extra sweetness. Read labels carefully to avoid canned fruits that contain additives, such as artificial color or flavor.

Opened canned fruit, whole or puréed, may be stored in the refrigerator for up to one week. It may also be frozen in food cubes for future use.

**Dried Fruits** are a good source of minerals, especially iron. They are high in sugar, but lower in vitamin C than other forms of fruit. Dried fruit can be introduced around five months or at the same time that the same cooked fruit is given. Dried fruits include apples, apricots, dates, peaches, pears, prunes, and raisins. They also make excellent "finger foods."

Buy well-sealed, clean containers and try to feel if the fruit is pliable. Many dried fruits have sulfur dioxide added as a preservative and may have a laxative effect, so use these sparingly. Try to buy dried fruits that are packed without preservatives and added sugar. Store dried fruits in tightly covered containers at cool room temperature or in the refrigerator for up to six months.

## ● APPLES

**Nutrition:** A well-balanced, good source of vitamins and minerals.

**Introduce cooked** at six–eight weeks. Raw at five months.

A peeled whole apple, given as a finger food, is useful in cleaning your baby's teeth and massaging sore gums.

**Buy** firm apples of any variety for cooking, ranging from tart to sweet. They are most plentiful in fall and winter months. Avoid apples which have a shriveled appearance from too-long storage, soft apples, and those with large bruised areas.

**Store** apples in a cool pantry for several weeks; or wash, dry, and store uncovered in the refrigerator.

**Instant Use:** Applesauce.

**Finger Food:** Peeled, whole apple.


## RAW APPLESAUCE

Jonathan, Grimes Golden, Delicious, McIntosh, Cortland, and Northern Spy are good varieties to use raw. Always prepare just before using or sprinkle with lemon juice to prevent browning.

> 1 medium apple
> 1 teaspoon lemon juice

1. Peel if necessary, core, blend on high speed. (Add 1 tablespoon fruit juice if apple is very dry) or grate with a rotary grater.
2. Add lemon juice.
3. Store in refrigerator for 1 day or freeze larger amounts.
YIELD: ½ cup purée or 3 food cubes.


## RAW APPLE/CARROT PURÉE

> ½ medium apple (cored, peeled if necessary)
> ½ carrot (wash, do not peel)
> 2 tablespoons fruit juice
> 1 teaspoon lemon juice

1. *Purée* all ingredients in blender or *grate* apples and carrot. Mix with juice.
2. Store in refrigerator for 1 day or freeze in food cubes.

YIELD: ½ cup purée or 3 food cubes.

## APPLESAUCE

**8 medium apples (2 pounds)**

1. Preheat oven to 350° F.
2. Wash and core apples.
3. Wrap single apples in a square of aluminum foil, twisting the corners over the top of the apple so it is tightly sealed. Or, place apples in tightly covered baking dish with a little water.
4. Bake ½ hour for the softer varieties; 45 minutes for harder apples.
5. *Purée* with food mill or strainer to remove skin, or scrape out pulp for a single serving with a spoon. Use blender to *purée* apple and skin.
6. Store up to one week or freeze in food cubes.

YIELD: 3 cups or 15 food cubes.

**VARIATION:**

Steam apples in steamer for 12–15 minutes. You can leave the apples whole and then remove the skin and cores with a food mill.

## STEWED DRIED APPLES

**1 cup dried apples**
**2 cups water**

1. Soak apples in water for 30 minutes.
2. Bring apples and water to a boil.

3. Cover and simmer 20–30 minutes.

4. Cool.

5. To *purée,* the stewed apples should be soft enough to mash with a fork. Use a food mill or blender for large quantities.

8. Store or freeze as for applesauce.

YIELD: 2 cups or 10 food cubes.

● APRICOTS

**Nutrition:** A very good source of vitamin A.

**Introduce cooked** around two months; raw at five months.

**Buy** apricots that are plump, with a uniform golden-orange color. Ripe apricots should yield to a gentle pressure on the skin. They are in season during June and July. *Do not buy* apricots that are dull, soft, or mushy (overripe); or very firm, pale yellow, or greenish-yellow (immature).

**Store** unripe apricots uncovered at room temperature, not in the sun, for several days until ripe. Store *ripe* apricots uncovered in the refrigerator for 3–5 days.

## RAW APRICOT PURÉE

**1 pound ripe apricots\***

1. Remove skins of apricots by plunging them in boiling water for 30 seconds, then run cold water over them while you rub off the skins. Or, remove skins by puréeing in food mill.

2. Remove the pits.

3. Very ripe apricots can be mashed with a fork. For large quantities or the smoothest purée, use food mill or blender.

4. Store purée in refrigerator for one day. Or, freeze in food cubes for up to one year.

YIELD: 2 cups or 10 food cubes.

\* (1 apricot is usually adequate for a single feeding.)

## STEWED APRICOTS

**1 pound ripe apricots**
**2 tablespoons fruit juice**

1. Wash. If it is necessary to remove skin, dip in boiling water, then rub off skin under cold water. Or, remove skins by puréeing in food mill.
2. Bring apricots and juice to a boil. Cover and simmer for 10 minutes or *steam* for 10 minutes; do not add juice.
3. Cool, pick out pits.
4. *Purée* in blender or food mill for smoothest purée. You can mash with a fork for a coarser texture.
5. Store in refrigerator for 5–7 days or freeze.

YIELD: 2 cups or 10 cubes.

### VARIATION: BAKED APRICOTS

**1 pound ripe apricots**

1. Preheat oven to 375° F.
2. Place washed apricots in covered baking dish, adding a small amount of water. Or, wrap tightly in aluminum foil (good for a single serving).
3. Bake for 20 minutes.
4. Proceed as for *Stewed Apricots*.

## STEWED DRIED APRICOTS

**1 cup dried apricots**
**1½ cups water**

1. Soak apricots in water for 1 hour.
2. Bring apricots and water to a boil.

3. Cover and simmer 15–25 minutes.

4. Cool. Mash with fork, or use a blender for large quantities or a finer purée.

5. Store and freeze as for *Stewed Apricots*.

YIELD: 1½ cups or about 8 food cubes.

## • AVOCADOS

**Nutrition:** A good source of unsaturated fat, some protein. High in linoleic acid, an essential fatty acid.

**Introduce** raw around six months. They are not suitable for cooking.

**Buy** avocados that are either light green with smooth skins; or dark green or brown with rough, leathery skins. Both varieties are good eating and are in season from November through May.

*Do not buy* fruit with dark, sunken spots or cracked surfaces, both signs of decay.

**Store** unripe avocados at room temperature, out of sun, for 3–5 days until they have ripened, so that they yield to gentle pressure on the skin. *Ripe* avocados may be held in the refrigerator for 3–5 days.

**Instant Use:** See recipe below.

### RAW AVOCADO

¼ very ripe avocado
1 teaspoon milk or citrus juice

1. Wash avocado.

2. Cut through skin to pit to remove ¼ of the fruit.

3. Peel back skin and mash avocado with a spoon, thinning with liquid if necessary.*

* Most babies will eat avocado purée without any thinning; so that the fruit can be mashed or scraped with the back of the spoon as it is removed from the skin.

To store leftover purée in the refrigerator for up to one day, sprinkle with lemon juice to prevent browning and tightly cover. Store the rest of the avocado in the skin, tightly wrapped, in the refrigerator for up to three days.

YIELD: 1 serving.

## FROZEN AVOCADOS

**2 medium avocados**
**4 tablespoons lemon juice**

1. Wash and peel avocados.
2. Mash fruit with the lemon juice. If a blender is used, push mix down with rubber spatula for smooth blending.
3. Pour immediately into ice cubes; cover and freeze.
4. Keep frozen for 4–6 weeks.

YIELD: 2 cups or 10 food cubes.

## • BANANAS

**Nutrition:** High in carbohydrates, good source of vitamins A and C. High caloric value.

**Introduce** raw, very ripe, or baked bananas as one of your baby's earliest foods, at around six weeks.

**Buy** fruit with firm bright skins, either greenish, yellow, or brown, depending on the stage of ripeness. *Do not buy* fruit that is bruised or shows soft spots, since it will spoil quickly; or fruit with discolored skins, or a dull, grayish appearance which shows that the bananas have been exposed to cold and will not ripen properly.

**Store** unripe bananas (green to solid yellow skins) at cool room temperature (60°–70° F.), away from sun. They will not ripen in the refrigerator and the cold will cause a loss of quality. Bananas will ripen in 3–5 days and the best eating quality is reached when the skins are solid yellow with brown spots or streaks. The riper the banana, the more digestible it is for a baby; so you may use bananas with completely brown skins as long as the fruit itself is unbruised. *Ripe* bananas should be stored in the warmest part of the refrigerator for up to two days.

**Instant Use:** See following recipe.

**Finger Food:** Cut in small pieces.

## RAW BANANAS

This is one of the easiest fruits to prepare.

1. Use a very ripe banana.

2. Remove only the peel of the part of the banana that you will be using in one feeding. For a very young infant, start with ¼ of the fruit.

3. Mash the banana with a fork or the back of a spoon until it is smooth.

4. It is not necessary to add any liquid or sugar.

5. The banana purée should not be saved, since it browns quickly. The unused portion of the banana should be wrapped, in the skin, and can be stored in the refrigerator for up to two days. Ripe bananas can also be peeled, wrapped tightly in aluminum foil, in meal-sized portions, and frozen for several months. Thaw in the foil and use immediately.

## BAKED BANANAS

If you must use greenish or yellow bananas that are not yet ripe, they should be baked to improve their digestibility.

1. Preheat oven to 450° F.

2. Peel banana.

3. Place in buttered baking dish, or wrap tightly in aluminum foil.

4. Bake about 10 minutes until tender.

5. *Mash* enough for one feeding with a fork or spoon.

Store whole baked banana in baking foil, tightly wrapped, in the refrigerator for one day.

VARIATION: BROILED OR SAUTÉED BANANAS

Unripe peeled bananas may also be sautéed in a small amount of butter, or broiled 3 inches from the heat until slightly browned. Prepare and store as for *Baked Bananas*.

● BERRIES

**Nutrition:** Blueberries, raspberries, blackberries, cranberries, etc., contain fair amounts of many nutrients. Strawberries are very high in vitamin C, almost as high as the citrus fruits.

**Introduce** raw and cooked at about seven months. Since berries sometimes cause allergic reactions, give only small amounts at first.

**Buy** firm, dry fruit which is in season from May through August. *Do not buy* berries which are crushed or show a white fuzzy mold. Avoid boxes which are wet or stained with berry juice.

**Store** berries whole, uncovered in a flat pan, for 1–2 days in the refrigerator. Remove any spoiled berries, since decay spreads quickly. Do not wash or stem the berries before storing.

**Finger Food:** Whole berries for babies over one year.

RAW BERRIES

1 quart box of berries*
½ teaspoon honey

* Do not use cranberries.

1. Wash berries just before using.

2. For a purée, press the berries through a strainer or food mill to remove the skin and seeds.

3. Mix with honey. (For a single serving, use only a few drops of honey to sweeten.)

4. Cover tightly and store in refrigerator for 1 day. Or, freeze in food cubes.

YIELD: 2 cups or 10 food cubes.


## STEWED BERRIES

Cooking will destroy the vitamin C in strawberries.

**1 quart box of berries**

1. Wash berries.
2. Put berries in top of double boiler.
3. Cook 15 minutes.
4. Cool and mash. Strain out skin and seeds.
5. Store purée in refrigerator for up to one week or freeze in food cubes.

YIELD: 2 cups or 10 food cubes.


VARIATION:

Since berries contain a high proportion of juice, they are good to combine with other fruit purées, either raw or cooked. The juice will serve as a natural thinner.


## CRANBERRY SAUCE

**1 pound cranberries**
**¼ cup water (or fruit juice)**
**¾ cup honey**

1. Wash and sort cranberries.
2. Bring water and honey to a boil.
3. Add fruit, cover and simmer 5–10 minutes until berries pop.
4. Use food mill or strainer to *purée* and remove skin.
5. Store purée in refrigerator for up to one week. Freeze in food cubes, or can.

YIELD: 3 cups or 15 food cubes.

## • CHERRIES

**Nutrition:** Sweet cherries are quite high in natural sugar. **Introduce** cooked at four months, raw at seven months.

**Buy** firm, dark cherries with shiny skin. They are in season during June and July. *Do not buy* shriveled fruit with dry stems or brown discoloration which indicates decay.

**Store** *unripe* cherries at room temperature to ripen in 3–5 days. Put ripe cherries, uncovered, in refrigerator for 1–2 days. Do not stem or wash.

**Finger Food:** Sweet cherries are a messy fruit and the pits must be removed; but babies love them. Serve after baby is one year old.

## RAW CHERRIES

**1 quart or pound ripe eating cherries** (Royal Anne, Napoleon, Bing, Black Tartarian, Republican, Lambert, Windsor)

1. Wash cherries and remove stems. If purée is to be prepared with a food mill or blender, remove the pits with the metal end (with eraser removed) of a pencil.
2. Mash cherries using strainer, food mill, or blender. The skin is thin enough to be digestible for older babies, if a blender is used.

3. Store purée in refrigerator, tightly covered, for one day. Or, freeze in food cubes for up to one year.

YIELD: 2 cups or 10 food cubes.

VARIATION:

Since cherries contain a large amount of juice, they are a good fruit to combine with more solid fruits such as apples or bananas.

## STEWED CHERRIES

**1 quart or pound sweet or cooking cherries (Montmorency or English Morello), or 30-ounce can sour cherries\***
**½ cup honey (use only with sour cooking cherries)**

1. Wash, stem cherries.
2. Place honey and cherries in double boiler or heavy saucepan.
3. Simmer over low heat for 15 minutes.
4. Cool, and remove pits with a fork or slotted spoon (easier than pitting raw cherries).
5. Mashes well with fork. Use food mill or blender for quantities and when first introducing fruit.
6. Store cooked purée in refrigerator for up to one week. Or freeze for up to one year.

YIELD: 2 cups or 10 food cubes.

VARIATION:

Since cherries contain a large amount of juice, they are a good fruit to stew in combination with a more solid fruit; just omit the liquid recommended for stewing the particular fruit.

\* Sour cherries are one of the few canned fruits that should be stewed to sweeten them.

## • CITRUS FRUITS

**Nutrition:** All the citrus fruits—oranges, grapefruits, lemons, tangerines, limes—are excellent sources of vitamin C. The pulp is also a source of certain vitamins and minerals.

**Introduce** as juice as early as two weeks. (See *Beverages* chapter 12.) Raw purées can be given by five months. Since vitamin C is destroyed by heat, citrus fruits should not be cooked. To prevent a rash, wash your baby's face immediately after feeding him a citrus fruit or drink.

**Buy** citrus fruits that are firm and well shaped. Select the heaviest fruits for the size, since the weight indicates the amount of juice in the fruit. Select those fruits with smooth skins, another indication of juice. If the skin is rough or wrinkled, the skin is likely to be thicker with less flesh to the fruit, with a large amount of pulp. Russeting, a tan or blackish mottling or specking on the skin, does not affect the quality of citrus fruit. These fruits are most plentiful and inexpensive during the winter months.

*Do not buy* citrus fruits that show signs of age (dull, dry, or hardened skin) or signs of decay (soft, discolored areas on the peel, water-soaked areas, or punctures).

*Oranges:* The *Parson Brown, navel* (*seedless*), and *pineapple* oranges are best for purées or as *finger food*. The *valencia* orange is better for juice. The seedless variety is more convenient for making purées. Oranges are required by state regulations to be well matured before picking, so skin color should not be used as a guide to quality. Oranges with a greenish cast, or spots, are as good as those which show a deep orange color (often more expensive). Some of those oranges with the brightest color have had artificial color added and must be so marked. There is some question as to the health hazards of this practice, but in any case it is unnecessary and may add to the cost of the orange.

*Grapefruit:* As with oranges, grapefruits are picked ripe and are ready for eating. There is little difference between the white or pink varieties. The seedless types will save you some time when preparing purées.

*Lemons* should have a rich yellow color. Those with a pale or greenish-yellow color will be more sour.

*Limes* must be mature when marketed and should be a dark green color. The small Key limes may have a yellowish color.

*Tangerines* should have a deep yellow or orange color. Very pale yellow or greenish fruit may be lacking in flavor. This is the one citrus fruit where the skin should feel loose and puffy. Since the skin peels easily and the fruit is usually quite sweet, tangerines make a good finger food.

**Store** citrus fruits at cool room temperature (60°–70° F.) for about one week. They may be stored for a short while in the refrigerator.

**Finger Food:** Wash orange, slice into sections.

If you own a blender, the following recipes will allow you to make full use of all the nutrition in a citrus fruit, both in the juice and the pulp.


## RAW APPLE/GRAPEFRUIT

**1 medium apple**
**½ medium grapefruit**

1. Wash, peel, and core apple.
2. Cut rind from grapefruit, remove seeds.
3. *Purée* apple and grapefruit in blender only.
4. Store in refrigerator for three days or freeze for one year.
YIELD: ¾ cup or 4 food cubes.

VARIATIONS:

*Apple/Orange.* Use 1 apple, 1 orange.
*Banana/Grapefruit.* Use 1 banana, ½ grapefruit.
*Banana/Orange.* Use 1 banana, 1 orange.
*Carrot/Orange.* Use 1 carrot, 1 orange.

## ● GRAPES

**Nutrition:** Grapes are high in sugar and low in vitamin C.
**Introduce** cooked at four months, raw at five months.

**Buy** well-colored, firm grapes that are strongly attached
to the stem. The green seedless variety are sweetest when they
have a yellowish cast to them.

*Do not buy* soft or wrinkled grapes (indicative of freezing
or drying), grapes with bleached areas around the stem end (indicative of poor quality), or leaking fruit which shows decay.

Grapes are most plentiful in late summer and fall. The
Thompson variety is thin-skinned, sweet, and seedless, which
makes it ideal as a finger food. You can also buy this variety
canned.

**Store** grapes at room temperature, out of the sun, until
ripe. Keep ripe grapes uncovered in the refrigerator for 3–5
days. Do not wash before storing.

**Finger Food:** Serve whole after one year old.


### RAW GRAPES

**1 pound grapes**
**2 tablespoons wheat germ**

1. Wash grapes.
2. *Purée* with food mill or strainer to remove skin. There is so
much skin in proportion to the pulp, that a blender will still
leave pieces of skin in the purée. It would also be too difficult
to digest.
3. Mix in wheat germ to thicken.
4. Store, tightly covered, in the refrigerator for two days or
freeze in cubes.

YIELD: 2 cups or 10 cubes.

Grapes contain a large amount of juice and are very sweet; so they are a good fruit to combine with hard, sour fruits.

## STEWED GRAPES

1. Follow instructions for raw purée.
2. Stew in double boiler or simmer over low heat for 10 minutes.

## • MELON/CANTALOUPE

**Nutrition:** Cantaloupes are the most common and generally the least expensive of the melons. They are an excellent source of vitamin A and a good source of vitamin C.

**Introduce** raw cantaloupe at six months. It should never be cooked.

**Buy** cantaloupes that are mature, either unripe or ripe. Since proper selection is considered to be an art, it is worth while to go into some detail. A well-chosen cantaloupe is sweet, juicy, and highly nutritious. A *mature* cantaloupe shows three signs: 1) The stem should be gone, leaving a smooth, symmetrical stem scar. If the scar is jagged or torn, the melon was picked before it was mature. 2) The netting, or veining, should be thick, coarse, and corky, and should stand out in bold relief over some part of the surface. 3) The skin color (ground) between the netting should have changed from green to a yellowish-gray, or pale yellow.

A *ripe* cantaloupe will have a yellowish cast to the rind, a pleasant odor when held to the nose, and will yield to light thumb pressure on the blossom end (opposite the scar or stem end).

An *overripe* cantaloupe should be avoided, since the flesh will be soft, watery, and tasteless. Signs of overripeness are a strong yellow rind color, softening of the entire melon, or mold growth in the stem scar.

**Store** mature, unripe melons at room temperature, out of the sun, for 2–4 days until ripe. Use immediately when ripe.

**Finger Food:** Sticks of cantaloupe are an excellent finger food, since they are sweet and juicy. It is a good substitute for carrots as a source of vitamin A.

**Instant Use:** Cantaloupe can also be used as an easy single serving of fruit. Just cut a slice and scrape the melon with a spoon as you feed your baby.


## CANTALOUPE PURÉE

½ very ripe cantaloupe
2 tablespoons wheat germ

1. Cut rind from melon, make sure that all the green is removed.

2. Cut melon into cubes and *purée* in blender, adding wheat germ.

3. Serve at once or freeze immediately. The purée spoils very quickly.

YIELD: 1 cup or 5 cubes.


VARIATION:

Cantaloupe purée is very sweet and thin because of the large amount of juice in a melon; so it is a good fruit to combine with a sour or hard fruit or vegetable.

## • NECTARINES/PEACHES

**Nutrition:** An excellent source of vitamin A.

**Introduce** cooked at two months, raw at five months.

**Buy** peaches or nectarines which are firm, but beginning to soften. The skin color should be yellow or creamy. The freestone variety are best for raw purées or for eating fresh. The clingstones are used mainly for cooking. Some good varieties are Elberta, Hale, Hiley, and Golden Jubilee.

*Do not buy* fruit that is very hard or has a green ground color. These are immature and will not ripen properly. Also avoid very soft fruit or those with large flattened bruises, since these are signs of decay.

**Store** unripe fruit at room temperature until ripe. Keep ripe fruit uncovered in the refrigerator for 3–5 days.

**Finger Food:** Peel and cut in pieces. Since nectarines have thinner skins, it is not necessary to peel for an older baby.

**Instant Use:** Cut in half and scrape with a spoon.

### RAW PEACHES/NECTARINES

**1 pound freestone peaches**

1. Wash and remove skin by dipping in boiling water for 1–2 minutes, then rub off in cold water.
2. Remove pits.
3. *Purée,* using any equipment. A blender should be used when making purée for a young infant.
4. Store in refrigerator for 1–2 days, or freeze for one year.
YIELD: 2 cups or 10 food cubes.

## COOKED PEACHES/NECTARINES

**1 pound peaches (any variety)**

1. Wash fruit. When mashing peaches with a fork or blender, remove skin. Otherwise, leave whole. The skin of nectarines is thin enough to *purée* in a blender.
2. Steam 15–20 minutes or bake—in covered dish with a little water or wrap in aluminum foil—for 20 minutes at 375° F.
3. Cool.
4. Remove pits and *purée*. (For a single serving, cut in half and scrape with a spoon.)
5. Store cooked purée in refrigerator for 5–7 days, or freeze for one year.

YIELD: 2 cups or 10 cubes.


## STEWED DRIED PEACHES

**1 cup dried peaches**
**1½ cups water or juice**

1. Soak peaches in water for one hour.
2. Simmer peaches, covered, in soaking water for 30–40 minutes.
3. *Purée* with any equipment.
4. Store as for cooked purée.

YIELD: 1½ cups or 8 food cubes.


## ● PEARS

**Nutrition:** Pears are high in natural sugar and fair in vitamins A and C.

**Introduce** cooked at two months and raw at 4 months.

**Buy** firm pears that have begun to soften, so that you can be sure that the pear will ripen. The color of the pear depends on the variety, and the best pears for using raw are: Anjou, or Comice (light to yellowish green); Bosc (greenish to brownish yellow with russeting); Bartlett (pale or rich yellow, red); or Winter Nelis (medium to light green). These varieties are in season from August until April.

*Do not buy* fruit that is wilted, shriveled, has dull skin, or weakening of the flesh near the ends (signs of immaturity). Soft spots on pears indicate that decay has begun and the fruit is overripe.

**Store** unripe fruits at room temperature until they begin to soften. Keep ripe washed pears in the refrigerator for 3–5 days.

**Instant Use:** Ripe pears can be halved and scraped with a spoon. Canned pears can be mashed with a fork.

**Finger Food:** Remove skin and cut in pieces.

## RAW PEARS

1 pound (3–4) pears (Bartlett, Bosc, Anjou)
1 tablespoon citrus juice

1. Wash fruit.
2. If using blender, peel and remove core.
3. *Purée,* and add citrus juice to prevent browning.
4. Use in one day, or freeze immediately.

YIELD: 2½ cups or 12 cubes.

## COOKED PEARS

1 pound pears (any variety)

1. Prepare as for Raw Pears.
2. Bake whole in a covered dish, with a little water in the bottom (or wrap in aluminum foil), for 20 minutes in a 350° F. oven, or *steam* firm whole pears for 20 minutes, or *broil* halved

pears, adding a little butter, for 7 minutes (good for single serving).

3. *Purée* in blender (or mash with a fork).

4. Store in refrigerator for five days, or freeze for up to one year.

YIELD: 2½ cups or 12 food cubes.

## ● PINEAPPLE

**Nutrition:** Pineapple contains a good amount of natural sugar and balanced amounts of several vitamins and minerals.

**Introduce** cooked at three months, and raw at six months.

**Buy** mature pineapples, either ripe or unripe. Mature fruit will have a pineapple odor, a very slight separation of the eyes or pips, and the spikes or leaves at the top can be easily pulled out. The fruit should also be firm and shiny, with heavy weight for its size. The mature, unripe fruit will be dark green in color, which will change to orange or yellow as it ripens.

*Do not buy* fruit with sunken or slightly pointed pips, dull yellowish-green color and a dried look. These are immature and will never ripen properly. Also avoid bruised fruit with discolored or soft spots, or traces of mold—all signs of decay which will spread quickly.

**Store** unripe pineapples at cool room temperature (60°–65° F.) 3–5 days until ripe. Never ripen in the sun. Ripe pineapple should be tightly wrapped to contain the odor and stored in the refrigerator for up to two days. Ripe fruit will spoil quickly, so plan its use carefully.

### RAW PINEAPPLE

**1 medium pineapple (2 pounds)**

1. Wash, cut off crown end and stem end.
2. Stand upright and cut off skin from the top to bottom.

3. Remove the eyes with a sharp knife.

4. A few sweet grapes or pieces of cantaloupe can be added as sweeteners.

5. Cut fruit in small chunks and *purée only in blender.* (If your blender is not powerful, cook fruit first.)

6. Store in refrigerator for one day, or freeze at once.

YIELD: 2 cups or 10 food cubes.

## COOKED PINEAPPLE

**1 medium pineapple**

1. Prepare pineapple as for raw purée.

2. Place cut fruit in steamer and cover. Steam for 10–15 minutes.

3. Cool and *purée in blender only.*

4. Store in refrigerator for up to five days or freeze for up to one year.

YIELD: 2 cups or 10 food cubes.

VARIATION:

Pineapple contains an enzyme which has some tenderizing action; so combine this fruit or use the juice in cooking any meat or poultry.

Canned pineapple that is packed in its own juice is available. Since it only requires blender puréeing, the canned fruit can save you time.

## ● PLUMS/PRUNES

**Nutrition:** Plums are a good source of natural sugar. The Italian prune plums can have a laxative effect.

**Introduce** cooked at two months, raw at five months.

**Buy** any variety of plum for cooking. For eating—the Red Beaut, Burmose, Laroda, Duarte, President, or Queen Anne are the sweetest and juiciest. Prunes are purplish to bluish black. They are in season from June through October. Look for fruit with good color and shiny skins that are firm but beginning to soften. *Do not buy* fruits with skin breaks, or brownish discoloration. The immature fruit is hard, poorly colored, and often shriveled.

**Store** plums at room temperature until ripe, then refrigerate uncovered for 3–5 days.

**Finger Food:** Slices of plums are good finger food, but the baby should be old enough to digest the skin, since peeled plums can be very messy. Whole plums should not be given, since the pits are quite small and might cause swallowing or choking. Dried pitted prunes are also excellent as a finger or teething food.

## RAW PLUMS

> 1 **pound ripe eating plums (about 15)**
> 1 **tablespoon citrus juice**

1. Wash fruit and remove pits.
2. *Purée* in food mill or strainer to remove skin. (The skin is usually too sour or tough to purée in blender.)
3. Add citrus juice to prevent browning.
4. Store in refrigerator for one day or freeze at once.

YIELD: 2 cups or 10 cubes.

*Note:* Some varieties may be very juicy and require some thickening—use wheat germ or cereal.

## COOKED PLUMS

**1 pound plums—any variety (good for hard fruit)**

1. Wash fruit.
2. *Steam* whole for 15 minutes or *bake* in covered dish or aluminum foil for 20 minutes at 375° F.
3. Cool and remove pits.
4. *Purée* in blender unless skin is very sour. Any other equipment can also be used.
5. Store cooked purée in refrigerator for five days, or freeze for one year.
*Note:* Some varieties may require thickening, or cook down the liquid.
YIELD: 2 cups or 10 cubes.

## STEWED DRIED PRUNES

**1 cup dried prunes**
**3 cups water**

1. Simmer prunes, covered, in water for 30–40 minutes.
2. Cool and remove pits.
3. *Purée* with any equipment.
4. Store as for *Cooked Plums.*
YIELD: 3 cups or 15 cubes.

## ● RHUBARB

**Nutrition:** Rhubarb has balanced amounts of vitamins and minerals. It is technically a vegetable, but is served as a fruit. Use only the stalks—the leaves are poisonous.

**Introduce** cooked at six months. Never use raw.

**Buy** fresh, firm stems with a bright, shiny look, and a large amount of pink or red color. It is most plentiful in May and June.

*Do not buy* stalks which are either very thin or very thick (likely to be tough or stringy). Also avoid stalks that are wilted or flabby, since they are not fresh.

**Store** rhubarb in refrigerator for 3–5 days.

## RHUBARB

**2 pounds rhubarb**
**¼ cup honey or brown sugar**

1. Wash rhubarb, cut in 2-inch pieces.
2. *Bake* covered or in aluminum foil for 30 minutes at 375° F. or *stew* in top of double boiler, or over low heat, for 15 minutes.
3. Add sweetening.
4. Use either strainer or food mill to *purée* and remove fibers for the smoothest purée, or *purée* in blender.
5. If purée is too thin, thicken with wheat germ or cereal.
6. Store in refrigerator for one week, or freeze for one year.
YIELD: 2½ cups or 12 cubes.

## ● TROPICAL—MANGO, PAPAYA, GUAVA

**Nutrition:** The tropical fruits are often ignored, yet are highly nutritious. Mangoes and papayas are an excellent source of vitamin A and good in vitamin C. Guavas are as high as orange juice in vitamin C and may be a substitute if your baby is allergic to orange juice.

**Introduce** raw at six months.

**Buy:** Unfortunately, these fruits are difficult to find and are expensive away from their growing area. Mangoes are in season from May to July, and the other fruits vary. Select fruit that is firm and free from bruises.

**Store** tropical fruit at room temperature until ripe. Mangoes and papayas should be very soft. The ripe fruit can be wrapped in waxed paper and refrigerated for 2 days.

**Instant use:** These fruits can be halved and scooped out with a spoon. They are also available canned and can be easily mashed with a fork.

**Finger Food:** Halve; cut out small pieces or strips.


## RAW TROPICAL FRUIT

If you find a quantity at reduced prices, take advantage of it. As with melon, cut in half, scoop out, and *purée*. Freeze at once for up to one year.

# 9
## VEGETABLES

VEGETABLES are an essential part of your baby's menu. They supply many vitamins, minerals, and carbohydrates. Fresh vegetables in season have the highest nutritional value, with frozen vegetables almost as high. As with fruits, canned vegetables are lower in some vitamins, but are more convenient and still supply adequate amounts of nutrients. Color is the most essential key to the amount of vitamins in vegetables, with the *deep yellow, orange, or dark green* vegetables containing the largest amounts. You should include at least one of these vegetables every day, along with a serving of some other vegetable.

One of the greatest advantages in preparing your own vegetables is the large variety that you may choose from. Many of the most nutritious vegetables, especially the green leafy ones, are unavailable in the commercial baby foods. If your baby dislikes one vegetable, you will have a wide range from which to select a substitute. The chances are that your baby will love the vegetables that you prepare yourself, with their natural flavors and textures. One of the reasons that so much salt is added to the commercial baby-food vegetables is to disguise a taste that the manufacturers consider unacceptable to mothers. Since studies have shown that babies have no preference for the taste of salt, it seems logical that babies may object to the highly processed, salted vegetables. These dislikes can continue through childhood and your child may never eat enough of the vegetables that are so important to his health. But, if he acquires as an infant, a taste for natural vegetable flavors, the battle is over before it has begun.

Another reason to prepare your own vegetables is their economy and ease of preparation. Buying in season and taking advantage of specials can amount to large savings. Very often you will be able to use vegetables that you have prepared for the rest of the family and might have thrown away as leftovers. Only simple cooking is required for most fresh or frozen vegetables and all of the purées can be frozen as food cubes. Most canned vegetables require no cooking, only puréeing. You should spend the most time and care in selecting and storing vegetables, so that you get the most nutritional value and flavor.

**Fresh Vegetables.** You should use these whenever possible for the most nutrition, flavor, and economy.

► Buy those that are in season and freshly picked for the maximum nutrition and flavor.
► Grades on vegetables are not required. Where you do find them, the U. S. Fancy grade is given on the basis of appearance which is not essential in baby food. The lower and usually less expensive U. S. Grade No. 1 is adequate. Your best guide to quality will be your own judgment on the appearance and maturity of the vegetables.
► If the official USDA grade shield does appear on a package, it indicates that the product was inspected during the packing and that at the time of packing, it met the requirements of the grade shown on the package.
► Plan the use of what you buy, since most vegetables lose their freshness and quality within 2–5 days.

Most vegetables should be stored in plastic bags in the crisper section of your refrigerator. This will prevent drying and wilting which causes a loss of vitamins, especially vitamin C. Root and tuber vegetables should be stored at cool room temperature for a short while, and in basements for a month or more. Before storing, cut out any decayed parts or sort out spoiled vegetables to prevent the spread of decay.

There are a few vegetables that a baby can eat raw. Do serve those frequently, since they will be highest in food value, and your baby will acquire a liking for the taste of raw vegetables. If a baby cannot digest raw vegetables, pieces will appear in the bowel movement and you should then postpone them for a while.

To preserve nutrients, always cut or peel raw vegetables just before serving, and do not soak any raw vegetable. You can use a blender to liquefy the raw vegetable with water or juice. You may also grate small amounts of raw vegetables and moisten them with vegetable oil or juice.

**Cooked vegetables.** There are several ways that you can cook vegetables; however, the ones that are easiest and retain the most nutrients are the *steam* and *bake* methods.

To *steam* almost any vegetable, use a steamer/blancher or an equivalent. (See chapter 4.) The main principle is to suspend the vegetables above a small amount of boiling water in a pot with a tightly fitting cover. Many vegetables can and should be steamed in the skin, and you can combine different vegetables in the same pot. If a vegetable requires lengthy steaming, add water as it boils away. Any liquid remaining in the pot can be used as a thinner.

*Bake* any vegetable that has a thick skin, such as potatoes or winter squash, in the skin. This is a convenient method when you are already using the oven for a regular family meal. Most succulent or juicy vegetables can be baked, at 325° F., by wrapping them tightly in foil, or by placing them in a tightly covered dish with a tablespoon or two of water. Then, the vegetables will steam in their own juices.

To *boil* the root and tuber vegetables that require lengthy cooking, place them in boiling water that just covers, in a tightly covered pot. If at all possible, bake instead of boiling these vegetables. Do boil down the cooking water and save it as a thinner, since it will contain vitamins and minerals.

To preserve nutrients, with any cooking methods, do not cut the vegetables. Most of the recipes give cooking times for whole vegetables. If you really are in a hurry, you can usually reduce the cooking time in half by slicing the vegetables. Never add salt or soda to the cooking water. If you must salt your family's vegetables, do it after cooking.

The cooking times given in the recipes are only guides. Remember that you want to cook to the minimum for easy purée-ing. If you are using a blender, the vegetables may require less time. If you are mashing by hand or with a food mill, you will have to cook them longer so they become more tender. Young or small vegetables will be more tender using less cooking time.

Remember that vegetables that are cooked, saved, and reheated will lose some vitamins, especially vitamin C. They may be stored for up to three days in the refrigerator; however the best way to store cooked purées is to freeze them in food cubes.

To can vegetables, you will need a pressure canner. You must follow detailed canning instructions to prevent the growth of botulism, a serious food poison, in canned vegetables. (See chapter 5.)

**Frozen vegetables** can be substituted for fresh in any of the recipes. You can save considerable time by using them, since the washing and cutting are already done. These are almost as nutritious as fresh vegetables, and offer a wide range from which to choose, especially during the winter months when many vegetables are not in season.

They will be more expensive than fresh vegetables in season, but there are several ways that you can save money. Buy cut vegetables instead of whole ones, and avoid fancy cuts or mixtures. Buy *Grade B* or *Extra Standard* vegetables which are as nutritious, but more mature and less uniform than the highest *Grade A*. *Grade C* or *Standard* is the lowest grade which usually indicates vegetables with the strongest flavor and firmer texture. Your baby may object to this taste, especially when the vegetable is first introduced. If not, using *Grade C* will result in considerable savings.

Do not buy packages that are damp or sweating (signs of defrosting) or stained (defrosted and refrozen). Frozen vegetables will maintain their quality for as long as eight months if the freezer temperature is kept at 0° F.

In general, you may follow the cooking times on the package, but use your steamer instead of boiling them in water as is usually suggested. Do not defrost the vegetables before cooking.

Most vegetables are sold in 10-ounce packages, which will yield 1–1½ cups of purée, or 5–8 food cubes. The large bags of vegetables are very economical, and you can either make a large amount or pour out only as much as you need.*

**Canned vegetables** are not as nutritious as fresh or frozen, but you do have a wide selection, and they are very convenient to use as an instant food. You can save money by buying the cut or diced styles and also the *Grade B* or *Extra Standard* grades for use in purées.

Do not buy cans that are leaking, badly dented, or bulging. If you buy the vacuum-pack jars, make sure that there is a popping sound when you open one. If not, the jar may have been opened and the food spoiled. Thoroughly wash cans or lids before opening.

These canned vegetables will require very little preparation. They are already cooked and only need puréeing. Most will require a food mill or blender for the smoothest consistency, but you can mash them with a fork to the texture of "junior" foods. The important thing to remember in using any canned vegetable is that the *liquid that it is packed in contains ⅓ the nutrients* in the vegetable. To use this liquid, drain the vegetables, then boil down the liquid. It can then be used to thin the vegetables, or in other purées. You can also strain it and serve it as a beverage. The *exception is the salt brine* that some vegetables may be packed in. Try to avoid buying this style, but if you do use it, discard the liquid. Never boil canned vegetables, since you will lose additional vitamins and minerals. You should only warm them slightly, even serve them cold.

*For most vegetables, a 15- or 16-ounce can will yield about 1½ cups purée, or 8 food cubes.* This can be refrigerated for up to three days or frozen for one month.

**Consistency.** Most vegetables, when first introduced, will require a little thinning; however, the least amount is the most desirable in terms of nutrition. *You can start with 1–2 table-*

---

* You may *cook raw* frozen vegetables, then purée and freeze the purée.

*spoons of liquid for each cup of vegetable.* The liquid should either be cooking water or canning liquid (reduced), juice, or undiluted evaporated milk. A small amount of butter, 1 teaspoon for each cup of purée, can be added to any vegetable to improve the consistency, and this is a good way to add fat to your baby's diet if he is drinking skim milk. Wherever possible, combine a thin vegetable, such as tomatoes or summer squash, with a thick one, such as potatoes or cooked dried beans. Here is where you can be most creative in selecting vegetable combinations for your baby. You can also combine vegetables with fruits. (See *Food-Combination Guide* in chapter 6.)

Very few vegetables will require thickening, but when it is necessary, use about 1 tablespoon of wheat germ or cereal to each cup of vegetable.

You will soon find the consistency that your baby prefers. It is important not to thin with water or thicken with starch.

Since the storage times are the same for most vegetables, I have listed them here for easy reference. Any variations will be given under the specific vegetable.

| REFRIGERATOR | | FREEZER |
|---|---|---|
| *Fresh* | *Canned or Cooked* | Fresh: 8 months |
| Whole: 3–5 days | Whole or | Raw purée: 1 month |
| Purée: 1 day | purée: 3 days | Cooked purée: 1 month |

## ● ASPARAGUS

**Nutrition:** Asparagus is a fair source of vitamins A and C. Babies love its mild taste and smooth texture.

**Introduce** only cooked at four months.

**Buy:** Asparagus is very expensive unless it is in season—April and June. Buy rich green spears with closed, compact tips.

*Do not buy spears* that are ribbed with up-and-down ridges or tips that are open, spread out, or decayed. These are all signs of aging, which means toughness and poor flavor. Very thin or thick stalks also indicate toughness. Avoid very sandy asparagus, since the sand can lodge in the tips and is very

difficult to remove. Frozen and canned asparagus are available
. . . the latter may have stannous chloride added as a color
preservative.

**Store** asparagus in a plastic bag, in the coldest part of the
refrigerator, for up to two days.

**Finger Food:** A steamed stalk of asparagus is tender and easy
to handle.

## ASPARAGUS

**1 pound asparagus**

1. *Prepare* asparagus by breaking off each stalk as far down as
the green. Remove scales with a knife and scrub in water to remove the sand.

2. *Steam* for 12–18 minutes or *bake* for 20 minutes in dish
or foil, at 325° F.

3. You will make the smoothest purée by removing the fibers
with a strainer or food mill. A blender gives a slightly coarser
consistency.

4. The *purée* should not require thinning or thickening.

YIELD: 1½ cups purée or 8 food cubes.

## • BEANS, GREEN AND WAX

**Nutrition:** Both varieties are equally high in vitamin A and
calcium.

**Introduce** cooked at three months.

**Buy** young, tender beans with firm and crisp pods. Avoid
wilted, flabby pods, serious blemishes, decay, or thick pods, which
indicate overmaturity.

**Store** covered in refrigerator for 3–5 days.

**Finger Food:** A whole steamed bean is tender and easy to
handle.

## GREEN/WAX BEANS

**1 pound beans**

1. Wash beans and remove ends and strings, if any.
2. *Steam* 20–30 minutes or *bake* in dish or foil for 30 minutes, at 325° F.
3. *Purée* with any equipment. Beans should require little, or no, thinning.

## • BEANS, LIMA

**Nutrition:** Incomplete proteins, B vitamins, carbohydrates.
**Introduce** cooked only at six months.
**Buy** well filled, clean, shiny, dark green pods. Hard or discolored skin indicates overmaturity. Canned baby limas of Grades A and B are the most tender and least starchy.
**Store** in pods in refrigerator 1–2 days.

## LIMA BEANS

**1 pound lima beans**
**½ cup liquid**

1. Snap open pods and remove beans. Or cut off a strip from the inner edge of the pod and push out the beans.
2. *Boil* lima beans, not pods, for 20–30 minutes or *steam* beans for 25–35 minutes.
3. *Purée* with strainer or food mill to remove skin for the smoothest purée. A blender will result in a coarser texture.
4. Thin with about ½ cup of cooking liquid, juice or milk.
YIELD: 1½ cups purée or 12 food cubes.

## ● BEETS

**Nutrition:** Fair amounts of most vitamins and minerals, good carbohydrates in sugar. The green tops are highly nutritious. (See *Greens.*)

**Introduce** cooked at five months, raw at seven months. Beets will cause bowel movements and urine to have a red color, and this is harmless.

**Buy** beets that are firm and round, with a rich red color and fairly smooth surface. Badly wilted or decayed tops may indicate long storage, but the roots are still usable if they are firm.

*Do not buy* long or large beets with round, scaly areas around the top—these are signs of toughness, fibers, and a strong flavor. Wilted and flabby beets have been too long in storage and are not fresh.

Canned and frozen beets are also available. They are called *Harvard* beets when they are packed in a thick, sweet vinegar sauce, and these should not be used.

**Store** beets, after removing root tips and most of the green tops, in the refrigerator, covered, for 1–2 weeks.

### COOKED BEETS

**1 pound beets (4–6)**

1. Wash beets, do not peel. Leave 1 inch of stem.
2. *Boil* for 35–60 minutes or *steam* for 40–65 minutes or *bake* for 40–60 minutes, at 325° F. (The older and larger the beet, the longer the cooking time.)
3. Rub off the skins and remove the stems from the beets.
4. *Purée* with any equipment.

YIELD: 1¾ cups purée or 8 cubes.

*Purée* equal amounts of beets and pineapple.

## RAW BEETS

**2 medium beets**
**½ teaspoon vegetable oil (corn, safflower)**
**1 teaspoon lemon or orange juice**

1. Wash beets and remove a thin paring.
2. Grate or *purée* in a blender, adding juice and oil to improve the consistency.

YIELD: ½ cup or 3 food cubes.

## ● BROCCOLI

**Nutrition:** Excellent source of vitamins A and C. Good source of calcium and potassium. The leaves contain the highest amounts of nutrients and should be cooked with the broccoli or saved and used as *greens*. It is one of the most valuable vegetables.

**Introduce** cooked only at four months. Some babies may react with gas to broccoli. If so, postpone it for another month and try again in small amounts. If your baby has this reaction to broccoli, also postpone the introduction of the leafy green vegetables.

**Buy** broccoli that has a firm, compact cluster of the small, dark green flower buds. None should have opened enough to show the yellow flower. The stems should be thin and free of decay.

*Do not buy* broccoli with spread bud clusters, yellowish-green color, or wilted. These are all signs of overmaturity and too-long storage. Avoid thick stems since these will be tough. Soft, water-soaked spots on the bud clusters are signs of decay.

Frozen broccoli is available in several styles. The chopped variety is nutritious and more economical for use in baby food.

**Store** broccoli covered, in the coldest part of the refrigerator for up to two days.

**Finger Food:** The small bud clusters of cooked broccoli are tender and easy to handle.

## BROCCOLI

**1 pound fresh or 10-ounce package frozen broccoli**
**⅓ cup liquid (evaporated milk is good)**

1. Cut off lower end of stalk. Do not remove leaves. Wash well. Slit the stalks if they are thick.
2. *Steam* 10 minutes. Remove cover for first few minutes for a milder flavor or *bake* for 20 minutes in dish or foil, at 325° F.
3. *Purée* with strainer or food mill for the smoothest texture. Add liquid. A good blender will also produce a smooth purée. Add liquid while blending.

YIELD: 1½ cups or 8 food cubes.

## • BRUSSELS SPROUTS

**Nutrition:** Brussels sprouts have fair amount of vitamin C and potassium.

**Introduce** cooked only, at eight months. This vegetable is part of the cabbage family (they look like very small cabbages) and may cause gas.

**Buy:** They are in good supply from October through December. Look for a bright green color with tight outer leaves.

*Do not buy* sprouts with yellow or yellowish-green leaves, or those which are loose, soft, or wilted. These are signs of overmaturity and too-long storage. Small holes or ragged leaves indicate worm injury.

**Store,** covered, in the coldest part of the refrigerator for two days.

**Finger Food:** Whole small sprouts are an interesting food.


## BRUSSELS SPROUTS

**1 pound fresh or 10-ounce package frozen Brussels sprouts**

**¼ cup liquid (evaporated milk is good; it dilutes the taste)**

1. Wash and remove any damaged leaves.
2. *Steam* for 10–12 minutes or *bake* for 15 minutes in covered dish or foil, at 325° F.
3. Cool and *purée* with any equipment, adding liquid.

YIELD: 2 cups or 10 cubes.


## • CABBAGE

**Nutrition:** Cabbage, both red and green varieties, is a fair source of vitamin C, and is high in vitamin K.

**Introduce** cooked only at eight months. Cabbage contains a high amount of roughage and may produce gas. If your baby has had reactions to broccoli or green leafy vegetables, he may also have a reaction to cabbage.

**Buy** firm, hard heads of cabbage that are heavy for their size. The outer leaves should be a good red or green and without serious blemishes.

*Do not buy* new cabbage with wilted or decayed or yellow outer leaves. Worm-eaten outer leaves often indicate that the worm injury extends into the rest of the cabbage. If the leaves on cabbage are discolored, dried, or decayed, or the stems of the leaves are separated from the base, the cabbage is overaged. Canned cabbage is usually pickled and not suitable for a baby. **Store** cabbage covered, in the refrigerator, for up to two weeks.

## CABBAGE

**1 pound cabbage**

1. Remove any wilted leaves and wash.
2. *Steam* cabbage for 15 minutes. Remove cover for first few minutes for a milder flavor.
3. *Purée* with any equipment.
YIELD: 2 cups or 10 food cubes.

**VARIATION:**

*Lemon Cabbage.* Add 1 tablespoon lemon juice.

## CARROT/CABBAGE

The flavor of carrots sweetens the cabbage taste.

**½ pound carrots**
**½ pound cabbage**
**2 tablespoons evaporated milk (undiluted)**

1. Scrub carrots. (Do not peel.)
2. *Steam* whole carrots 15 minutes. Add cabbage and steam another 15 minutes.
3. *Purée,* adding evaporated milk.
YIELD: 2 cups or 10 food cubes.

## • CARROTS

**Nutrition:** Carrots are a highly nutritious vegetable, high in vitamin A, carbohydrates, and potassium. They are a fair source of vitamin C.

**Introduce** cooked at three months, raw at five months. Cooked carrots actually supply more carotene, which the body turns into vitamin A. They are easily digestible and babies love the flavor. Carrot purée may be useful in the treatment of diarrhea.

**Buy** carrots which are smooth, well colored, and crisp. The smaller the carrot, the more tender and milder flavored. However, the deeper the color, the more vitamin A.

*Canned* baby carrots are especially tender.

*Do not buy* carrots with large green areas at the top, since the trimming will be wasteful. Also avoid carrots which are flabby, wilted, or show spots of decay. These have been in storage too long and have lost much of their nutritional value.

**Store** carrots, covered, in the refrigerator for one week. Remove root tips and tops before storing.

### COOKED CARROTS

**1 pound carrots (4–5)**
**¼ cup liquid (milk, orange juice, cooking juice)**

1. *Prepare* carrots by scrubbing well with a brush.
2. *Steam* whole for 20–30 minutes (you can shorten the time by slicing the carrots) or *bake* in covered dish or foil for 35 minutes at 325° F.
3. Cool and rub off skin if preparing for a young baby or when first introducing. Otherwise the skin can be puréed with a blender.
4. *Purée,* adding liquid, with any equipment. A strainer or food mill will also remove the skin.

## RAW CARROTS

Introduce raw carrot in small amounts by mixing it with a fruit. (See *Apple/Carrot Purée.*)

## • CAULIFLOWER

**Nutrition:** Cauliflower is a good source of vitamin K.

**Introduce** cooked only at six months. It may cause gas. If so, wait a month or two, then offer again.

**Buy** cauliflower heads that are white, compact with clean tops or curd. It is in season from September through January. *Frozen* Grade B cauliflower may look slightly gray or brown, but is usable.

*Do not buy* heads where the curd is spread, shows severe wilting or discolored spots. These are signs of aging or overmaturity. Also avoid curd with a smudgy or speckled appearance, which are signs of insect injury, mold growth, or decay.

**Store** cauliflower, covered, in the refrigerator for 3–5 days.

**Finger Food:** Small cooked flowerets are easy to handle.

## CAULIFLOWER

**1 pound fresh or 10-ounce package frozen cauliflower**
**⅓ cup liquid (milk or cooking water)**

1. Remove any spots on head, base or stem. Wash thoroughly and cut in chunks.

2. *Steam* for 10–18 minutes. Remove cover for first few mintes for a milder flavor, or *bake* in covered dish or foil for 20 minutes, at 325° F.

3. *Purée,* adding liquid, with strainer, food mill, or blender.
YIELD: 1½ cups or 10 food cubes.

VARIATION:

A small amount of grated cheese will add a good flavor.

## ● CELERY

**Nutrition:** Celery is a good source of sodium and cellulose. It contains a large amount of liquid and is a good vegetable to mix with a more solid one such as carrots or peas.

**Introduce** cooked at four months, raw at eight months. Cold, raw celery stalks are an excellent teething food.

**Buy** celery that is fresh and crisp. The surface should be shiny with light or medium green color. Good celery is available year round.

*Do not buy* wilted celery with flabby upper branches or leaf stems. These are signs of overlong storage, toughness, and lower nutritional value. Also avoid celery with hollow or discolored centers in the branches. A sign of this internal discoloration is gray or brown on the inside surface of the larger branches. In general, the larger the stalks, the less tender.

**Store** celery, covered, in the refrigerator for 3–5 days.

## COOKED CELERY

**1 pound celery**

1. Remove any leaves and trim the roots. Separate the stalks and wash well. Scrape off any discolorations. If a blender is used, remove the strings from the large outer stalks or cut in short pieces.*

2. *Steam* 30–35 minutes or *bake* in covered dish or foil for 35 minutes, at 325° F.

3. *Purée* with food mill or strainer for the smoothest purée,

* Do not purée long stalks of celery in blender. It may tangle in blades.

since the strings will be removed. A blender may also be used.
YIELD: 2 cups purée or 10 food cubes.

VARIATION:

*Celery/Carrots:* Use ½ pound carrots, ½ pound celery.
*Celery/Peas:* Use ¾ pound celery, ⅓ cup peas.

## ● CORN

**Nutrition:** Corn is a good source of carbohydrates and phosphorous.

**Introduce** cooked only at four months.

**Buy** fresh corn in season during May through September. Look for fresh husks with good green color, silk ends without decay or worm injury and stem ends that are not too discolored or dried. The small kernels and the white variety are usually the most tender and juicy.

*Do not buy* husks that are yellowed, wilted, or dried, or corn with stems that are discolored or dried out. These are signs of too-long storage. Corn with very large kernels or of dark yellow color is overmature and will be starchy and tough.

*Frozen* whole corn and kernels are available and are useful for baby food if good fresh corn is out of season.

*Canned* corn is available in several styles. The creamed corn is packed in a thick, creamy sauce made from corn, salt, sugar, water, and often starch. Here you are paying for preparation and ingredients that are not necessary or desirable in baby food. Only use this style when nothing else is available.

Corn is also canned in a clear liquid or in a vacuum pack with little or no liquid. The latter is usually the more tender. Only Grade A canned corn should be used in puréeing, since it is the sweetest, most tender, and juicy.

Canned corn does not require cooking, but if you are puréeing the hulls, it will be more tender if you simmer it for a while.

Use a food mill to prepare a smooth purée and remove hulls.

**Store** fresh corn in the husks, uncovered, in the refrigerator for 1–2 days.

**Finger Food:** Cook corn, then, with a sharp knife, cut off only the tops or slice down the middle of each row of the kernels. Your baby will love holding the cob and sucking the corn from the kernels.

## CORN

**4 ears fresh corn or 10-ounce package frozen**
**3 tablespoons milk**

1. Remove husk, all silk, and any bad spots.
2. *Steam* corn 10 minutes or *boil* for 7–10 minutes.
3. Cool and, with a sharp knife, cut the kernels off as close as possible to the cob.
4. You will prepare the *smoothest* purée by using a strainer or food mill to remove the hulls of the kernels. A high-speed blender will also prepare a purée that older babies can digest.
   YIELD: 1½ cups or 8 food cubes.

## • CUCUMBERS

**Nutrition:** Cucumbers contain only fair amounts of vitamins and minerals. However, they have a high liquid content and can be puréed with other vegetables as a thinner.

**Introduce** raw only at seven months.

**Buy** firm cucumbers with good green color and fairly thin.

*Do not buy* cucumbers that are overgrown, large in diameter, with dull color, or turning yellowish. Other signs of toughness and bitter flavor are withered or shriveled ends.

**Store** cucumbers, washed and covered or in crisper, in the refrigerator for 3–5 days.

## CUCUMBERS

**¼ medium cucumber**

1. Peel. Cut in half lengthwise and scoop out the seeds with a spoon.
2. *Purée* only in a blender.
YIELD: ¼ cup or 1 food cube.
*Note:* Cucumber does not store or freeze well. It is best combined with another vegetable for a single serving.


## • EGGPLANT

**Nutrition:** Eggplant has only fair amounts of nutrients.
**Introduce** cooked only at eight months.
**Buy** firm, heavy eggplants with smooth, dark purple skin.
*Do not buy* those which are poorly colored, soft, shriveled, or show decay with soft, dark brown spots.
**Store** at cool room temperature (60° F.) for 2–3 weeks. At room temperature, only one week. Do not store in refrigerator.


## EGGPLANT

**1 medium eggplant**

1. Wash, do not peel.
2. *Steam* for 10–15 minutes or *bake* for 15–25 minutes, at 325° F.
3. *Purée* with any equipment.
YIELD: 2 cups or 10 food cubes.

## ● GREENS

**Nutrition:** The various leafy green vegetables are some of the best sources of all the vitamins and minerals, especially iron. They are also very inexpensive and easy to prepare as baby food. The various greens include:

*Spinach*—potassium, vitamin A, magnesium

*Kale*—vitamins A, C, magnesium

*Collards*—vitamins A, C, and riboflavin, niacin

*Turnip Greens*—vitamins A, C, iron, B-complex

*Beet Greens*—vitamin A, iron, magnesium

*Chard*—iron, magnesium, potassium, sodium, vitamin A

*Mustard Greens*—high iron, potassium, vitamin A, B-complex

*Broccoli Leaves*—vitamins A, C, potassium

*Dandelion Greens*—high iron, potassium, vitamins A, B-complex

*Parsley*—vitamins A, C

*Watercress*—vitamins A, C

**Introduce** cooked at four months, raw at seven months. If your baby has reactions of gas or rashes to any of these greens, postpone them a month. It is important to keep trying, since they are so nutritious. Parsley, watercress, and dandelion greens have a strong flavor, so introduce them in very small quantities, mixed with eggs, white sauce, or a favorite vegetable.

When your baby reaches the trying stage of eating paper, give him some large pieces of raw leafy greens, such as spinach or lettuce, to chew on. He may not actually eat any, but at least they are better than paper.

**Buy** greens that are fresh, young, tender, free from blemishes, with a good green color. Beet greens and some chard will have a reddish-green color. The spring months are the best time to buy young greens.

Frozen greens are also available and can save preparation and cleaning time. Use the Grade A for the most tender greens.

*Do not buy* leaves with coarse, fibrous stems, yellow-green color, softness, or wilting. If greens show signs of insect damage, the insects may be hidden in the leaves and are very difficult to wash away.

**Store** greens in plastic bags in the refrigerator for 1–2 days.

## COOKED LEAFY GREENS

**1 pound fresh greens***
**1 tablespoon butter (optional)**
**3 tablespoons milk or fruit juice**

1. Wash the leaves thoroughly. Cut off any blemished areas. If the leaves have large or tough center stems, you may discard them without losing nutritional value. These stems will produce a coarser purée.

2. *Steam* most greens for 5–15 minutes depending on the thickness of the leaves. You may leave the cover off for the first few minutes for a milder flavor. *Boil* strongly flavored greens, such as dandelion, for 20 minutes in an uncovered pot.

3. *Purée* with blender for the smoothest texture, adding the butter and milk or juice. *Do not use cooking water.*

YIELD: 1¾ cups or 9 food cubes.

**VARIATION:**

If your baby objects to cooked greens, try introducing them in small amounts in *Vegetable Soufflé*, and *Vegetable Custard*. (See also *Eggs*.)

\* (A 10-ounce package of frozen greens will yield 1¼ cups purée; use only 2 tablespoons liquid.)

## RAW SCRAMBLED GREENS

When your baby is eating eggs, you can use them as a way of introducing raw greens. The main problem is the texture of the greens, since they tend to stick to his mouth and are difficult to swallow. Mixed with eggs, they go down quite easily. This can be a Protein/Vegetable serving.

¼ cup raw greens (cooked can also be used)
1 egg
1 tablespoon milk

1. Wash and prepare raw greens as for cooking.
2. Put egg, milk, and greens in blender (the Mini-Blend jar is perfect) and *purée*. The mixture will be bright green.
3. Scramble the eggs to a soft consistency.
YIELD: 2 servings or ½ cup.

VARIATION:

Raw chopped greens may also be added to cereal, or mixed with cooked egg yolk. Chop the greens in a blender with a small amount of water. Mix in the greens and use a little liquid to thin the cereal or egg yolk.
*See also:* Jellied Vegetables
Vegetable Custard
Vegetable/Egg Yolk Custard

## ● KOHLRABI

**Nutrition:** Good source of vitamin C and potassium. This is a little-used vegetable that is part of the cabbage family, although the edible portion looks like a turnip. The tops may also be used as greens.

**Introduce** cooked at six months.

**Buy** small or medium-size roots with smooth surfaces and fresh tops.

*Do not buy* large vegetables, since they will be more fibrous and tough, or those with blemishes or cracks.

**Store** kohlrabi, covered, in the refrigerator for up to one week.


## KOHLRABI

1 pound kohlrabi
3 tablespoons liquid (evaporated milk is good)

1. Wash and remove skin. Cut into large pieces.
2. *Steam* for 30–40 minutes or *bake* in covered dish or foil for 1 hour, at 325° F.
3. *Purée* with any equipment, adding liquid.
YIELD: 1½ cups or 8 food cubes.


## ● LEGUMES: DRIED PEAS, BEANS, LENTILS

**Nutrition:** The legumes (dried peas, beans, and lentils) are very economical sources of protein (incomplete), and contain high amounts of iron, phosphorous, calcium, magnesium, potassium, and the B-complex vitamins. They are also low in fat. Soybeans are a source of complete protein and are included in the *Protein Foods* chapter.

The various legumes include: *Peas* (green, split, black-eyed, cow, and yellow); *Beans* (navy, kidney, pinto, lima); *Lentils*.

They are similar in nutrition and can be substituted for a serving of cereal grains. Cooked peas and beans are very thick and are good to combine with juicy fruits and vegetables. They can also be thinned with milk, to supplement their incomplete protein, or combined with a small amount of other protein foods and served as a low-cost meat substitute. Another means of supplementing their protein is to soak these dried legumes in skim milk instead of water, then cook them slowly in the milk. As you can see, they are a very good buy in terms of their nutritional cost.

**Introduce** cooked at seven months. They can be served as a finger food if cooked until very soft.

**Buy:** *Dried* peas, beans, and lentils keep well and can be bought in large quantities. *Canned cooked* beans are also available in different varieties—baked beans, limas, or kidney beans—often with sauces. This is the most convenient way of using these beans since they require little, if any, cooking but they are much more expensive than preparing your own. For an older baby, they can be mashed directly from the can. Remember to read the labels—if they are packed in a salt brine, *drain the beans and do not use the liquid.* U. S. Grade B canned beans are adequate and economical.

**Store** dried peas, beans, and lentils in tightly covered cans or plastic bags at cool room temperature for up to two years. Cooked purées will keep in the refrigerator for three days and can be frozen for one month.

**Cooking:** You may feel that dried peas, beans, and lentils require lengthy cooking time. They do, but little of your time and effort is involved. A timesaver is to cook a large quantity, then freeze them. If you have a good blender, you can also shorten the cooking time in half by first grating the dried legumes.

The packaged soup mixes of dried peas, beans, noodles, and vegetables are convenient and require a shorter cooking time. Remember to omit the seasoning packet and reduce the amount of cooking water to about half of that stated on the package—you are not preparing soup.

## COOKED DRIED PEAS/BEANS/LENTILS

**1 cup any legume**
**3 cups water or skim milk**
**1 tablespoon butter or oil**
**¾ cup milk**

1. Rinse legumes briefly. Soak in water or milk overnight. Or, you may bring them to a boil for 2 minutes, cover, and allow them to sit for 2 hours. (This presoaking or cooking is unnecessary if you are using a pressure cooker.)

2. Add the butter or oil to prevent foaming over.

3. *Simmer* about 2 hours with the cover partly ajar to prevent foaming over. (Lima beans cook in about 1 hour; black-eyed peas in ½ hour.)

4. When cooking some beans, the skins will float to the top. You should skim these off for the smoothest purée.

5. *Purée* with any equipment, adding ¾ cup milk.

*Note:* If you are cooking beans or peas for the rest of your family, do not add salt until the last few minutes of the cooking. If it is added at the start of the cooking, the beans will take much longer to soften. For the same reason, do not add acid foods, such as tomatoes, until the end of the cooking time.

YIELD: 2½ cups or 12 food cubes.

## ● LETTUCE

**Nutrition:** The dark-green leafy lettuce has fair amounts of vitamin A and iron. The iceberg variety has very little nutritional value.

**Introduce** cooked at four months, raw at seven months. As with the other green leafy vegetables, lettuce can be used as a substitute when your baby shows a desire for chewing paper.

**Buy** romaine or leaf lettuce, which is dark green and crisp. *Do not buy* lettuce with considerable discoloration or decay of the outer leaves. Avoid wilted lettuce, which is a sign of over-long storage and lower nutritional value.

**Store** lettuce in plastic bag, in refrigerator, for 1–2 days.

**Use** lettuce raw or cooked as a green leafy vegetable. (See *Greens.*)

## • MUSHROOMS

**Nutrition:** Mushrooms are very high in niacin and have fair amounts of other vitamins and minerals. They have a high liquid content and are good in combinations with other vegetables or meats.

**Introduce** cooked only at eight months.

**Buy** young mushrooms that are small to medium. The caps should either be closed around the stem or slightly open with pink or light-tan gills. The surface of the cap should be white, creamy, or light brown depending on the variety.

Canned mushrooms are available, with the "stems and pieces" style less expensive.

*Do not buy* mushrooms with wide-open caps, dark gills, or pitted and discolored caps. These are all signs of overripeness and decay.

**Store** in plastic bag, in the refrigerator, for 1–2 days. They are very perishable, often expensive, but freeze well. So, if you come across a sale, prepare a purée and freeze at once.

**Finger Food:** This is one of the few vegetables that is *not* a good finger food. The small pieces tend to be tough, but slippery. This encourages the baby to swallow the pieces whole, and they are not digested.

## MUSHROOMS

1 **pound fresh mushrooms**
2 **tablespoons wheat germ, rice, or instant cereal**

1. *Prepare* mushrooms by washing thoroughly. Cut off tough ends of the stems, but leave the stems.

2. *Steam* the caps and stems in the top of a double boiler for 5–10 minutes (do not use a steamer, or you will lose the juice), or *sauté* in a little butter or oil for 5–10 minutes or *bake* in covered dish or foil for 15 minutes, at 325° F.

3. *Purée* mushrooms and juice with blender for the smoothest texture. Add thickener. A food mill may also be used, then add the liquid and thickener.

YIELD: 2½ cups or 12 food cubes.

## • OKRA

**Nutrition:** Okra has only fair amounts of vitamins and minerals.

**Introduce** cooked only at five months.

**Buy:** Fresh okra is the immature seed pod of the okra plant and should be small, no more than 4 inches long. On tender pods, the tips will bend with a slight pressure. They should have a bright green color and be free from blemishes. Frozen okra can also be used.

*Canned* okra is usually pickled and salted and is not suitable for a baby.

*Do not buy* fibrous pods with stiff tips, hard bodies, or pale, faded green color.

**Store** fresh okra, covered, in the refrigerator for 3–5 days.

### OKRA

**1 pound okra**

1. Wash and scrub the pods thoroughly. Cut off the stem end. If the pods are large, cut them in half. Do not peel.

2. *Steam* okra for 15–20 minutes or just until tender (when

okra is overcooked, it will become gummy), or *bake* in covered dish or foil for 30 minutes, at 325° F.

3. *Purée* with any equipment.

VARIATION:

Okra produces a thin purée, so it is good combined with vegetables such as carrots, or in stews.

## ● ONIONS, LEEKS

**Nutrition:** Onions and leeks contain fair amounts of many nutrients. They have a high liquid content and are good to combine with less juicy vegetables or stews.

**Introduce** cooked only at eight months. If you want to *purée* a family dish which contains a small amount of onions for flavoring and the other ingredients have been introduced, you can try it as early as five or six months.

**Buy** onions that are firm and dry. They should be fairly free of green sunburn spots or blemishes. Bermuda and Spanish onions are the sweetest and mildest flavored. Leeks should have crisp green tops.

**Canned** onions are usually packed in a salt brine, and should not be used.

*Do not buy* vegetables that are wet, with soft spots or necks. These are either immature or decayed inside. Also avoid onions with thick, hollow, woody centers in the neck, or with fresh sprouts.

**Store** onions at cool room temperature for 2–3 months. They should either be spread out or piled in open mesh containers.

Moisture or high temperature will cause sprouting or decay.

## ONIONS

1 pound onions
2 tablespoons wheat germ, cooked rice, or instant
   cereal

1. *Prepare* onions under water to prevent your eyes from watering. Wash and remove outer peel and any blemishes.
2. *Steam* whole 30–40 minutes, sliced 10 minutes, or *bake* in covered dish or foil, whole for 30 minutes, sliced 10 minutes. (Overcooking will produce a strong flavor.)
3. *Purée* with any equipment, add thickener.
YIELD: 2 cups or 10 food cubes.

## ● PARSNIPS

**Nutrition:** Good source of carbohydrates and potassium, fair amounts of other minerals and B vitamins.
**Introduce** cooked at five months.
**Buy** parsnips that are small to medium size, well formed, smooth, firm, and free from major blemishes. They look like white carrots and are sweetest during late winter.
*Do not buy* large parsnips which will have tough, woody centers, or badly wilted or flabby ones that will be tough and fibrous.
**Store** parsnips, covered, in the refrigerator for up to one week.

## PARSNIPS

1 pound parsnips
¼ cup liquid (evaporated milk or apple juice is good)

1. Scrub well with brush.

2. *Boil* whole parsnips in water to cover for 10–20 minutes, or *bake* 45 minutes in covered dish or foil, at 325° F.

3. Plunge in cold water and rub off skins.

4. *Purée* with any equipment, adding liquid and a teaspoon or two of butter.

YIELD: 2 cups purée or 10 food cubes.

VARIATION:

*Baked Apple/Parsnips.* Prepare ½ pound parsnips; combine and bake with 1 cup chopped raw apples or applesauce.

## ● PEANUTS, OTHER NUTS

**Nutrition:** Peanuts and other nuts are excellent sources of protein (incomplete), fat, linoleic acid (essential fatty acid), magnesium, phosphorous, niacin, folacin, and vitamin E. They also have fair amounts of other minerals and the other B vitamins. As with legumes, the protein of nuts is the most useful when it is combined at the same meal with an animal protein. Milk is the most practical source and can be used as a thinner in preparing the nut butter.

**Introduce** at seven months. Although peanut butter is a nutritious staple for many toddlers, I thought twice about giving it to my baby. Properly thinned, she loved it!

**Buy:** There are many commercial peanut butters on the market, so read the labels carefully to find the one with the least additives and salt. It is amazing what can be added to such a simple food—mono-diglycerides, hydrogenated vegetable oil, dextrose, sugar, and salt. Avoid the peanut "spreads" which contain a lower amount of peanuts. All the commercial peanut butters will require thinning with milk or they will never get past the roof of your baby's mouth. The consistency is probably the major reason we never think of feeding peanut butter to babies.

If you live near a health food store, you will be able to buy raw unsalted nut butters that require little, if any, thinning; however, they are quite expensive. You will find it most nutritious and economical to make your own peanut butter with raw or toasted peanuts. You must use a good blender, and the Mini-Blend jar is ideal. Your baby will prefer both the consistency and the taste of homemade peanut butter.

*Do not buy* nuts that are preserved with BHT.

**Store** unopened commercial peanut butter for nine months at cool room temperature; opened peanut butter for up to six months in the refrigerator. Homemade peanut butters do not have preservatives and will not keep as long. These may be kept for two months in the refrigerator. They may also be frozen for 4–6 months. If you thin with milk, only store for 2–3 days. Whole peanuts should be kept in a tightly covered can, in the refrigerator, for up to four months.

## PEANUT/NUT BUTTERS

**1 cup peanuts or other nuts (raw or toasted)**
**3 tablespoons milk or safflower, corn, or olive oil**

1. If you are using toasted salted peanuts, wash them to remove the salt.

2. *Purée* the milk, or oil, and the peanuts in the blender at a medium speed. If you do not use a Mini-Blend jar, you must push the mixture down as it blends.

YIELD: ¾ cup.

VARIATION:

*Peanut Butter Custard*
*Peanut Butter Cookies*

## ● PEAS

**Nutrition:** Peas supply good amounts of iron, B vitamins, especially niacin, and carbohydrates.

**Introduce** cooked peas at three months.

**Buy** pea pods that are crisp, green, and unspotted, with a velvety surface, and well filled with peas.

*Do not buy* pods which are swollen light in color, or spotted with gray. These will contain tough and poorly flavored peas. Immature peas will have dark green, or wilted flat pods. Wilting or flabbiness is also a sign of overlong storage.

*Canned* and *frozen* peas are available in several sizes and grades. *Grade A* or *Fancy* peas will have the tenderest skins and sweetest taste. These will produce the smoothest purée. *Grade B* or *Extra Standard* peas will be more mealy, but have a good flavor. *Grade C* should not be used for baby food. Canned peas that have been graded for size will be more expensive; but the smaller the peas, the more tender they will be. Tenderness is important since peas are one of the first vegetables introduced.

**Store** fresh pea pods, covered, in refrigerator for 1–2 days. Like corn, peas will lose sweetness and tenderness as they are stored. Remove from pods just before using.

### PEAS

    **2 pounds peas (in pods)**
    **3–4 tablespoons liquid (milk or cooking water)**

1. Just before cooking, shell peas.
2. *Steam* 10–20 minutes.
3. For the smoothest purée, use food mill or strainer, which will also remove the skins. Add liquid.

## ● PEPPERS

**Nutrition:** Peppers are very high in vitamin C and are fair in other vitamins and minerals. They have a high liquid content and are good combined with a thicker vegetable or in stews.

**Introduce** cooked at eight months, raw at nine months.

**Buy** either green or red sweet peppers that are shiny, heavyweight, and have firm walls or sides.

*Do not buy* those with thin walls, lightweight, and are wilted or flabby. (The vitamin C will have been reduced due to overlong or improper storage.) Also avoid peppers with soft watery spots which are signs of decay.

**Store** peppers, washed and covered, in the refrigerator for 3–5 days.

### COOKED PEPPERS

They have a high juice content and are good combined with thick vegetables such as potatoes, or in stew. Allow about 10 minutes of cooking when combining with other recipes. Use only the outer shell.

### RAW PEPPER

Since the main value of peppers is vitamin C, and this vitamin is destroyed by heat, peppers should be used raw.

1. *Prepare* by removing stem, seeds, and membranes.
2. *Purée* in blender in equal amounts with other raw, hard vegetables such as carrots.

## • POTATOES, WHITE

**Nutrition:** High carbohydrates and potassium, good source of vitamin C if cooked in skins.

**Introduce** cooked at six months.

**Buy** a variety of potatoes, depending on your cooking method. The *new* potatoes are good for boiling and should not be baked. They are available in late winter and early spring. They should be well shaped, firm, and without green sunburn discoloration. Some amount of skinned surface is normal. *General purpose* potatoes are better for boiling but can be baked. *Baking* potatoes are used for baking in the skin. These types of potatoes are available year round and should be firm, well shaped, free from blemishes, sunburn, and decay spots.

*Do not buy* potatoes with large cuts or bruises which must be cut away or those with green sunburn spots. Sprouted and shriveled potatoes have been kept too long in storage and they are lower in nutritional value.

Canned and frozen potatoes are available in many styles. Avoid those canned styles that are packed in a salt brine. Dehydrated or "instant" potatoes can be used as an instant food, but they have large amounts of additives and should not be served often.

They are a very thick, bland vegetable and are good in combination with leafy greens.

**Store** potatoes, unwashed, in a dark dry place with good ventilation and a temperature of 45–50° F. for 2–3 months. Exposure to light will cause greening or lower eating quality. High temperatures will speed sprouting and shriveling. Potatoes stored at room temperature should be used within 1–2 weeks.

## MASHED POTATOES

1 pound potatoes
½ cup liquid (milk is good)

1. Wash well and scrub with brush. Remove eyes and blemishes. Do not peel.

2. *Boil* in water to cover, in covered pot, for 20–40 minutes, or *steam* 30–45 minutes or *bake* in skin or wrapped in foil for 40–60 minutes, at 400° F.

3. Rub off skin (boiled) or scoop out (baked). *Purée* with fork, strainer, or food mill, or mixer. Add liquid and a little butter. *Do not* mash in blender.

YIELD: 2 cups purée or 10 food cubes.

VARIATION:

Add a little grated cheese for flavoring.

## STEWED APPLES AND POTATOES

6 medium potatoes (1½ pounds), peeled
1 cup milk
2 medium cooking apples, cored, peeled, diced

1. Cut potatoes into thin slices, or chop.
2. Place potatoes and milk in pan.
3. Bring to a boil, cover and simmer for 20 minutes.
4. Add apples and cook for another 15 minutes. Add more milk if the mixture is very thick.
5. *Purée* with any equipment. It should be soft enough for even a fork or spoon.
6. To serve as a family dish, just add a little salt and pepper.
YIELD: 4 cups or 20 food cubes.

## • SQUASH, SUMMER

**Nutrition:** High in potassium, good amounts of vitamins A and C, and niacin.

**Introduce** cooked only at four months. This is a juicy vegetable, so it is good combined with more solid vegetables or in stews.

**Buy** any of the varieties—yellow are *Crookneck, Straightneck,* greenish-white *Patty Pan,* or green *Zucchini, Italian Marrow.* Look for squashes that are well developed, firm, with glossy skin.

*Do not buy* overmature or aged squashes which have dull skins and a hard surface. These will have enlarged seeds and dry, stringy flesh.

Canned and frozen summer squash is available and useful.

**Store** summer squash, covered, in the refrigerator for 3–5 days.

## SUMMER SQUASH

**1 pound squash**
**2 tablespoons wheat germ (optional)**
**2 teaspoons butter or oil**

1. Wash well, remove slice from both ends. For the smoothest purée, cut in half lengthwise and remove seeds.

2. *Steam* 15–20 minutes or *bake* in covered dish or foil for 25–30 minutes, at 325° F.

3. *Purée* with any equipment. A strainer or food mill will also remove the seeds and skin. Wheat germ may be added as a fortifier thickener. A small amount of butter may be added for flavor.

YIELD: 1½ cups purée.

## • SQUASH, WINTER

**Nutrition:** The winter squashes are high in carbohydrates, potassium, and vitamin A. They also contain some iron, magnesium, and riboflavin.

**Introduce** cooked only at three months.

**Buy** any variety that is in season. *Acorn* is green and available all year. Other varieties are *Butternut, Hubbard, Delicious,* and *Banana* which are in season from early fall to late winter. Buy squash with a hard, tough rind, and heavy for its size. Variations in skin color do not affect the flavor.

*Do not buy* squash with cuts, sunken spots, or mold on the rind—these are signs of decay. A tender or soft rind indicates immaturity and poor eating quality.

**Store** winter squash at cool room temperature (around 60° F.) for several months. Keep them at room temperature for only 1–2 weeks. Do not store them in the refrigerator.

**Instant use:** Canned and frozen squash is already cooked and mashed. The only preparation might be the addition of a little milk.

### WINTER SQUASH

**1 pound squash**
**1 tablespoon milk (optional)**
**2 teaspoons brown sugar or honey (optional)**
**1 tablespoon butter (optional)**

1. Wash well. Cut acorn squash in half; other varieties, cut in large pieces. Remove seeds and stringy centers. Do not remove skin.

2. *Steam* for 25–30 minutes or *bake* for 45–55 minutes. (Place

halved squash cut side down on dish or foil; put pieces of squash in covered dish or wrap in foil to shorten the baking time.)

3. Scoop out of skin and *purée* with any equipment. Add milk for a thinner purée. Add butter or brown sugar for a family dish.

YIELD: 1 cup purée or 5 food cubes.

## ● SWEET POTATOES, YAMS

**Nutrition:** Sweet potatoes and yams are high in carbohydrates, and vitamin A. They contain fair amounts of other vitamins and minerals.

**Introduce** cooked only at six months.

**Buy** well-shaped, firm sweet potatoes with smooth, bright orange skins that are free from signs of decay. Yams have white to reddish skins and are more moist when cooked. However, they are a tropical vegetable and are difficult to find fresh. Frozen yams and sweet potatoes are available in several styles, including cooked and mashed. Canned sweet potatoes should be bought in a vacuum pack without any syrup. The canned solid pack may have a small amount of liquid.

*Do not buy* sweet potatoes with worm holes, cuts, or any injury which penetrates the skin. These defects will increase the spoilage. Even if you cut away the decayed spot, the rest of the flesh will have a bad taste. Sweet potatoes decay easily, so look for such signs as wet, soft spots; discolored or shriveled ends; or sunken, discolored spots on the sides.

**Store** sweet potatoes at cool room temperature (around 60° F.) for a month or two. Keep them for only one week at room temperature. Never store them in the refrigerator.

**Instant use:** Some styles of canned and frozen sweet potatoes are already cooked and mashed. It is only necessary to thin with milk.

## SWEET POTATOES

1 pound sweet potatoes
⅓–½ cup liquid (milk, orange, or apple juice is good)
1 tablespoon butter (optional)

1. Scrub and wash potatoes. Trim roots and any bad spots. Do not peel.
2. *Steam* 30–35 minutes or *bake* for 40 minutes at 400° F. or 60 minutes at 350° F.
3. Scoop potato out of skins and mash with food mill, mixer, or strainer, adding liquid. *Do not use* blender.
YIELD: 1½ cups purée or 8 food cubes.

## BAKED SWEET POTATOES AND APPLES

¾ cup cooked sweet potatoes
¼ cup liquid (milk or fruit juice)
½ pound apples or 1 cup applesauce

1. Preheat oven to 350° F.
2. Remove skin and slice. Prepare apples: Remove skin and core. Slice.
3. Mix sweet potatoes and apples in buttered baking dish and pour liquid over.
4. Bake covered for 30 minutes.
5. To *purée,* mash with fork.
YIELD: 2 cups or 10 food cubes.
*Note:* This is a good family dish.

## • TURNIPS, RUTABAGAS

**Nutrition:** Fair amounts of carbohydrates, vitamins, and minerals.

**Introduce** cooked only at five months.

**Buy** turnips (white flesh) and rutabagas (yellow flesh) year round. Look for small or medium-size firm vegetables that are heavy for their size. If the tops are attached on turnips, they should be green and fresh. These greens are high in nutritional value and should be used. (See *Greens.*) *Do not buy* large vegetables which tend to be fibrous and tough, or those with skin punctures or signs of decay.

Frozen turnips and rutabagas are available and convenient.

Store turnips at cool room temperature (60° F.) for up to five months. Keep them only one week at room temperature.

## TURNIPS/RUTABAGAS

1 pound turnips
2 tablespoons evaporated milk

1. Wash and remove skin. Cut into large pieces.
2. *Steam* 20–30 minutes or *bake* 35–45 minutes, at 350° F.
3. *Purée* with any equipment, adding milk. A small amount of butter may be added for flavor.

YIELD: 2 cups purée or 10 food cubes.

## • TOMATOES

**Nutrition:** Tomatos contain good amounts of vitamins A and K. They contain about half the vitamin C as oranges and can be used as a substitute, if your baby is allergic to orange juice. Remember to double the serving. Their high juice content makes tomatoes a good vegetable to combine with other foods as a thinner.

**Introduce** cooked at three months, raw at five months.

**Buy** tomatoes either picked unripe or ripe; the latter will have better flavor and more nutrition. They are most plentiful from July to October. Look for tomatoes that are smooth, well formed, and reasonably free from blemishes. Marks around the top of a ripe tomato are harmless and sometimes indicate excellent flavor. Fully ripe tomatoes should yield to slight pressure and should have a rich red color. Underripe tomatoes will be hard and have a pink to light red color.

*Do not buy* overripe and bruised tomatoes or those with green or yellow areas, or deep growth cracks near the stem scar. Also avoid decayed tomatoes with soft, water-soaked spots, depressed areas, or surface mold.

**Store** ripe tomatoes in the refrigerator for several days. Ripen tomatoes at room temperature for 3–5 days. Do not place them in the sun.

**Instant Use:** Both canned and raw tomatoes are good instant foods. With raw tomatoes, cut them in half, remove the seeds, and scrape out the flesh. Buy canned tomatoes that are packed without added water, salt, or preservatives. *Do not give tomato purée or paste to a baby, as these are concentrates.*

**Finger Food:** Small pieces of raw, peeled tomato are juicy and nutritious.

Greenish or very hard tomatoes can be kept for several weeks around 50° F.

## COOKED TOMATOES

**1 pound tomatoes (4–5)**
**3 tablespoons wheat germ, instant cereal**
   *or*
**2 tablespoons whole wheat flour**
   *or*
**2 tablespoons cooked rice or cereal**

1. Wash tomatoes. If a blender or fork will be used, remove the seeds and skins. (An easy way is to dip the tomatoes briefly in boiling water, then plunge them in cold water.) However,

a strainer or food mill will *purée* the skins and seeds. This seems the easier preparation.

2. *Steam* 5 minutes in a pot with a tightly fitting lid or in the top of a double boiler, or *bake* in a covered dish or foil for 8 minutes at 325° F. (Do not use a steamer/blancher or you will lose the juice.)

3. *Purée* with fork, strainer, food mill, or blender, depending on your preparation.

4. Add one of the thickeners. (If flour is used, heat until thickened. If rice is added, *purée* with the tomatoes.)

YIELD: 1½ cups or 8 food cubes.

*Note:* This is the only vegetable purée that can be canned in the same way as fruit. (See *Home Canning,* chapter 5.)


# RAW TOMATOES

This is very economical in season and very nutritious, since all the vitamin C is preserved.

**1 pound ripe tomatoes (4–5)**
**3 tablespoons wheat germ, or 2 tablespoons rice or cereal**

1. *Prepare* and *purée* as for cooked tomatoes. Omit the cooking step.

2. Do not thicken with flour. Use rice, cereal, or wheat germ.*

3. Store in refrigerator for 2–3 days, or freeze in food cubes.

YIELD: 1½ cups or 8 food cubes.


# GENERAL VEGETABLE RECIPES

The easiest way to prepare vegetables is to serve them plain or in combinations. For variety, with strong-tasting vegetables or

---

* You can also freeze the purée without thickening, then use the individual cubes as a thinner for meats, etc.

those with consistency problems, such as greens, you may do a little extra work and use one of the following recipes for variation. Where an egg or cereal is used, remember to increase the serving so that it counts as an all-in-one meal of vegetable, protein, and/or cereal. These recipes can be prepared for the rest of the family and used as a vegetable dish.

Good vegetables to prepare this way are: *Asparagus, Broccoli, Carrots, Cauliflower, Leafy Greens, Mushrooms, Peas, Winter Squash,* and *Sweet Potatoes*.

## VEGETABLE SOUFFLÉ

½ cup cooked or canned vegetable, mashed
½ cup Medium White Sauce
2 eggs, separated
⅛ teaspoon cream of tartar

1. Preheat oven to 325° F.
2. Mix vegetables, White Sauce, and egg yolks. (With a blender you can do this at the same time you are mashing the vegetables.)
3. Cool mixture if necessary.
4. Beat egg whites. Add cream of tartar. Beat until stiff.
5. Fold into vegetable mixture.
6. Bake 40 minutes in greased casserole, or individual dishes. The mixture may also be steamed in the top of a double boiler for 1½ hours.
7. Serve at once. This may be kept for 1–2 days—the texture will not be the same, but the baby probably won't know the difference.

YIELD: 3–4 servings.

## VEGETABLE CUSTARD

1 teaspoon butter or margarine
1 teaspoon whole wheat or enriched flour
1 tablespoon non-fat dry milk
¼ cup hot milk
  *or*
⅓ cup Medium White Sauce
1 beaten egg
½ cup mashed vegetable

1. Preheat oven to 350° F.
2. Grease two custard cups.
3. Melt butter, blend in flour, wheat germ, or cereal.
4. Gradually add hot milk and non-fat dry milk.
5. Stir sauce until thickened.
6. You can substitute ⅓ cup White Sauce for steps 3–5.
7. Stir a small amount of hot sauce into egg, then mix egg with rest of sauce.
8. Add vegetables.
9. Pour into custard cups and place in pan of hot water that comes up to level of mixture.
10. Bake 30 minutes or until a knife comes out clean. The custard may be stored, covered, in the refrigerator for 2–3 days.
YIELD: 2–3 servings.

## EASY VEGETABLE CUSTARD

Follow the above recipe; however, substitute for the White Sauce any of the following: *¼ cup milk, ¼ cup cooking or canning liquid plus 2 tablespoons non-fat dry milk, ¼ cup fruit juice.* Skip steps 3–5.

## VEGETABLE/EGG YOLK CUSTARD

This is a good supper dish that counts as a serving of vegetables and egg yolk, if you double the amount given. You can make this as soon as your baby has been introduced to egg yolk, and it is also very useful if he shows an allergy to egg whites.

> ¼ cup vegetable purée (Asparagus, broccoli, carrots, leafy greens, peas, and sweet potatoes are good. See specific vegetable for preparation of purées.)
>
> 1 egg yolk, beaten
> ¼ cup milk (whole or skim)
> ½ teaspoon honey or brown sugar

1. Preheat oven to 350° F.
2. Blend together vegetable, egg yolk, milk, and honey.
3. Pour into 2 custard cups and place in pan of water.
4. Bake for 30 minutes or until a knife comes out clean. (The cups may also be placed in a pan of simmering water for 10 minutes.)
5. Refrigerate for up to 3 days.

YIELD: 2 servings.

## JELLIED VEGETABLES/FRUIT

You can combine almost any food or raw grated vegetable or fruit with gelatin to improve the "swallowability" or add variety. It is an especially good way to serve leafy green vegetables, raw carrots, raw beets, and is very easy to make with a blender.

> ½ envelope plain gelatin (The dessert gelatins can also be used, but they contain sugar and preservatives.)
>
> ½ cup boiling water (or vegetable cooking water)
> ⅓ cup fruit or vegetable juice
> 1 cup cubed fruit or vegetables
>   *or*
> ¾ cup puréed fruit or vegetables

1. Dissolve gelatin in hot water.

2. If you have a blender, combine cold water or juice with the vegetables until they are finely puréed. Or, finely grate raw vegetables.

3. Drain the vegetables and add ⅓ cup of the liquid to the gelatin.

4. Chill until the mixture is very thick (about ½ hour).

5. Fold in the fruit or vegetables.

6. Pour into mold and chill until firm.

7. Cover and store in refrigerator for 4–5 days. Do not freeze.

YIELD: 1½–1¾ cups.


## MEDIUM WHITE SAUCE

This sauce can be used to improve the texture of leafy green vegetables, or in custards and soufflés.

**1½ tablespoons butter, margarine, or vegetable oil**
**2 tablespoons whole wheat or enriched flour***
**1 cup hot milk**
**⅓ cup non-fat dry milk (optional)**

1. Heat oil or butter.

2. Blend in flour until smooth.

3. Gradually add hot milk and stir until blended and thickened. Add dry milk if desired.

4. Keep for 2–3 days.

YIELD: 1 cup.

* Instant White Sauce can be made by substituting 4 tablespoons dry infant cereal for the flour. You can mix it with oil without heating.

## MAYONNAISE

You can use a small amount of mayonnaise to improve the texture or flavor of raw vegetables, the green leafy vegetables, and meat purées. It is also a way to add fat to your baby's diet if he is drinking skim milk.

**2 egg yolks, beaten**
**2 tablespoons lemon juice**
**1 cup oil (corn, safflower, olive)**

1. Put the egg yolks and lemon juice in a blender, mixer, or bowl (use an egg beater).
2. Blend on a low speed, slowly adding the oil.
3. Cover and store in the refrigerator for up to 2 weeks.

# 10

## PROTEIN FOODS

At least two servings of a good source of complete proteins should be included in your baby's daily diet. They also supply some vitamins and minerals, especially iron, that are lacking in milk. Included in this group are Meats (beef, lamb, veal, pork), Organ Meats (liver, kidney, brains, sweetbreads), Poultry, Fish, and Eggs. Soybeans are also a good source of high-quality protein. Some of these protein foods are less expensive than others and some are easier to prepare as baby food. However, as long as you balance your selection, you can count any of these foods as an equal serving of a protein food.

### ● MEATS: BEEF, LAMB, VEAL, PORK

**Nutrition:** Meat is one of the essentials in your baby's diet. Veal is meat from young cattle. It is grayish-pink with very little fat. Beef comes from mature cattle, lamb from young sheep, and pork from young hogs. The different meats, or cuts of meat, contain nearly the same high amount of complete protein. Meat is especially valuable as a source of iron, with beef and veal supplying the highest amounts.

**Introduce:** When your baby is five months old you can introduce lean meat purées of veal, beef, and lamb. Pork and ham are usually given a month later. After meat is introduced, your baby should be eating several servings weekly.

**Buy:** Since meat is probably the most expensive but necessary food that you will feed your baby, it is important to know how to get the best value for your money. According to law, all meats and meat products, which are shipped between states, must be inspected for wholesomeness, proper labeling, and to make certain the meat has not been adulterated or contaminated. Each state must supply the same inspection service for meat sold only within that state. The inspection seal is a circle with the words: "U. S. Inspected and Passed by Department of Agriculture." Only buy meat that carries the seal. (See *U. S. Grades* in chapter 2.)

The government has also published this handy chart so that you can easily compare the serving cost of different meats and cuts of meat at various prices:

Cost per Serving of Red Meat and Poultry

| Retail cut | Servings per pound | Price per pound / Cost per serving | | | | | | | | | | | |
|---|---|---|---|---|---|---|---|---|---|---|---|---|---|
| | | 29 | 39 | 49 | 59 | 69 | 79 | 89 | 99 | 109 | 119 | 129 | 139 |
| **BEEF:** | | | | | | | | | | | | | |
| Sirloin Steak | 2½ | 12 | 16 | 20 | 24 | 28 | 32 | 36 | 40 | 44 | 48 | 52 | 56 |
| Porterhouse, T-bone, Rib Steak | 2 | 15 | 20 | 25 | 30 | 35 | 40 | 45 | 50 | 55 | 60 | 65 | 70 |
| Round Steak | 3½ | 8 | 11 | 14 | 17 | 20 | 23 | 25 | 28 | 31 | 34 | 37 | 40 |
| Chuck Roast, bone-in | 2 | 15 | 20 | 25 | 30 | 35 | 40 | 45 | 50 | 55 | 60 | 65 | 70 |
| Rib Roast—boneless | 2½ | 12 | 16 | 20 | 24 | 28 | 32 | 36 | 40 | 44 | 48 | 52 | 56 |
| Rib Roast—bone-in | 3 | 15 | 20 | 25 | 30 | 35 | 40 | 45 | 50 | 55 | 60 | 65 | 70 |
| Rump, Sirloin Roast | 3 | 10 | 13 | 16 | 20 | 23 | 26 | 30 | 33 | 36 | 40 | 43 | 46 |
| Ground Beef | 4 | 7 | 10 | 12 | 15 | 17 | 20 | 22 | 25 | 27 | 30 | 32 | 35 |
| Short Ribs | 2 | 15 | 20 | 25 | 30 | 35 | 40 | 45 | 50 | 55 | 60 | 65 | 70 |
| Heart, Liver, Kidney | 5 | 6 | 8 | 10 | 12 | 14 | 16 | 18 | 20 | 22 | 24 | 26 | 28 |
| Frankfurters | 4 | 7 | 10 | 12 | 15 | 17 | 20 | 22 | 25 | 27 | 30 | 32 | 35 |
| Stew Meat, boneless | 5 | 6 | 8 | 10 | 12 | 14 | 16 | 18 | 20 | 22 | 24 | 26 | 28 |
| **LAMB:** | | | | | | | | | | | | | |
| Loin, Rib, Shoulder Chops | 3 | 10 | 13 | 16 | 20 | 23 | 26 | 30 | 33 | 36 | 40 | 43 | 46 |
| Breast, Shank | 3 | 15 | 20 | 25 | 30 | 35 | 40 | 45 | 50 | 55 | 60 | 65 | 70 |
| Shoulder Roast | 2½ | 12 | 16 | 20 | 24 | 28 | 32 | 36 | 40 | 44 | 48 | 52 | 56 |
| Leg of Lamb | 3 | 10 | 13 | 16 | 20 | 23 | 26 | 30 | 33 | 36 | 40 | 43 | 46 |
| **PORK—FRESH:** | | | | | | | | | | | | | |
| Center Cut or Rib Chops | 4 | 7 | 10 | 12 | 15 | 17 | 20 | 22 | 25 | 27 | 30 | 32 | 35 |
| Loin or Rib Roast | 2½ | 12 | 16 | 20 | 24 | 28 | 32 | 36 | 40 | 44 | 48 | 52 | 56 |
| Boston butt—bone-in | 3 | 10 | 13 | 16 | 20 | 23 | 26 | 30 | 33 | 36 | 40 | 43 | 46 |
| Blade Steak | 3 | 10 | 13 | 16 | 20 | 23 | 26 | 30 | 33 | 36 | 40 | 43 | 46 |
| Spare Ribs | 1⅓ | 22 | 29 | 37 | 44 | 52 | 59 | 67 | 74 | 82 | 89 | 97 | 104 |
| **PORK—CURED:** | | | | | | | | | | | | | |
| Picnic—bone-in | 2 | 15 | 20 | 25 | 30 | 35 | 40 | 45 | 50 | 55 | 60 | 65 | 70 |
| Ham—fully cooked: | | | | | | | | | | | | | |
| bone-in | 3½ | 8 | 11 | 14 | 17 | 20 | 23 | 25 | 28 | 31 | 34 | 37 | 40 |
| boneless and canned | 5 | 6 | 8 | 10 | 12 | 14 | 16 | 18 | 20 | 22 | 24 | 26 | 28 |
| shankless | 4¼ | 7 | 9 | 12 | 14 | 16 | 19 | 21 | 24 | 26 | 28 | 30 | 33 |
| center slice | 5 | 6 | 8 | 10 | 12 | 14 | 16 | 18 | 20 | 22 | 24 | 26 | 28 |
| **POULTRY:** | | | | | | | | | | | | | |
| Broiler, ready-to-cook | 1⅓ | 22 | 29 | 37 | 44 | 52 | 59 | 67 | 74 | 82 | 89 | 97 | 104 |
| legs, thighs | 3 | 10 | 13 | 16 | 20 | 23 | 26 | 30 | 33 | 36 | 40 | 43 | 46 |
| breasts | 4 | 7 | 10 | 12 | 15 | 17 | 20 | 22 | 25 | 27 | 30 | 32 | 35 |
| Turkey, ready-to-cook: | | | | | | | | | | | | | |
| under 12 lbs. | 1 | 29 | 39 | 49 | 59 | 69 | 79 | 89 | 99 | 109 | 119 | 129 | 139 |
| 12 lbs. and over | 1½ | 22 | 29 | 37 | 44 | 52 | 69 | 67 | 74 | 82 | 89 | 97 | 104 |

The government also supplies a voluntary grading service which is widely used for beef. The grade shield is marked on the wholesale cut and may appear on the meat you buy or on the label. If you are not sure of the grade, ask the butcher. The main basis for the grade is the tenderness which results from liberal marbling or fat in the meat. *There is no difference in wholesomeness or nutrition among the grades.* You can use the less expensive grades for a considerable saving of money in buying meat for purées.

The most expensive grades are *USDA Prime* and *USDA Choice;* the latter is the grade sold by most supermarkets. The next grades are *USDA Good* which has even less fat, and *USDA Standard* with the least amount of fat. These two lower grades will cost less and contain more lean meat. What an opportunity for a bargain! After the meat is braised and puréed your baby will never know how tender the original piece of meat was.

You can also save money in your choice of the cut of meat that you use. The boneless chuck roasts, the various round roasts, and stewing meat are easy to prepare and are very tender when braised. You should look for the cuts with the least amount of fat and take advantage of sales. Remember that stewing chuck meat has at least the same amount of protein, possibly even more, than prime sirloin steak.

*Ground meat,* if you do not have a blender, is easier to purée with a food mill. Select a lean piece of boneless meat—beef, veal, or lamb—and ask the butcher to grind it. Even if the whole cut is more expensive than the packaged preground meat, you will still get more value for your money, since ground meat can legally contain as much as 30 per cent fat. If you must buy preground meat, make sure it is bright red, and is as lean as possible. Dark red or brownish-red meat is not fresh.

Another type of meat that is easy to purée without a blender is the *precooked meat* that is sold sliced in many delicatessens. *Roast beef* and *baked or boiled ham* are usually available. These meats are quite expensive, but they can be puréed with a grater or food mill—quite handy when you are short of time or are traveling. They also make good finger foods since the thin slices are very tender. The ham, because of its high salt content, should not be served too frequently.

*Do not give your baby* the *precooked luncheon meats.* They contain salt, additives, and fillers, and are also expensive in terms of nutritional cost.

*Frankfurters* will be discussed in the chapter on *Finger Foods.*

*Bacon,* a salted meat which contains a high percentage of saturated fat, is very expensive for a small amount of protein and should not be counted as a serving of protein.

The meat purées that you make at home will be less expensive than the commercial purées. However, the major advantage in making your own purées is that you know exactly what you are feeding your baby. At present there is a good deal of controversy over the high amount of salt (as much as twenty times the normal amount) that is added to the commercial meat purées, and the use of preservatives such as sodium nitrate. Until recently, MSG was included in all commercial meat purées, but was removed after research showed it might be harmful to infants. Meats are a staple in your baby's diet, and there is no reason to risk his health by including these unnecessary ingredients.

**Store:** Since meat is expensive, you should store it properly. *Uncooked* meat should be stored in the coldest part of the refrigerator. Meat can be kept in the store wrapper for 1–2 days; just put a couple of holes in it for the air to circulate. If the surface of the meat is dry, the bacteria will grow less quickly. Large cuts of meat can be wrapped loosely and stored up to five days. However, ground meat spoils quickly and should be used within 1–2 days. Cured or smoked meats can be kept for one week. Uncooked meat can easily be frozen if it is wrapped properly. Remove any excess fat and wrap the meat tightly in plastic or foil freezer wrap. Label and date the packages if you plan to freeze them for a long period. Freeze the meat quickly, at 0° F. or lower. Here are suggested times for different meats and cuts.

Lamb, beef (roasts and steaks): 12 months
Veal, pork (roasts): 8 months
Veal, lamb, pork (chops or cutlets): 4 months
Cured or smoked meats (such as ham): 2 months
Ground and stew meat of any kind: 3 months

Meat should be thawed in its wrappings, in the refrigerator, before cooking. Meat may also be cooked frozen—allow twice as much cooking time.

*Cooked* meats should be covered, refrigerated promptly, and can be kept in the refrigerator for 2–3 days. Cooked purées can be frozen up to 2–4 months without losing quality. (See chapter 5.)

## MEAT PURÉE

You can use any meat that you have cooked for your family, or you can cook a month's supply of meat, 3–4 pounds, only for use as baby food. (*Each pound of meat will yield about 1½ cups of purée or 8–10 food cubes, depending on the cut of meat you use.*) Always cook meat at low to moderate temperature for as short a time as possible. If you overcook meat or use a high heat, the meat will shrink and become tough and tasteless. When meat is done properly, it will be tender and easy to purée. Pork and veal must be thoroughly cooked until well done. If you are using the less tender cuts, or lean grades, you should always cook the meat with the *braising* or *stewing* method.

**Braising** or cooking the meat with steam and a small amount of liquid or in the meat's own juices.

1. If you are using the oven, preheat to 350° F.
2. Cut away as much fat as you can.
3. Brown the meat evenly in a heavy pan. If the meat is very lean, use a little oil. Flouring the meat will cause it to brown better, but it is not necessary. The browning seals in the meat juices and helps prevent shrinkage. (You can also wrap any meat

tightly in aluminum foil and braise it in the oven. It will cook in its own juice.)

4. Add a small amount of liquid (½ cup for a roast).

5. Cover the pan tightly and cook in the oven or simmer on the top of the stove. You can also use your steamer for braising.

6. Add water if the liquid cooks away before the meat is done.

7. See *Puréeing Meat*.

### TIMETABLE FOR BRAISING MEATS

| | | |
|---|---|---|
| Beef roasts | 3–5 pounds | 3–4 hours |
| Beef steak | 1–1½ inches | 2–2½ hours |
| Short ribs | 2–2½ pounds | 2–2½ hours |
| | | |
| Veal shoulder | 3–5 pounds | 2–2½ hours |
| Veal chops | ½–¾ inch | 45 minutes |
| | | |
| Lamb chops | ½–¾ inch | 30–45 minutes |
| Lamb shanks | 1 pound each | 1½–2 hours |
| Lamb shoulder | 3–5 pounds | 2–2½ hours |
| | | |
| Pork chops | ½–1 inch | 45–60 minutes |
| Pork roast | 3–5 pounds | 3–4 hours |

Near the end of the cooking time, you can poke the meat to test for tenderness. If it looks stringy, the meat is getting overcooked. You can easily braise a small amount of *cut-up* meat or chops. Just remove the fat and place the meat in aluminum foil and place in a 350° oven for 45–60 minutes. This is practical if your oven is already in use.

**Stewing** is similar to braising. However, more liquid is used and the meat is cut into pieces or cubes. Here is a recipe for an all-purpose stew in which you may use pieces of veal, beef, or lamb. Stews are a good all-in-one meal; just serve 2–3 food cubes each feeding and omit other vegetables.

## ALL-PURPOSE MEAT STEW

⅓ cup flour
1½ pounds boneless stew meat, cut in 1-inch cubes
2 tablespoons fat or oil
3 cups liquid (water, vegetable or fruit juice)
4 medium potatoes
5 medium carrots
10-ounce package frozen peas (or any other green
   vegetable)

1. Heat fat or oil in the bottom of a heavy saucepan.
2. Coat meat in flour and brown in fat.
3. Add water and cover tightly.
4. Simmer about 1½ hours.
5. Add potatoes and carrots. Simmer 15 minutes.
6. Add frozen peas and simmer for 5 minutes.
7. See *Puréeing Meat.*

VARIATION:

Any vegetable can be substituted and ½ cup of rice may be substituted for the potatoes. Follow the cooking times for other vegetables in the chapter on *Vegetables.*

YIELD: 4–5 cups of purée or 20–25 food cubes.

## GROUND MEAT

You can also cook ground meat of any type to use in meat purées. It has the advantage of faster cooking and it can be puréed easily in a food mill or strainer, if you do not have a blender.

1. The easiest way to cook ground meat is to place it in a heated saucepan.

2. Cook over low heat, stirring to break up the meat.

3. Cook ground meat until it is thoroughly cooked, but not browned. If it is crunchy, it will not make a smooth purée. Be sure to cook pork thoroughly.

4. Drain off fat.

**Puréeing Meat.** Cooking meat for use in baby food is very easy. The difficulty comes in puréeing the meat to a very smooth consistency, so that a young baby can swallow it. If you have a high-speed blender, you can easily purée any cut or grade of meat, whether it is roasted, broiled, stewed, or braised. If you don't have a blender, try to use a neighbor's to make a month's supply at a time. Other alternatives are:

► Use a food mill to *purée* meat that has been braised until very tender. The meat will have a fairly coarse mixture, and it is time-consuming. Ground meat can be puréed to a smooth texture with a food mill.

► You can grate small amounts of chilled meat in a hand grater, such as the Mouli. This will make a very smooth purée and is an economical way to use leftovers such as steak.

► Thin the meat purée with the meat cooking juices and the juice that runs out when cutting the meat. If stewing or braising, cook the liquid down. You can remove excess fat from the cooking liquid by chilling it quickly in the refrigerator or freezer, then skimming off the fat that has solidified on the top.

► You can also use vegetable juice as a thinner, or add a juicy vegetable or fruit to the meat while it is cooking.

► *For a purée with a smooth consistency, one cup of cooked meat requires about ¼ cup of liquid.* A little butter or mayonnaise can be added for a smoother consistency.

► Cool the purée quickly and freeze into food cubes immediately. Or, store in refrigerator for two days.

## ● ORGAN MEATS: LIVER, KIDNEY, BRAINS, SWEETBREADS

**Nutrition:** Organ meats are some of the most nutritious and *economical* meats that you can easily prepare. Your baby will probably love the taste, even if you do not. So, serve with a smile!

*Liver* (calves, beef, lamb, pork, and chicken) and *kidneys* are some of the highest sources of iron, phosphorous, sodium, vitamin A, thiamine, riboflavin, and niacin. They contain the same amount of high-quality protein as meat.

*Sweetbreads* are high in protein but lower in the other nutrients. *Brains* contain only ½–⅓ the protein in meat or the other organ meats, and lower amounts of the other nutrients. Unless you prepare brains or sweetbreads for your family, their nutritional value is not high enough for the effort (and on my part, the mental anguish) involved in their preparation. There are other organ meats such as tripe, tongue, and heart that I choose to ignore completely.

**Introduce** beef liver or kidney at five months, other organ meats at six months.

**Buy** fresh meats and plan to cook them the same day.

**Store** uncooked meats, loosely covered, in the coldest part of the refrigerator. *Uncooked* meats can be frozen for 2–3 months. The *cooked* purées can be frozen for one month, or refrigerated for two days.

### LIVER PURÉE

Liver is one of the easiest protein foods that you can prepare for your baby, and you do not need a blender to make a smooth purée. Beef or lamb liver costs quite a bit less than calves' liver and is fine for baby food. You should always keep a supply of frozen cubes on hand and can serve it two to three times a week. It is especially valuable for its high iron content.

*A warning:* Steamed or braised liver has a very strong odor, so make it on a day when you aren't having company and can open a window!

> 2 pounds liver
> 1 cup liquid (milk or vegetable juice, or cooking liquid)

1. Rinse the liver under cold water.
2. If you are using a blender to purée, remove the outer skin and any large veins.
3. *Steam* liver for 10 minutes, covered, in steamer; or in a pot with a little water, or *broil* liver for 3–4 minutes on each side.
4. *Purée,* adding the liquid to thin. A food mill or a blender will give the smoothest purée. Cooked liver is also one of the few meats that can be scraped with a spoon or dull knife to prepare a purée. Chicken livers can be mashed with a fork.

YIELD: 3 cups or 15 food cubes.

VARIATION:

*Liver Stew:* Combine equal amounts of liver, carrots, and green beans, or broccoli, to make a complete dinner dish. You can steam them all together, just follow the individual cooking times.

## KIDNEY/CARROT STEW

Kidneys are more difficult to prepare than liver, and they also give off a very strong odor when cooking. But babies like them. They are inexpensive and highly nutritious, so take an hour one day and make enough for a month.

> 1 pound kidneys
> 4 medium carrots, scrubbed
> ½ cup liquid (milk, juice, or cooking liquid)

1. Preparing the kidney is the most work. Remove the outer membrane, split the kidney lengthwise through the center, and remove the inner fat and tubes.

2. Soak it in cold water for 1 hour, drain.

3. Place kidneys in a pot, cover with cold water, and simmer for 1 hour.

4. Drain the water. Add enough new water to cover.

5. Add carrots.

6. Simmer for another 15–30 minutes until tender.

7. *Purée,* adding liquid to thin. A blender or food mill will produce a smooth purée, but the food mill takes a longer time. A hand grater will produce a coarser texture.

YIELD: 2½ cups or 12 food cubes.

VARIATION:

The kidney can be prepared without any vegetable, or you can add any other vegetable—tomatoes are good.

## SWEETBREADS OR BRAINS

I am including general cooking instructions in case you do want to prepare them for your baby. They are considered delicacies. The recipe is untested due to my own squeamishness.

1. Wash under cold running water. Soak in salted water for 15 minutes and drain.

2. Remove the membrane on brains with the tip of a knife.

3. Add 1 teaspoon of salt and 1 tablespoon of vinegar or lemon juice to a quart of water.

4. Bring water to a boil. Drop in brains or sweetbreads and cover.

5. Simmer brains 15–20 minutes.
   Simmer sweetbreads 25–35 minutes.

6. Rinse thoroughly in cold water.

7. Hold the sweetbreads under cold water and slip off the

membrane. Cut out the dark veins and thick connective tissue.

8. *Purée* as for liver and kidneys, thinning if necessary.

## • POULTRY

**Nutrition:** Poultry, either chicken or turkey, offers the same amount of high-quality protein as meat and can be substituted often. It is also an excellent source of niacin, with good amounts of thiamine, riboflavin, and linoleic acid. Turkey supplies the most iron. Some types of poultry, which are very adequate for use in baby food, can be considerably less expensive than meat.

**Introduce** chicken and turkey at five months.

**Buy** any poultry that carries the U. S. Department of Agriculture inspection seal. Federal inspection of poultry is compulsory and it is your guarantee of wholesomeness, both while the bird was alive and during processing. The grading is voluntary. However, most of the poultry sold carries the *U. S. Grade A.* The lower grades are not usually available to the consumer and are used in processed foods where the appearance is not important. If you can buy the lower grade, you will be able to save money, and the cooked poultry will be fine for baby-food purées. Any *poultry product,* frozen or canned, must also carry the U. S. "Inspected for Wholesomeness" seal on the label.

You can use any type of poultry—roasters, fryers, or broilers—which you usually buy for your family meals. However, you can save money by using the lower-priced mature chickens or turkeys that may be labeled "Mature," "Old," or "Stewing." These terms refer to the age of the bird when killed and not the freshness when sold. These older birds are not tender enough to be broiled, fried, or roasted, but they are perfect for stewing or braising.

If you want to save time, buy the frozen boned chicken and rolled-turkey roasts. However, you are paying a premium for the preparation, as they are more expensive. Look for sales on these. Also, dark meat is as nutritious as white meat and may be less expensive.

As a rule, whole chickens are more economical than cut-up parts. Breast sections should not be priced more than 40 per cent higher than the whole chicken. Leg and thigh sections should not cost more than 30 per cent higher. For example, if the whole chicken is $.39 per pound, the breast sections should be $.55 per pound, and the leg and thigh sections only $.50 per pound. If they are priced higher, you will save money by buying the whole chicken, and it is just as easy to use in preparing baby food. Large turkeys are usually more economical than smaller ones. The self-basting variety is very costly for the little time you save and up to 6 per cent of the weight can be injected vegetable oil used in the basting.

**Store uncooked** poultry in the coldest part of the refrigerator and use within 1–2 days. Do not store in butcher paper, but rewrap it in wax paper or plastic, first removing the giblets.

*Frozen uncooked* poultry, tightly wrapped, can be kept at 0° F. for as long as 12 months for chicken and turkey, and 3 months for livers and giblets.

*Cooked* purées can be stored, tightly covered, in the coldest part of the refrigerator for two days. You may also freeze it in food cubes or store for 1–2 months.

*To thaw* frozen poultry, either raw or cooked, place it unwrapped in the refrigerator or in cold water. *Do not thaw it at room temperature.* If you allow additional cooking time, you can cook poultry still partially frozen. Frozen food cubes should be heated while frozen, just before a feeding. Thawed poultry spoils quickly, so do not save leftovers.


## CHICKEN/TURKEY PURÉE

The easiest way to cook poultry for baby food, either whole or in parts, is to *braise* or *stew*. Always cook the poultry completely; that is, do not partially cook it one day and finish it the next day. As a rule, *you will obtain 1 cup of cooked poultry (without the bone) from each 1½ pounds of a whole chicken or turkey.* For each 1 pound of a boneless turkey roast, you will obtain 1 cup of cooked turkey. (Since there is some indication that chemical steroids, used in poultry food, tend to accumulate in the skin, you should remove most of the skin before cooking.)

To braise poultry, you will cook it in a small amount of liquid in a tightly covered pot.

1. For oven braising, preheat the oven to 325° F.

2. Put the poultry in a heavy, covered roasting pan. You may need to add additional liquid during cooking. Place in oven or simmer on top over a moderate heat.

3. Allow 45 minutes per pound for whole birds up to 4 pounds.

For larger birds, cook about ½ hour per pound.

►You can also braise small parts such as drumsticks or breasts in the oven by tightly wrapping the pieces in *aluminum foil.* They will cook in 30–45 minutes.

►If you have a *large steamer,* you can use it to braise small birds or parts. Braising is really the same method as steaming. Depending on the size of the poultry, the cooking time should be 30–60 minutes.

►You can test for doneness by piercing a fleshy part and noting the color of the juice that runs out. If it is at all pink, the poultry is not done. You may also be able to tell by pressing the flesh and moving the drumstick. However, these are rather subjective tests with which I have never been too successful. Just be sure the juice and the flesh show no sign of pinkness. The flesh should also be separating from the bones.

Stewing poultry is a good way of tenderizing the more mature poultry. You can leave the chicken whole or cut it into parts. Remove the skin.

1. Place poultry in a deep pot. Add enough water to

half cover the whole bird or, if cut up, to completely cover the parts.

2. Cover the pot tightly and simmer: 2–3 hours for a 3–4 pound stewing chicken; ½ hour per pound for a larger chicken or turkey; 45–60 minutes for a broiler fryer.

3. Check for doneness. It should be well separated from the bones, thus saving you time and effort.

*Note:* When you have stewed the poultry, you will have a considerable amount of cooking liquid with a mild flavor and some nutrients. Cool, skim off fat, and freeze it as food cubes. You can then use it as thinner, or serve it to your baby as soup if he is sick or unable to eat solids.

## MEAL-IN-ONE POULTRY STEW

VARIATION:

Cooked poultry can be combined with vegetables, cereals, rice, etc., or you can save pots and time by adding vegetables or rice to the poultry while it is stewing. Just check the cooking time for the individual vegetable. You can also thin the cooked poultry with a juicy vegetable such as tomatoes, raw or cooked. If you use equal amounts of poultry, a yellow vegetable, and a green vegetable, you will have a balanced stew to use as a complete all-in-one meal.

For example:

  1½ pounds poultry
  10-ounce package frozen greens (last 15 minutes)
  ½ cup of rice (last 45 minutes)
  3–4 medium carrots (last 30 minutes)

YIELD: about 4 cups of purée, or 20 food cubes.

**Puréeing poultry.** If you have braised or stewed the poultry, it should be falling away from the bones. Just pull it off, making sure you remove all the small bones.

►For each 1 cup of cooked chicken, *purée* with about ⅓ cup of liquid. Use the cooking juices or vegetable juice.

►You can use a food mill or blender for a very smooth purée.

►To prepare small amounts with a coarser texture, you can chill the poultry and use a hand grater.

►You can add a small amount of butter, or oil, to improve the texture and flavor—about 2 teaspoons for 1 cup purée.

## • FISH

**Nutrition:** Fish is one of the most valuable foods that is also easy to prepare and to purée. It can be an inexpensive source of high-quality protein, containing the same amount as the more expensive meats. Salt-water fish is also one of the few good sources of iodine. Other nutrients that are found in good amounts in fish are vitamins A and D (higher in fatty fish), thiamine, riboflavin, niacin, calcium phosphorus, and iron (although a smaller amount than in meat).

**Introduce** *lean* fish at six months, *fatty* fish at eight or nine months, and *shellfish* after your baby is one year old. Although fish is not commonly served as a baby food in America, it is widely used in Europe and other areas. One reason might be that we eat considerably less fish than meat and poultry. Most babies love the soft texture and the mild flavor of fish, so try and feed your baby fish at least twice a week as a protein dish.

Fish, especially shellfish, may cause an allergic reaction in some babies, usually in the form of a rash. Introduce fish in a very small amount, about a teaspoon, and wait four days to make sure there is no reaction. If there is, wait a month and try it again.

## LEAN FISH

| | | |
|---|---|---|
| Bass, Black | Perch | Smelts |
| Carp | Pickerel | Snapper |
| Catfish | Pike | Sole |
| Cod | Pollack | Spot |
| Flounder | Redfish | Suckers |
| Fluke | Red Snapper | Sunfish |
| Grouper | Robolo (Snook) | Tautog |
| Haddock | Rockfish | Walleyed Pike or Perch |
| Hake | Rosefish | Weakfish (Sea Trout) |
| Herring, Lake | Sheepshead | Whiting (Silver Hake) |
| Kingfish | | |

## FATTY FISH

| | | |
|---|---|---|
| Alewife | Mullet | Shad |
| Bonito | Pompano | Striped Bass |
| Butterfish | Porgies | Sturgeon |
| Eels | Salmon | Tuna |
| Halibut | Sablefish | Whitefish |
| Herring, Sea | Sardines | Yellowtail |
| Mackerel | Sea Bass | |

## SHELLFISH

| | |
|---|---|
| Shrimp | Crayfish |
| Lobster | Scallops |
| Crab | |

**Buy** fish either whole, as steaks, or in fillets, fresh or frozen. If your family eats fish, you can use whatever type of fish that you usually cook. If you are buying fish only to prepare as baby food, the steaks and fillets will be the easiest type to use.

*Fresh Fish.* Whole fresh fish should have clear, bright eyes; reddish gills, shiny scales, firm flesh that is not separated from the bones; and a fresh, mild odor. If you notice a distinct fishy smell in any type of fresh fish, do not buy it. Steaks and fillets should be moist, white, and free from brown, yellow, or dried spots. If you plan to freeze the uncooked fish, make sure that it was not already frozen and defrosted. You should not refreeze thawed fish. You can test by placing the fish in water; if fresh it will float, if thawed the fish will sink.

*Frozen Fish* is available whole, in steaks, and fillets. Look for the U. S. *Grade A* or *B* on the package. The "U.S." means that the fish was processed and packed under continuous in-plant inspection by the U. S. Department of the Interior. This inspection and grading is done on a voluntary basis, and many products may be packed without this control which is your guarantee of a wholesome product.

If, when you open or thaw the frozen fish, it has a cottony look, darkened or yellow areas, a fishy smell, or an excess of liquid, do not use the fish, but return it to the store. The signs indicate that the fish has been thawed and refrozen.

*Frozen Fish Products* such as sticks, portions, etc., should not be used as food for your baby, since they usually contain various additives and fillers.

**Store** fish carefully, since it does spoil easily. The faster you use fresh fish, the better the taste and texture.

*Fresh* fish should be stored, tightly wrapped in plastic or foil, in the coldest part of the refrigerator for 1–2 days. Do not store in butcher wrap or newspaper.

*Frozen Uncooked* fish should be tightly wrapped in freezer wrap and kept frozen at 0° F. for 4–6 months.

*Cooked* fish should be tightly covered and stored in the refrigerator for no longer than two days.

*Cooked Frozen* fish purées can be kept for up to one month.

**Thaw** frozen fish in the refrigerator or under cool running water. You can always cook fish frozen or partially thawed.

**Cooking Fish.** Fish is one of the easiest foods to prepare. The main thing to remember is not to overcook fish since it will become tough. Fish is done when the color changes from translucent, or watery, to white, and the flesh flakes easily and separates from the bones.

►Prepare the fish as baby food as soon as possible after cooking, and freeze the purée at once.

►The best way to cook fish for baby food is to bake, poach, or steam it. If your family eats fish prepared by these methods, just make some extra for the baby. (Do not give a young baby fried fish.)

►One pound of fish fillet yields about 1½ cups purée or 8 food cubes. Prepare and freeze a month's supply at one time.

## BAKED FISH

1. Preheat oven to 350° F.

2. Place the fish on a buttered pan or aluminum foil. Dot with butter. You can also wrap the fish in foil, but this is actually steaming it.

3. Bake dressed whole fish (about 3 pounds) for 30–45 minutes; fillets or steaks (about 2 pounds) for 20–25 minutes. It is not necessary to turn the fish.

4. See *Puréeing Fish*.

## POACHED FISH

This method is good for thin fillets, steaks, and small whole fish. It is quick, easy, and the cooked fish is very digestible.

1. If you have a steamer, it is perfect for poaching, or use a shallow pan. In the steamer or pan place enough court bouillon, water with a little lemon juice, or milk to cover the fish.

3. Bring the liquid to a boil and reduce heat to a simmer.

4. Lower the fish into the steaming basket (or place in the pan of cooking liquid).

5. Cover and simmer for 5–15 minutes, depending on the thickness of the fish.

6. You can boil the liquid down and use it as a thinner.

7. To steam the fish, use only enough water to cover the

bottom of the steamer and keep it boiling for 10–15 minutes.

8. Test for flakiness.

9. See *Puréeing Fish*.

## MEAL-IN-ONE FISH STEW

Fish can be combined with most vegetables to make an all-in-one stew. If you are steaming vegetables, just add the fish during the last 10–15 minutes. Cooked fish can also be used in custards and soufflés, but you needn't bother just for the baby.

**Puréeing Fish.** Although fish is easily and quickly cooked, you must be especially careful to remove all bones before you prepare it as a purée. Even fillets, which are considered boneless, should be checked.

▶ When the fish has been thoroughly flaked and the bones removed, you can purée it with a blender or food mill for the smoothest purée; or simply mash it with a fork for coarser texture. Fish is an easy food to chew, so it is a good way to start introducing coarser texture. Larger flakes can be used as one of the first *finger foods*.

▶ For each 1 cup of fish, *purée* with about ¼ cup of liquid, either milk, cooking juice, or vegetable juice. You can also add a little butter or mayonnaise for a smooth texture.

## ● SOYBEANS

**Nutrition:** Although soybeans are a vegetable, they supply almost the same amount of high-quality complete protein as meat or poultry, and can be counted as a serving of a protein food. They are also high in linoleic acid, iron, potassium, thiamine, and fat. As you can see, soybeans are quite a nutritional bargain at $.28 a pound—and that is the *dry* weight. Although we do not usually consider them as desirable a food as sirloin steak, your baby will never know the difference.

**Introduce** at seven months. They are easily digested and are a very *un*allergenic food. If your baby is drinking skim milk, serve soybeans to supply some fat to his diet.

**Buy:** If you cannot find soybeans in your local supermarket, try the nearest "health" food store. Buy them in quantity, since they keep well. Soybeans are also a major ingredient of imitation bacon chips which are sold in most supermarkets.

**Store** dry soybeans in tightly covered cans or plastic bags, at cool room temperature for up to two years. Cooked purées will keep in the refrigerator for up to three days and can be frozen for two months.

## SOYBEAN PURÉE

1 cup dry soybeans
3 cups water
1 tablespoon butter or oil
¾ cup liquid (milk or tomato juice is good)

1. Rinse the soybeans, then soak them in water overnight. You can also bring them to a boil for 2 minutes, cover, and allow them to sit for 2 hours. The presoaking or cooking is not necessary if you are using a pressure cooker.

2. Add the butter or oil to help prevent the beans from foaming while cooking. Do not add salt.

3. Return the pot to a moderate heat and *simmer* about 2 hours. Leave the cover ajar to prevent foaming and spilling.

4. When the skins float to the top, you can skim them off to prepare the smoothest purée.

5. *Purée* with any equipment, adding ¾ cup liquid to thin.

YIELD: 2½ cups or 12 food cubes.

VARIATION:

If you do not thin the mashed soybeans, you can use the purée as a nutritious thickener for juicy fruits and vegetables.

## • EGGS

**Nutrition:** Eggs should be one of the staples of your baby's diet. They are nutritious, inexpensive, and easy to cook and purée. Eggs contain a good amount of complete protein, iron, riboflavin, vitamins B₆, B₁₂, and A, and are one of the few foods that contain natural vitamin D. They also supply saturated fat which is important to your baby's diet if he is drinking skim or non-fat dry milk. The *yolk* has most of the fat, iron, and vitamins A and D in the egg. The *white* contains half the riboflavin and protein of the whole egg. So, if you want to use only the egg yolk, you can double the amount and come out ahead nutritionally. At $.60 a dozen for large eggs, the cost comes to about $.40 per pound. Very economical for a high-protein food!

**Introduce:** The cooked egg yolk can be introduced in small amounts at four months. The cooked egg white is a possible source of allergy and should not be introduced until your baby is six to seven months old. Always use the cooked egg yolk or white when first introducing; raw yolk can then be used in beverages. Most doctors recommend that a baby eat one egg per day, but no more than nine to ten per week. You may use it occasionally as the second daily protein serving. Some doctors limit eggs because of their cholesterol content, but this has been criticized as unnecessary. If your baby is drinking skim milk, eggs are an important source of fat and cholesterol. (*See Nutrition,* chapter 1.)

**Buy:** The grade, size, and color of an egg does not affect its nutritional value. The important thing to look for in buying eggs is freshness. In some areas, the last date of sale must be stamped on the carton. Another guarantee of freshness is the *Grade AA* or *Fresh Fancy* which shows that the eggs have been produced under the U. S. Department of Agriculture's Quality Control Program. This grade must be dated with the last day of sale, which is ten days after the eggs were inspected. The main difference in the grades is the appearance of the eggs. *Grade AA* or *A* eggs have a better appearance and are good for frying or poaching. Since your baby won't be concerned with the appearance and will be eating his eggs well cooked and mixed, you can save money by buying the *Grade B* eggs. Just be sure they are fresh!

The *size* on the egg carton refers to the minimum weight for the dozen eggs and ranges from 30 ounces for *jumbo* eggs to 18 ounces for *small* eggs. If you are buying eggs specifically to feed your baby, the *medium-size* egg should be adequate for one feeding without wasteful leftovers. You can easily figure out which size is the most economical by the $.07 rule: *If the difference in price between two sizes of eggs is less than $.07, buy the larger size.*

The nutritional value of brown and white eggs is exactly the same. Since some people prefer the white eggs, you may find the brown eggs less expensive.

Besides freshness, the important sign to look for in buying eggs is a clean, uncracked shell. If the shell is cracked or dirty, the egg might contain the bacteria that causes the food poisoning, Salmonella.

**Store**

*Whole eggs* in the refrigerator with the large end up. Do not wash them or you will remove the protective coating. They should be used within one week, or else they may develop off-flavors and lose some of their thickening ability.

*Whole hard-cooked* eggs in the shell for up to one week.

*Cooked yolks* and/or *whites* should be covered and can be saved for 2–3 days.

*Raw yolks* should be covered with water in a tightly lidded container and stored for 1–2 days.

*Raw whites* should be tightly covered and stored for 1–2 days. If your baby is eating only yolks, you can use these whites in cakes, meringues, soufflés, and whipped in many desserts. You can also beat an egg white and use it as an inexpensive facial masque!

*Frozen raw eggs* (whole, yolk, or whites) may be stored for 6 months. If you are freezing the whole egg, first mix the white and yolk together. Do not freeze raw or cooked eggs in the shell.

*Cooked egg yolks* may be frozen in food cubes for up to one month. Other cooked egg dishes should not be frozen.

**Using Eggs:** You can prepare eggs in many ways and this is one area in which you can really use your ingenuity.

Both the egg yolk and the white are useful as a way of smoothly binding together many nutritious foods that would be difficult for your baby to swallow, such as leafy green vegetables, wheat germ, etc. Almost any food can be combined with eggs.

As a binder you can cook eggs in the form of custards, soufflés or just plain scrambled—the easiest.

If you are using only the egg yolk, remember to substitute 2 yolks for each whole egg that a recipe calls for. Yolks only can be substituted for whole eggs in any custard recipe and in most baked goods. The main exception is a soufflé which depends on the beaten egg white for its lightness.

► Eggs will separate easily if they warm to room temperature.
► When you are cooking any dish with eggs as the main ingredient, use a low to moderate heat, to prevent the egg from becoming tough or hard.
► You will also find hard-boiled egg yolks useful as a highly nutritious thickener for juicy fruits and vegetables, or when you have overthinned a purée.
► Finally, you can combine a small amount of eggs, with their complete protein, with many inexpensive foods that contain incomplete proteins, such as dried peas, beans, lentils, cereals, noodles, and rice.

The following recipes cover the basic and easiest ways to prepare eggs that your baby will enjoy eating.

## EGG YOLK PURÉE

This is the easiest food to cook and mash. There should be no reason for you to buy the commercially prepared egg yolks. It is also a food on which you can save considerable money by preparing yourself. The yolks of two *large* eggs, thinned to the same consistency, make the same amount of purée (3½ ounces) as in a jar of commercial egg yolks. The cost of the eggs, at $.55 a dozen, is $.09 (and you will still have the whites to use), as compared with an average cost of $.27 for a jar of egg yolks. (The jar states that it contains 3 egg yolks, but it does not state the size.) The commercial egg yolk is also thinned with water and contains a very high proportion of salt, which is unnecessary and may be harmful to your baby's health. Now, see how easy it is to prepare your own!

   4 large eggs
   ¼–⅓ cup liquid (milk, fruit, or vegetable juice)

1. Wash eggs.
2. Place eggs in a pan and cover with cold water.
3. Bring water to a simmer and cook for 15–20 minutes. Do not let the water boil.
4. Plunge the eggs, in the shell, immediately into cold water.
5. Cut the eggs in half and remove the yolks.
6. With a spoon or fork, mash the yolks with the liquid.*
7. The purée may be frozen for up to one month, or covered and stored in the refrigerator for 2–3 days.
   YIELD: 1 cup purée or 5 food cubes.
   (You can use the hard-cooked white in sandwiches, salads, and casserole dishes; or, serve it to an older child.)

* If you are using the yolk as a thickener, store or freeze it without thinning.

VARIATION:

### *Egg Yolk/Wheat Germ Purée*

Mix 1 tablespoon wheat germ with 2 tablespoons of milk or fruit juice, and allow to soften for 10 minutes. Mix together with the cooked egg yolks and rest of liquid.

(For a single egg yolk, use about 1 teaspoon wheat germ and two teaspoons liquid.)

## SCRAMBLED EGGS

You may scramble the whole egg or only the yolk. The size of the egg to use for one serving depends upon your baby.

**1 medium egg (or 2 egg yolks)**
**1 tablespoon milk (vegetable or fruit juice)**

1. Melt a small amount of butter or oil in a pan.
2. Beat the egg and milk. (If you want to save a dish, you can do it quickly in the pan.)
3. Cook the egg slowly, stirring until it is loosely cooked. (If the egg is cooked too long, it will be dry and difficult to swallow.)
4. Serve at once. It should not be necessary to thin the eggs.
5. Leftover scrambled eggs become hard and should not be saved. Do not freeze.

VARIATION:

### *Meal-In-One Eggs*

You can add up to ¼ cup of almost any purée to a *medium* egg while you are beating it, or you can *purée* a food with the egg. Try fruit, vegetable, or meat purées, grated cheese, cottage cheese, leftover cooked cereal or rice, etc.

This is also a good way to feed your baby the highly nutritious *wheat germ.* Soften 1 teaspoon of wheat germ in 2 teaspoons of milk for a few minutes before beating it with the egg and milk. For a balanced meal, combine a *cereal grain* and *fruit/vegetable* with the eggs.

## SMOOTH EGGS

This is an easy way of preparing an egg dish with the consistency of custard.

> **2 eggs (or 4 yolks)**
> **½ cup milk**
> **2 teaspoons butter**

1. Mix the eggs and milk together.
2. Melt the butter (or oil) in the top of a double boiler.
3. Add the egg mixture, cover.
4. Cook 10–15 minutes without stirring.
5. Cool and store in the refrigerator for up to three days.
YIELD: 3 servings.

## BASIC BAKED CUSTARD

Custard takes more effort to make, and since the main ingredient is milk, it should not be counted as a serving of eggs. You may wish to make a custard for a family dessert, and the baby will also enjoy it as a good supper dish. You may find that custard is useful as a way of feeding your baby some valuable foods such as green leafy vegetables, wheat germ, etc.

> **2½ cups milk (whole, skim, or evaporated)**
> **4 eggs (or 8 egg yolks)**
> **⅓ cup brown sugar or honey or 2 tablespoons molasses**
> **1 teaspoon vanilla**

1. Preheat oven to 350° F.
2. Bring milk to boiling point and remove from heat.
3. Beat the eggs, adding vanilla and sweetening.
4. Pour a little hot milk into the eggs, and mix.
5. Pour the egg mixture into the rest of the milk, stirring until it is mixed.
6. Pour custard into cups or casserole and place in a pan of hot water that reaches to the level of the custard. The water will cook the custard evenly.
7. Bake in oven for about 40 minutes or until a knife inserted in the center comes out clean. If you overcook the custard, it will pull away from the sides of the cup, leaving liquid around it, and the custard will have a harder texture.
8. Cool, cover, and store in the refrigerator for up to three days.

YIELD: 4–6 servings.

VARIATIONS:

### Stirred Custard

1. Follow the recipe for *Baked Custard* until you have mixed the eggs and milk together.
2. Pour the custard into the top of a double boiler and cook over simmering water for about 5 minutes or until the spoon is well coated. Stir constantly.
3. The custard will have a smooth, creamy texture.

### Wheat Germ Custard

Add 1 tablespoon of wheat germ to the milk before heating it. Proceed as for *Baked* or *Stirred Custard*.

### Anything Custard

You can add ¼–½ cup of almost any purée—vegetable, fruit, cereal, meat, fish, etc.—for each whole egg used in a custard.

Mix the purée (or chopped food) with the eggs before mixing with the milk or liquid. Proceed as for *Baked Custard*. See also *Vegetable Custard, Easy Vegetable Custard, Vegetable/Egg Yolk Custard,* and *Fruit Custard*.

## Soufflés

A soufflé is a very light custard that often uses a *White Sauce*. The lightness is obtained by beating the egg whites separately and folding them carefully into the egg mixture. A soufflé takes even more time and dishes than a custard, and it must be eaten immediately. Most likely, the only time that your baby will eat a soufflé is when you have made one for the rest of the family. As with custard, you can add almost anything to a soufflé. (See *Vegetable Soufflé*.)

## ● YOGURT

**Nutrition:** Yogurt contains all the valuable nutrients in milk—complete protein, calcium, riboflavin, and others. If you make your yogurt with milk that has been fortified with vitamins A and D, they will also be present in the yogurt. Some brands of commercial yogurt are also fortified with vitamins A and D. In addition, the bacteria in yogurt stimulates the body to produce vitamin K, which is important in blood-clotting and liver functions. Breast milk contains an adequate supply of vitamin K, but cow's milk contains less. If your baby is bottle fed, yogurt can be an important supplement in his early diet.

**Introduce** plain yogurt as early as four weeks. It is easily digested and is easy to swallow. The fruited varieties can be used after the specific fruit has been introduced. When your baby is accustomed to the taste and consistency of yogurt, you can use it, mixed with meats and vegetables, as a way of introducing new tastes and textures.

**Buy** commercial yogurts without preservatives or fillers. See the *Yogurt* section in the chapter *Instant Food* for a full discussion of commercial yogurt. The purest yogurt will contain only fresh milk, non-fat dry milk, and yogurt cultures.

**Store** yogurt in the refrigerator for one week to ten days. It will develop a stronger flavor the longer it is kept. *Do not freeze.*


## HOMEMADE YOGURT

Yogurt is one of the easiest foods that you can make yourself. It will have a milder, less acid taste than the commercial yogurts. You can also save quite a bit of money! An 8-ounce container of plain yogurt costs an average of $.30. You can make yogurt, using non-fat dry milk, that costs $.04–$.05 for the same 8 ounces. Now see how easy it is!

> **1 quart milk (any kind—whole, skim, goat, soy, etc.)**
> **½ cup non-fat dry milk powder**
> **¼ cup plain yogurt (commercial or homemade)**

1. Mix the milk and milk powder together in a pot.
2. Bring the milk to a boil and remove from heat at once. This will destroy any bacteria already in the milk. Be careful not to allow the milk to scorch the pot.
3. Cool the milk to about 105°–110° F. You can use the same wrist test that is used in warming a baby's bottle. A few drops of milk on the inside of your wrist should feel warm.
4. Mix a spoonful of milk into the yogurt, then stir the yogurt into the milk, blending well.
5. Now you must find a warm place for the yogurt to sit for about 5 hours. There are several choices, but the main principle is to keep the yogurt at a temperature of around 105°–110° F. so that the yogurt bacteria will grow. Too hot or too cold a temperature will kill the bacteria and you will only have sour milk. But if you are off by a few degrees, it will just take

longer for the yogurt to set. So you needn't be too worried about thermometers and exact degrees.

▶ If you can easily replace the light bulb in your oven with a 100-watt bulb and can leave the light on with the door closed, you will have a good temperature.

▶ I have had good results by simply warming the oven at 150° F. for 5 minutes then turning it off. After 2–3 hours you may check to see whether it needs another minute or so of warming. The oven should feel warm, but not hot when you open the door. You can always use a thermometer, of course.

▶ Probably the simplest and oldest way of making yogurt is to mix it in a heavy warmed casserole, cover, and wrap it in a blanket for 12 hours or until set. A widemouthed thermos can also be used for a small amount.

▶ There are commercial yogurt makers that you can buy for about $12, but they really are not necessary.

6. Using the oven method, the yogurt should set in about 5 hours. The longer you allow it to set, the more sour the yogurt will be. Do not stir.

7. Chill the yogurt before dividing into smaller containers or transferring.

*Here is an even easier method* which can save cleaning a pot. In Step 1, bring 1 quart of water to a boil. Pour the water into yogurt container and add 1¾ cups non-fat dry milk. Proceed with Step 3. (Since non-fat dry milk is already sterile, you do not need to boil it.)

*Note:* You can feed your baby the yogurt cold or slightly warmed. Another way you can use yogurt is to mix it with foods that are difficult to swallow, such as green leafy vegetables, wheat germ, etc. When you are first introducing meat, you can mix it with a little yogurt as you are feeding your baby. The meat purée will be easier for him to swallow.

VARIATIONS:

There are many ways that you can add flavor and variety to your homemade yogurt.

*Before* heating the milk, add ¼ cup honey or brown sugar or 2 tablespoons molasses.

*After* heating the milk and cooling, add ⅓ cup of any cooked fruit (prunes, apricots, peaches), puréed or chopped, or even some vegetable purée such as squash. You can also add ½ cup of fresh chopped or puréed fruit.

*Before* serving, you can stir in any flavoring you happen to have around.

### Yogurt Cheese

You can make a tasty cream cheese by hanging yogurt in cheesecloth and allowing it to drain several hours.

## • CHEESE

**Nutrition:** Cheese contains the same nutrients as milk and is a valuable food. It does lack the iron that is in other protein foods. For example: a 1-inch cube of Cheddar cheese has the same calcium as ½ cup of milk; and ½ cup cottage cheese=⅓ cup milk.

As for protein, 1-ounce of hard cheese (Cheddar, Swiss, or American), or ¼ cup cottage cheese, equals the protein of 1 ounce of lean meat, fish, or poultry.

If your baby is drinking milk, there is no need to add large amounts of cheese to his diet. You will find small amounts of cheese useful as an easy way of improving the quality of protein in such low-cost foods as noodles, cereal, rice, dried peas, beans, and lentils.

**Introduce** all types of cheeses around four to five months.

**Buy** hard cheese—Swiss, American, Cheddar, etc.—that has not been diluted with various additives and fillers. See chapter 2 on *How to Read Labels*. In general, you should not buy any cheese that is labeled with the words "Imitation," "Spread," or "Food."

Cottage cheese varies as to the types of additives, so read labels to buy the brand with the least amount. Sorbic acid is usually added as a preservative. Also, try to buy a brand that carries a government or state *grade* or *inspection* seal. In some areas the containers will be dated with the last day of sale, so look for it.

**Store** *hard cheeses,* tightly wrapped, in the refrigerator for 2–3 weeks. Any mold spots can be cut away. Hard cheese may also be frozen for several months. *Cottage cheese* should be kept in the refrigerator for up to one week. It should not be frozen.

## USING CHEESE

► Grated hard cheese can be used as a protein supplement and as flavoring in many purées. It is especially good in rice and vegetable dishes.

► To grate, cut hard cheese into small cubes and grate in a blender or with a hand grater. Softer cheese will grate better if it is well chilled or frozen. (One-half pound of cheese makes 1 cup grated cheese.)

► Always cook cheese at low to moderate temperatures and add near the end of cooking.

► For one use of cottage cheese, see *Noodle and Cheese Pudding.*

► Creamed cottage cheese may be mashed with a fork or puréed in a blender, and fed directly to your baby. It is a good *instant* food that is readily available.

► See Bibliography for pamphlet on how you can make your own cottage cheese.

# • NON-FAT DRY MILK

**Nutrition:** Non-fat dry milk powder is an excellent source of complete protein and contains all the vitamins and minerals of fresh milk. Only the fat and water have been removed. At $.20 for the equivalent of a quart of milk, it is a very low-cost and convenient way to serve protein to your baby, especially as a supplement with the economical cereal grains and legumes.

**Buy:** The *U. S. Extra Grade* mark on the label indicates that the dry milk meets the government's standards of composition and wholesomeness. The label will also tell you whether vitamins A and D have been added as supplements.

**Store:** The unopened powder can be kept at cool room temperature for several months. The opened packages of powder should be kept dry and used within two weeks.

**Using Dry Milk:** You can add dry milk as a fortifier in any recipe that contains liquid. It is especially good in any fruit or vegetable purées that are naturally thin or have strong tastes. Added to baked goods, it supplements the incomplete protein in the flour. *Use 2–4 tablespoons of powder for each cup of liquid.* Remember that 1/3 cup of powder supplies the same nutrients as 1 cup of milk. You can also increase the amount of non-fat dry milk powder, when it is specified in a recipe, by up to 50 per cent.

# 11

## DESSERTS

DESSERTS are not a necessity in your baby's diet. The highly sweetened or starchy ones, such as puddings, can even be harmful. I have included some basic recipes for nutritious desserts that your family will enjoy and that you can also feed your baby as fruit, cereal, protein, or dairy servings.

## FRUIT MILK SHERBET

This is a different way to serve fruit and is something the rest of the family will enjoy. There are egg whites, a possible allergen, in this dessert, so be sure that you have already introduced your baby to whole eggs, probably around seven months. Any fruit that has been introduced can be used; bananas, peaches, apricots, pears, plums, berries are especially good.

> 1½ cups fruit purée (Use any basic recipe for purées
> in the *Fruit* chapter
> 2 tablespoons honey (optional, depending on tartness
> of fruit)
> 1 teaspoon plain gelatin powder
> 1 tablespoon water
> ¾ cup milk (whole or skim)
> 1 egg white

1. Soften the gelatin in the water. Blend into the purée.
2. Add honey, if used.
3. Add milk and blend thoroughly.

4. Pour into a metal ice cube tray without the dividers. Cover and freeze until it is frozen around the edges.

5. While the mixture is freezing, beat the egg white until stiff.

6. Pour the frozen mixture into a bowl or blender and blend slowly until it is smooth.

7. Fold in the egg white.

8. Return to the ice cube tray and freeze until it is solid.
YIELD: 2½ cups.

*Note:* All the steps may be done in a blender except for dissolving the gelatin and beating the egg white.

## CITRUS FRUIT SHERBET

Once citrus juices have been introduced, this dessert is a good way of feeding your baby the entire fruit which contains additional nutrients. This recipe requires a high-speed blender to *purée* the pulp finely.

> 1 tablespoon brown sugar or honey (omit if a sweet
> orange is used)
> 1 teaspoon plain gelatin powder
> 1 cup fruit juice
> 1 lemon, orange, or ½ medium grapefruit

1. Melt sugar (or honey) in fruit juice. Dissolve in the gelatin.

2. Remove the fruit peel.

3. In a blender, liquefy the fruit. Add the juice and blend.

4. Pour into metal ice cube tray with the dividers removed.

5. Cover and freeze until fairly firm—about one hour.

6. Pour back into blender, and blend at a slow speed until smooth.

7. Return to ice cube tray and freeze until firm.
YIELD: 1½ cups.

## FRUIT/EGG YOLK CUSTARD

This is a dessert that counts as a serving of fruit and egg yolk. It makes a good supper dish and can be given as soon as your baby has been introduced to egg yolk. You will find it especially useful if your baby shows an allergy to egg whites.

1 piece fruit* (banana, pear, or peach is good)
   *or*
¼ cup fruit purée
1 egg yolk, beaten
¼ cup milk (whole or skim)

1. Preheat oven to 350° F.
2. Blend together the fruit, egg yolk, and milk.
3. Pour into 2 custard cups and place in pan of water.
4. Bake for 30 minutes or until a knife comes out clean.
The cups may also be placed in a pan of simmering water for 10 minutes, if you do not have an oven available.
5. Refrigerate for up to three days.
YIELD: 2 servings.

## FRUIT CUSTARD

This is a highly nutritious dessert for the entire family. It contains eggs, so wait until you have introduced the whole egg to your baby's diet.

2 cups milk (whole or skim) plus ½ cup non-fat dry milk (optional)
3 beaten eggs
½ cup fruit purée, raw or cooked (banana, peaches, plums, or apricots are good)

* Use blender to purée fruit with yolk and milk.

1. Preheat oven to 350° F.

2. If you have a blender, the milk, eggs, and fruit can be slowly blended at the same time. Do not use a high speed because you will have too much foam. Otherwise, mix them together until they are blended.

3. Pour the mixture into 8 custard cups. Place in pan of hot water that comes to the level of the custard.

4. Bake for 30 minutes or until a knife comes out clean.

5. Cover and refrigerate for up to three days.

YIELD: 8 servings.


## PEANUT BUTTER CUSTARD

1⅓ cups milk (whole or skim)
⅓ cup peanut butter
2 eggs, beaten
3 tablespoons honey (optional)

1. Preheat oven to 325° F.

2. Add the milk gradually to the peanut butter, stirring until smooth.

3. Blend in the eggs and honey.

4. Pour into a small baking dish or custard cups. Place in pan of hot water to level of custard.

5. Bake for 30 minutes, until knife comes out clean.

6. Cover and refrigerate for up to three days.

YIELD: 2 cups.

# FRUIT CRUNCH

This is an easy family dessert that your baby can eat as a serving of fruit and cereal.

> 3 cups sliced fruit*
> ⅔ cup brown sugar (or less, depending on tartness of fruit)
> ½ cup quick-cooking rolled oats
> 3 tablespoons flour (whole wheat, unbleached, or enriched)
> 3 tablespoons melted butter or margarine or safflower oil

1. Preheat oven to 350° F.
2. Peel fruit if your baby does not eat skins and you are *puréeing* in a blender.
3. Place fruit in an 8-inch-square baking pan.
4. Sprinkle with the sugar.
5. Combine the dry ingredients.
6. Mix the fat or oil with the dry ingredients until crumbly.
7. Sprinkle the mixture over the fruit.
8. Bake 1 hour.
9. *Purée* baby's portion in blender for smoothest texture.

\* *Some good fruits are:* apples, peaches, plums, nectarines, blueberries, and rhubarb (2 cups, or 12 ounces frozen, with 2 cups of any other fruit).

## APRICOT WHIP

This dessert is high in iron and contains some protein. It is also a way to use leftover egg whites.

> **1 pound package dried apricots**
> **2 teaspoons orange or lemon juice**
> **¼ cup brown sugar**
> **3 egg whites**

1. Prepare the apricot purée as in *Stewed Dried Apricots.*
2. Add the juice and sugar, heating until the sugar is dissolved. Cool.
3. Beat the egg whites until stiff.
4. Fold the apricot mixture into the egg whites.
5. Cover and store in the refrigerator for up to three days.
YIELD: 6 servings (adult).

**VARIATION:**

You can also use other stewed dried fruits such as prunes or peaches.

## GELATIN DESSERTS

Gelatin contains no vitamins or minerals, but it does supply a good amount of protein. It also gives a thicker consistency to some thin or difficult to swallow foods. You can use it to give some variety to your baby's meals, either plain or combined with almost any puréed food. The gelatin dessert powders contain mainly sugar and a variety of preservatives, so do not use them. Instead, buy the envelopes of plain dry gelatin which are less expensive and just as easy to prepare. Here is a basic recipe.

**1 envelope plain gelatin**
**½ cup cool water**
**1½ cups fruit or vegetable juice**
**1 cup puréed fruit, vegetables (optional)**

1. Place cool water in a small pan. Sprinkle in gelatin and stir to dissolve.

2. Add juice and heat for a minute or so, stirring well.

3. Pour into 4 small cups and cool. If you are adding a purée, stir it in after the gelatin has begun to thicken, in about ½ hour.

4. Store in refrigerator for 3–4 days.

YIELD: 4 servings.

# *12*

## BEVERAGES

BEVERAGES ARE ESSENTIAL in your baby's daily diet. Milk is the most important, but fruits and vegetable juices also supply vitamins and minerals. Since there is a wide variety of milks and juices for you to choose from, I feel it is important for you to be aware of the differences. I have also included basic information on buying, storing, and using milk and juices.

## MILK FOR YOUR BABY

You will probably be feeding your baby some form of cow's milk, even if you breast feed during the early months. Milk is an almost complete food, inexpensive for the amount of nutrition, and indispensable for your baby's growth. By the time he is three months old he should be drinking 3 cups to one quart a day and should continue for the next few years. Milk contains high amounts of complete protein, calcium, phosphorous, and riboflavin. It is naturally low in vitamin D and loses most of the vitamin C during processing. The amount of butterfat depends on whether the milk is whole or skimmed.

**Whole Milk,** whether it is pasteurized, homogenized, or evaporated, contains at least 3.25 per cent butterfat if it is stamped *U. S. Grade A*. This grade also indicates that the milk was processed under sanitary conditions and is wholesome. The fresh milk has been heated to kill harmful bacteria, and this pasteurizing also destroys the vitamin C. The butterfat in this milk will rise to the top, and the bottle must be shaken, before pouring, to distribute the fat.

▶ *Homogenized Milk* is pasteurized fresh milk that has been processed to disperse the butterfat evenly through the milk. Read the label to see if a particular brand has been fortified with Vitamin D.

▶ *Evaporated Milk* is concentrated by removing half of the water. It is sterilized and sold in cans and is usually fortified with vitamin D. One advantage is that you can easily carry home a good supply and store the cans at cool room temperature for several months. It is also good to use when traveling, since it is readily available and of uniform composition throughout the world. It is also less expensive than fresh, whole milk.

You can easily prepare whole milk by mixing equal parts of evaporated milk and water. It is very convenient to mix it directly in your baby's bottle. Remember to wash the top of the can before opening. You can cover the opened can and store it in the refrigerator for up to five days. You can also use evaporated milk in concentrated form to thin purées, especially strong-flavored vegetables; and also in fruit and vegetable drinks to supply some extra nourishment.

**Skimmed Milk** is available in fresh, evaporated, and powdered form. It is whole milk that has had most of the butterfat removed. Since vitamin A is also removed with the fat, most skim milk is fortified with vitamin A. Otherwise, it has the same nutritional composition as whole milk.

▶ *Fortified skim milk* has vitamins A and D added, along with a small amount of non-fat milk solids.

▶ *Evaporated skim milk* has been concentrated by removing part of the water. It is sold in cans and is stored and used in the same way as evaporated whole milk.

▶ *Non-fat dry milk powder* is skimmed milk from which almost all the water has been removed. You can buy it in any store, packed in boxes or in premeasured one-quart envelopes. The *U. S. Extra Grade* on the label indicates that the milk meets the government's standards of composition and wholesomeness. The label also indicates whether vitamins A and D have been added.

This form of milk is very inexpensive, around $.20 a quart as compared with $.40 or more for a quart of fresh liquid milk. This can mean a saving of at least $6.00 each month, if your baby is drinking a quart a day.

I have found this milk very convenient, since I can carry home 20 quarts in one box, and never have to dash out on a late night search for a bottle of fresh milk.

You can store the unopened powder at cool room temperature for several months. The opened package of powder should be kept dry and used within two weeks.

You will find it very convenient to carry a small amount, when you are traveling or visiting, and mix up a bottle wherever you find water—even a park or a gas station.

To obtain liquid milk, you will usually mix 1⅓ parts non-fat dry milk powder to 4 parts water. For example:

1 cup (8 ounces)=⅓ cup powder+1 cup water
1 bottle (8 ounces)=3 ounces powder+8 ounces water
1 quart=1⅓ cups powder+1 quart water

You can also use non-fat dry milk as a fortifier, to add nutrients to whole or skimmed milk, or in any recipes. Just add up to 50 per cent more powder, for instance:

1¾ cups powder to 1 quart water
2–4 tablespoons powder for each 1 cup liquid in a recipe

As a way of saving money and moderating the amount of cholesterol, you can also mix equals parts fresh milk and liquid non-fat dry milk. If your baby is already drinking whole fresh milk, you can use this mixture to gradually accustom him to skim milk. Once non-fat dry milk has been mixed, it must be stored as fresh liquid milk.

SKIM MILK OR WHOLE MILK?

There is, at present, a controversy among doctors and nutritionists as to whether or not a baby should be fed whole milk or skim milk, which has had the fat removed. Some doctors feel that by feeding a baby skim milk and limiting the amount of other foods that are high in saturated fat, they can reduce the possibility of atherosclerosis, or hardening of the arteries, in adult life. (See *Nutrition—Fats* and *Oils*.)

Dr. Fomon and other experts on infant nutrition object to such a drastic manipulation of an infant's diet for several reasons. They feel that a moderate intake of saturated fat, or food cholesterol, is necessary for proper development of the brain and nervous system and may also enable the body to handle cholesterol in adult life. Another essential nutrient in butterfat is linoleic acid which is important in your baby's development. Skim milk also supplies only half the calories of whole milk, and calories are important for an underweight baby. A point to remember is that breast milk does contain butterfat.

However, besides the cholesterol question, there are some reasons why you might prefer to feed your baby skimmed milk. Some babies have difficulty digesting the butterfat in whole milk, and the result is the very messy and smelly habit of "cheesing." This may not happen if you use skim milk. You should also be able to take advantage of the convenience and economy of nonfat dry milk.

One answer, until more conclusive research is done, is to plan a well-balanced diet for your baby. A very young baby should be drinking whole milk. When your baby is eating solids, he will get an adequate amount of saturated fat in such foods as meat, liver, poultry, egg yolk, and butter, and you can then feed him skim milk as a regular beverage. You may also add to a bottle of skim milk two teaspoons of polyunsaturated safflower, corn, or olive oil, which will be equivalent in fat to whole milk and supply more of the essential linoleic acid.

If you are still feeding your baby whole milk, you should limit the amounts of high cholesterol foods or saturated fat. In any case this is an important question for you to discuss with your doctor, in view of your baby's own individual needs.

Of course, you can always use powdered milk for convenience, when traveling or visiting, and still use whole milk as your baby's main milk. A baby will not have difficulty in switching from whole milk to skim, since it is the fat in whole milk that usually causes digestive trouble.

## MILKS NOT FOR YOUR BABY

*Raw cow's milk* or *Certified raw milk* is one instance where an unprocessed food should not be used. All the original nutrients are there, but so are all the bacteria which can cause various illnesses and intestinal troubles. Since you must boil it to make it sterile, you have the same loss of vitamin C as in pasteurized milk, so it hardly seems worth the trouble and risk.

*Condensed milk* is sold in cans, usually on the same shelf as evaporated milk. Be careful not to confuse them. Since this milk is highly sweetened, it is not suitable for your baby.

*Filled, Diet, or Modified Skim milk* are various names for milk products that were developed for diet-conscious people who do not like the taste of skim milk. If the name confuses you, read the list of ingredients on the label. The different brands vary in composition but are usually some mixture of skim milk, non-fat dry milk, water, and vegetable fat.

While there is nothing harmful in these ingredients, the government has not set standards to insure that these milks have the same nutritional composition as cow's milk. The protein content may be higher or lower, and the vegetable fat is often coconut oil which is a saturated fat that lacks essential fatty acids. They are usually more expensive than plain whole or skim milk.

If this type of milk is the only one available, your baby will not be harmed by an occasional bottle, but he should not drink this milk regularly.

*Synthetic, Non-dairy, or Imitation milk* is also sold in dairy departments. This product has no relation to cow's milk. It is a combination of vegetable fat, sodium caseinate, soy solids, corn syrup, flavoring agents, emulsifiers, stabilizers, and water. Government standards have not been set for their nutritional value. Needless to say, do not give them to your baby.

*Chocolate milk* is also sold in dairy departments. It is sweetened and many babies are allergic to chocolate, so don't even try it in an emergency.

*Instant Breakfasts* are a form of milk drink, packaged in cans or in powder form. It is really a combination of sugar, flavorings, and some vitamin supplements. In an emergency, if milk is just not available, you can give your baby the liquid *vanilla* flavor. The powder form depends on being mixed with milk for its nutritional value. So don't just mix it with water and give it to your baby as milk.

*Buttermilk* is made from skim milk, and bacterial cultures have been added which gives it a sour taste. The name sounds healthy, but it is not suitable for your baby.

*Goat's milk and Soybean-based milk* are often given to babies who show an allergy to cow's milk. However, they do not have the same nutritional composition, so you should never use them without the advice of your doctor.

HOW TO STORE MILK

Fresh milk, and evaporated or non-fat dry milk that has been reconstituted, should be carefully handled to retain nutrients and prevent spoilage. I've always felt so guilty when I've had to throw away a quart of spoiled milk.

► Always buy fresh milk that is as fresh as possible. In some areas of the country the cartons must be clearly stamped with the date of the last day that the milk can be sold. In areas which do not have this law, the cartons are usually stamped with a coded date, and you can ask the owner of the store to interpret it. If you are buying more milk than you will use immediately, select those cartons with the latest date. If you find milk in the case that is past the legal selling date, you should not buy it—instead, notify the manager of the store to have it removed from the shelf.

► Cans of evaporated milk and packages of non-fat dry milk powder often are stamped with the packaging date. Buy the most recent date if you are buying large amounts. Store unopened evaporated and dry milk at cool room temperature.

► Keep liquid milk tightly covered and store it in the coldest part of the refrigerator. Remember that the door, which may have a shelf for milk, is usually the warmest area of the refrigerator, and milk should not be stored there.

► Plan to use milk within 3–5 days.

► Do not allow containers of milk to stand in the light, since light destroys the vitamin riboflavin. If you have your milk delivered, supply a box for the milk to be left in, so that it does not sit in the light. Since your baby's bottle may often be out for as long as an hour during a feeding, you can preserve the riboflavin by using opaque plastic bottles, or the disposable bottles which are used inside a solid holder.

► Do not pour unused milk back in the original container once it has been removed, or mix old milk in with fresh milk.

► You may freeze milk for up to a month, but it must be used soon after thawing.

## HOMEMADE FORTIFIED MILK

If your baby becomes balky at eating solids, or you want to add nutrients during his early months, here are some fortifiers that you can add to one bottle daily. You may even find a combination that you can give as an evening bottle to insure a wakeless night.

> 1 cup milk or formula
> 2 tablespoons non-fat dry milk powder
> 1–2 raw egg yolks* (raw egg white is difficult to digest)
> ¼ teaspoon molasses (laxative, iron)
> ½ teaspoon powdered brewer's yeast—(*not* baking yeast; B vitamins)
> 2 teaspoons vegetable oil (vitamin E, linoleic acid)
> 2 teaspoons plain yogurt (vitamin K)

1. Blend the ingredients with an electric blender or egg beater.

2. Allow it to settle for a few minutes so that there are no air bubbles.

3. Use a nipple with an enlarged hole. You can enlarge the hole by piercing it with a hot needle held in a pencil eraser.

## JUICES: FRUIT AND VEGETABLE

Fruit and vegetable juices supply vitamins and minerals while satisfying your baby's thirst. The juices sold especially for infants are expensive and highly sweetened. Instead, you should serve your baby any of the canned and frozen juices on the market, or you can easily prepare juice from fresh fruits and vegetables.

**Nutrition:** Juice is most valuable in your baby's diet as a source of vitamin C. This vitamin, although adequate in human milk, is destroyed in cow's milk by the pasteurization process. You can give your baby a vitamin supplement, but daily servings of certain juices will supply an adequate amount of vitamin

---

* Raw egg yolk should not be added until after cooked egg yolk has been successfully introduced.

C, together with other nutrients. Fruits and vegetables have different amounts of vitamin C.

▶ An orange a day keeps the doctor away" should replace the old proverb about the apple. The citrus fruits— oranges, grapefruits, lemon—are your highest vitamin-C fruits. One *three-ounce serving* each day of one of these juices, either fresh, dehydrated, or frozen, will give your baby enough vitamin C. When these juices are canned some of the vitamin is lost, so you should increase the serving to at least *4 ounces*. The orange and grapefruit juices sold in bottles in the dairy section have been pasteurized and are the same as canned juices.

▶ Guava juice, available in cans, is as high as the citrus fruits in vitamin C.

▶ Canned tomato or papaya juice will supply an adequate amount of vitamin C, if you double the serving to *6 ounces* daily.

▶ Never heat fruit juice before serving, since heat destroys vitamin C.

▶ Other fruits are low in vitamin C and should be considered only as beverages.

▶ Apricot nectar, papaya, and mango juices are very high in vitamin A.

**Introduce** orange juice, then other citrus juices at around two to three weeks. Orange juice is a possible allergy food, so when you first introduce it, dilute the juice with an equal amount of water. Begin with one ounce daily, then gradually increase to 3 ounces. If your baby does show an allergic reaction to orange juice, you can try guava or tomato juice or give him a vitamin-C supplement. Other juices can be given as beverages at around the same time you would introduce the fruit or vegetable.

**Buying:** The Federal Food and Drug Administration has set standards of identity for the various forms of fresh, frozen, and canned orange juice that require a high content of juice. Unless you live in a tropical climate or buy oranges in season, the frozen orange juice concentrates are the most economical source of vitamin C. Since the juice content is set by the government, you can take advantage of the lower-priced store brands or private labels.

Standards have also been set for canned pineapple, tomato, and prune juice. Any sweeteners and preservatives must be stated on the label, so you can select the brands without additional sweeteners.

If you buy fruit juice, other than orange juice, that has been fortified with vitamin C, read the label carefully to check the amount of vitamin C in a serving that your baby is likely to drink. Remember that he should have 40–50 mg. of vitamin C daily.

Please notice that I have been using the word *"juice."* There are many beverages, both canned and frozen, which cannot be legally labeled as "juice." These include the fruit *"punches,"* *"drinks,"* and *"ades"* and are clearly labeled with these descriptive words. The nutritional cost of these beverages is very expensive—you are paying for and filling your baby up with mainly water and sugar. (*This is equally true of the citrus drinks such as* *"orangeade"* *or* *"lemonade."*) Even if vitamin C is added, the amount is fairly small, and you are still missing the other vitamins and minerals in the original fruit. You would come out ahead, in terms of nutritional cost, if you diluted frozen orange juice concentrate, instead of the usual three-to-one dilution, with the same amount of water as in these drinks—often as high as nine parts water to one part juice. There are no government standards for these drinks, and the label does not state the percentage of real juice.

Other beverages that your baby should not drink are the *"instant breakfast-drink powders"* and the *"imitation orange juices."* Again, the label and list of ingredients are your warning. These drinks contain little or no real juice and instead are made up of a variety of fillers, artificial color, artificial flavor, vegetable oil, sugar, and preservatives. Some vitamin C is added, but they still lack the other nutrients found in orange juice. These imitation juices are usually sold in the same freezer section as frozen orange juice, so you must be careful not to confuse them. You can also buy dehydrated-juice crystals that are real juice and should not be confused with the breakfast-drink powders. If you are in doubt about a product, just read the list of ingredients.

**Store** canned juices at cool room temperature for several months. Before opening the can, shake it well and rinse the lid. The opened can may be covered and stored in the refrigerator for 2–3 days. The acid in citrus juices acts as a preservative and these juices keep the longest. Frozen juices may be kept solidly frozen for several months in a 0° F. freezer, or for one month in the freezer compartment of a refrigerator. Do not refreeze thawed juices; use them within 3–4 days. Fresh citrus juices can be refrigerated for 3–4 days or frozen. Other fresh fruit and vegetable juices should be prepared just before serving and should not be saved.

**Straining:** Until your baby is drinking from a cup you will have to strain citrus juices so the pulp will not clog the nipple of the bottle. Even enlarging the hole in the nipple will not help. You might as well strain a 2- or 3-day supply to save cleanup. If you serve the "nectars," or a banana milk shake, you can enlarge the hole in the nipple with a hot needle held with a pencil eraser. As soon as your baby is drinking from a cup, you can serve him citrus juices with the pulp (which contains nutrients), and any other fruit or vegetable juice you have liquefied in your blender.

Here are a few easy recipes for preparing fresh juices. For detailed buying and storing information, see *Fruits* (chapter 8) and *Vegetables* (chapter 9).

### FRESH ORANGE JUICE

The best juice oranges are the Valencia, Hamlin, and Parson Brown. Select oranges that have smooth skins, and are heavy for their size. Oranges with russet or greenish skin color are often less expensive, but just as nutritious as the oranges with a bright orange color.

**1 medium juice orange**

1. Wash the orange.
2. Cut in half and squeeze the juice with either a hand or electric juicer or if you have a good blender: peel the orange, cut in half, and liquefy. This is a good method if you are making a large quantity and do not have an electric juicer.
3. Strain the juice for bottle feeding.
4. Do not add any sweetener.

YIELD: 3 ounces or 2 food cubes (1 serving).

*Note:* It will save you clean-up time to make a large batch and freeze it in food cubes.


## FRESH GRAPEFRUIT JUICE

**½ medium grapefruit**

1. Prepare as for orange juice.

YIELD: 3 ounces or 2 food cubes (1 serving).


## FRESH LEMON JUICE

**2 lemons**
**½ teaspoon brown sugar or honey**

1. Prepare as for orange juice. Add sweetening.

YIELD: 3 ounces or 2 food cubes (1 serving).

## ALL-PURPOSE FRUIT JUICE

You can prepare almost any fruit as a juice with an electric blender. Here is a general recipe with suggestions for some specific fruits.

**½ cup chopped fruit**
**¾ cup liquid\* (water, fruit juice, or milk)**

1. Select ripe fruit. Take advantage of seasonal prices or sales.
2. Wash the fruit. Peel and remove seeds. (If you are straining the juice, do not bother to peel thin-skinned fruits such as peaches, apricots, pears.)
3. Place fruit and liquid in blender and blend on highest speed until the fruit is liquefied.
4. Strain for use in a bottle. Or, use a nipple with an enlarged hole. As soon as your baby starts drinking from a cup, leave the pulp in to make a thick, nutritious drink.
5. Serve at once; do not store.

*Note:* Do not add sugar. Fruits contain natural sugar.

YIELD: 1 cup juice.


VARIATIONS:

Combine thick fruits with juicy fruits such as *banana/orange*. Experiment with any fruit you may have on hand or left over from a family meal. This is a good way to use up a piece of very ripe fruit that you might throw away.

---

\* For very juicy fruits such as berries, decrease the liquid to ½ cup. Do not combine milk with citrus fruits.

# ALL-PURPOSE RAW-VEGETABLE JUICE

There are fewer vegetables that can be prepared and served as juices because of their generally stronger tastes; however, they do make highly nutritious drinks. Carrots are an excellent source of vitamin A, green leafy vegetables contain high amounts of vitamins and minerals, beets are high in natural sugar. See *Vegetables* (chapter 9) for specific information on any vegetable you prepare as a juice. Here is a general recipe for use with a blender.

½ cup chopped vegetable
1 cup liquid (water, milk, or fruit juice)

1. Wash the vegetable. Peel if necessary.
2. Place vegetable and liquid in blender and liquefy on highest speed.
3. Strain and serve at once. Do not store.
YIELD: 1 cup.

VARIATION:

This is another way of preparing vegetable juice if you do not have a blender. You can also make a large amount and freeze it.

2 cups chopped vegetable
1 quart water

1. Wash and peel vegetable if necessary. Chop or cut in small pieces.
2. Place in pot. Cover tightly and simmer for 1 hour.
3. Cool and strain. Store in refrigerator for 2–3 days, or freeze in food cubes.
YIELD: 3½ cups.

VARIATIONS:

You can combine many fruits and vegetables to make a variety of nutritious drinks. Here are some suggestions, but use your imagination and whatever you may happen to have on hand—either fresh, frozen, or canned.

*Carrot/Orange*
*Carrot/Pineapple*
*Pear/Green leafy*
*Orange/Green leafy*
*Tomato/Green leafy*
*Carrot/Apple*
*Beet/Pineapple*
*Carrot/Celery*

## FRESH CARROT JUICE

This is one of the first vegetable juices that you can serve your baby when he is three months old. It is also an old-fashioned treatment for diarrhea. You will need a blender to prepare this juice.

**1 medium carrot**
**¾ cup water (or skim milk)**
**1 tablespoon non-fat dry milk powder (optional)**

1. Wash carrot. Cut in half.
2. Place carrot, water, and dry milk in blender. Blend on highest speed.
3. Strain and serve at once. Do not save.
YIELD: 6 ounces juice.

## BOILED CARROT JUICE

This is really the same as raw carrot juice, but you will not need a blender and you can make enough for several servings.

    **1 pound carrots (4–5 medium)**
    **1 quart water (or 2 cups water plus 2 cups skim milk)**
    **½ cup non-fat dry milk powder (optional)**
    **1 tablespoon brown rice (optional)**

1. Wash carrots and cut in small pieces, or chop.
2. Place all ingredients in a pot. Cover tightly.
3. Bring to a boil. Simmer for 1 hour.
4. Cool and strain. Do not force the carrots through—you want a juice, not a purée.
5. Serve in a bottle with an enlarged nipple hole.
6. Store the juice, tightly covered, in the refrigerator for 2–3 days. Or, freeze in food cubes.

YIELD: 3½ cups.

## 13

## INSTANT BABY FOOD: HOW
## TO LIVE OFF THE LAND

THE FOODS that are described in this chapter form the basis of easy baby-food cookery. In fact, they can all be used without any cooking or can be purchased already cooked in stores or restaurants. You can feed your baby some foods directly from the container. Other foods require only a fork or spoon to prepare the smoothest purée. A few foods may require the use of a blender, food mill, or strainer to prepare a smooth purée; but can still be mashed to a coarse texture with a fork or spoon. Since you are preparing your own baby food, you can quickly accustom your baby to eating coarser textures. You can always try a food—a hungry baby can become very adept at swallowing!

Instant foods can be particularly valuable when you are traveling or visiting, since there is no need to carry or store especially prepared food for your baby. To make your life even easier, train your baby to eat any food cold. These foods may be found in any small store, restaurant, or home kitchen. You should also keep some of these foods on hand for quick use if you happen to run out of your frozen supply of food cubes, or if you do not have adequate freezer space to take advantage of the food-cube method.

You should keep a list of the more successful ones for use by baby sitters and for your own quick reference. Use your imagination in finding new instant foods that I have missed; just keep in mind the basic good buying principles as described in chapter 2—*How to Read Labels*. For more detailed information, look up any specific food in the preceeding recipe chapters. The instant foods are also organized according to their basic food group, i.e., *Cereal Grains, Fruits, Vegetables,* and *Protein Foods;* so you can easily select a well-balanced menu.

## CEREAL GRAINS

*Dry Infant Cereals* are easy to carry and prepare. They are usually mixed 1 part cereal to 5 parts cold milk or formula.

*Instant Cereals* can usually be ordered in any restaurant. The smoothest ones will be the "Cream of Wheat, or Rice." If your baby has been introduced to whole-grain cereals, order oatmeal, Ralston, or Wheatena.

*Graham Crackers* or other soft enriched or whole-grain crackers can be soaked in milk and mashed to a soft purée. Bread can also be soaked. Avoid those which use BHT as a preservative.

*Rice Pudding* is usually available in restaurants and can be mashed with a fork or spoon.

## FRUITS

*Fresh fruit* is one of your most convenient instant foods. It is easy to carry and is available in any store or restaurant. As soon as possible, you should introduce raw fruit to your baby. Bananas can be served as early as six weeks, and other raw fruits at four to five months of age. You will be able to easily prepare a very smooth purée with only a spoon from any of the following fresh fruits. You will not even need a feeding dish.

| | |
|---|---|
| APPLES | MANGOES |
| APRICOTS | NECTARINES |
| AVOCADOS | PAPAYAS |
| BANANAS | PEACHES |
| CANTALOUPE | PEARS |
| GUAVAS | PLUMS |

1. Select ripe fruit.

2. Wash the fruit. Do not peel—the skin will serve as the dish.

3. Cut the fruit in half, or cut as large a slice as your baby will eat. Peel one side of a banana.

4. Remove the pit or seeds.

5. As you feed your baby, mash spoonfuls of fruit by scraping the cut side with the front or back edge of a spoon. This method is easy and will make a smoother purée than mashing with a fork.

Whole fruit keeps well, but when mashed, it turns brown quickly. So only mash as much as you will use in one feeding. The unpeeled part of the fruit can be wrapped and will keep at room temperature until the next feeding. You can also store it in the refrigerator for 1–2 days.

*Canned or Stewed Fruits* are also convenient as instant fruits. You can keep a supply on hand in your pantry. Try to buy the brands that are packed in water, or their own juice, or in "light syrup." The heavier the syrup the more sugar it contains. Always drain the fruit before puréeing, since it should not require any thinning. Some good fruits are:

*Applesauce:* Use the plain variety. The applesauce that is combined with other fruits often contains artificial color, flavor, or other additives, and is more expensive. You can serve applesauce to your baby without puréeing.

*Baked Apples:* Mash with a fork or spoon for a smooth purée.

*Jellied Cranberry Sauce:* Can be mashed with a spoon for a smooth purée. Do not feed your baby the whole type which contains skins.

*Pears:* Can be mashed with a fork for a smooth purée.

*Peaches, Apricots, Fruit Salad, Prunes* can be mashed with a fork for a coarser purée.

*Pineapple* requires a blender to prepare a purée.

## VEGETABLES

There are many vegetables that you can keep on hand or order in a restaurant as instant food.

*Mashed Potatoes* require thinning with a little milk. The "instant" or dehydrated potatoes should be used only as a last resort, since they may be lower in nutrients and usually are loaded with additives and fillers.

*Canned Yams or Sweet Potatoes* are already cooked and can be mashed with a fork, adding a little milk. Buy the vacuum-pack instead of the type that is packed in sugar syrup.

*Beans, Baked or Kidney, and Peas* can be puréed to a coarse texture with a fork, and thinned with a little milk. Or use a blender for a smooth purée.

*Peanut Butter:* Thin with an equal amount of milk.

*Winter Squash (Acorn, Butternut, etc.):* The frozen squash is cooked and mashed. It only requires thawing, since it is already puréed. You can usually order this squash in a restaurant.

*Fresh Ripe Tomatoes:* Cut in half, remove the seeds, and scrape with a spoon.

*Any Canned Vegetable:* Since it is already cooked, you only need to purée it in a blender or food mill. (See *Vegetables* in chapter 9.) Most can be mashed with a fork to a coarse texture. Drain the canning liquid, then add a small amount for thinning if necessary. If the canning liquid is not salted, you can serve it as a nutritious beverage.

## PROTEIN FOODS

EGGS

One of the best and most convenient instant protein foods! They are included as an instant food since a boiled egg is so easy to make, stores well, and can be easily carried when traveling. You can always order an egg in any restaurant.

## Egg Yolk

► Keep the boiled egg in the shell until ready to use. It can be kept at room temperature for one day, or refrigerated for one week.
► Cut it in half and remove the yolk.
► Mash the yolk, adding about 1 tablespoon milk or juice to thin.

## Scrambled Eggs

Order or prepare an egg so that it is loose, or softly scrambled. Mash it with a fork or spoon, adding a little milk.

*Egg Custard* can be ordered in most restaurants and can be fed directly to your baby.

### LIVER

Either chopped chicken liver or a pâté can be thinned to make a very smooth purée. It is available in most delicatessens and restaurants. Since these pâtés are rich and highly seasoned, only use them as a last resort to feed an older baby. You can also order sautéed or broiled chicken livers in many restaurants and mash them with a fork, adding a little milk. The beef and calves liver is usually too tough to prepare with a fork, but you can scrape some off with a spoon or dull knife.

*Prepared spreads* such as deviled ham, chicken, and liver can be purchased in small cans. These can easily be thinned to make a smooth purée, but they are also highly seasoned and often contain additives.

### PRECOOKED MEAT AND POULTRY MEALS

There are many canned and frozen prepared dishes that contain meat, poultry, cheese, vegetables, rice, pastas, beans. While they are more expensive than the same dishes that you can prepare yourself, they are easily stored and very convenient. For a quick meal, just open the can (or defrost) and put the food through the blender.

Some dishes such as spaghetti or macaroni and cheese can also be mashed with a fork or food mill to a coarser purée. These dishes can often be ordered in a restaurant.

The amount of protein depends on the type of dish and the specific brand; however, most contain more protein and other solids than the corresponding commercial baby-food dinners.

Read the labels carefully and buy those which list protein foods first, as the major ingredient. Avoid those brands which contain many additives and fillers. Remember that these foods should only be served occasionally when convenience is important.

*Stews* (usually the highest in protein)

*T. V. Dinners* (Choose one with a plain meat and two vegetables)

*Chicken and Noodles*

*Spaghetti and Meat Balls*

*Macaroni and Cheese*

*Chile con Carne* (for an older baby)

*Do not use* the frozen chicken or meat potpies, since they contain very small amounts of protein.

Leftovers can be stored in the refrigerator for two days. The canned foods can be frozen in food cubes for up to one month. *Do not* refreeze the frozen foods.

DAIRY FOODS

These dairy foods can also be used as sources of protein, and they contain the same nutrients as milk. They are very convenient and readily available instant foods.

*Yogurt* can be one of your baby's earliest foods. There is a wide variety of brands and flavors.

► Buy the brands, such as Dannon, that do not contain fillers and additives. The simplest list of ingredients is: fresh milk, non-fat dry milk, and yogurt cultures.

► You should introduce *plain* yogurt first, then *prune whip*.
► Older babies will enjoy the various fruit flavors. The Swiss-style yogurts have small pieces of fresh fruit which are easily mashed.
► Do not feed your baby the *chocolate* or *coffee* flavors.
► You can feed your baby yogurt directly from the container, at refrigerator temperature.
► Unused yogurt must be stored in the refrigerator and can be kept up to one week.
► See chapter 10 for instructions on how you can easily make your own yogurt.

*Cottage Cheese* is easy to prepare.

► Use the creamed variety or add a little milk. Mash with a spoon for a smooth purée. It is also good when mixed with a little fruit such as applesauce.
► Avoid those brands which contain fillers and preservatives.
► Cottage cheese spoils easily, so try to buy by the date, or taste it yourself before feeding it to your baby.
► You can store it in the refrigerator for up to one week.

*Ice Milk or Cream* is readily available and is a favorite of most babies.

► Ice milk is more easily digested by young infants.
► Introduce *vanilla* first and then fruit flavors. Remember to mash or remove any large pieces of fruit.
► Do not feed your baby *chocolate* or *nut* flavors.
► Sherbet is mostly water and sugar.

*Puddings,* if they are homemade, can be served occasionally as an instant food. The canned and frozen puddings are highly sweetened and contain a high percentage of fillers and additives, so don't bother feeding them to your baby.

## 14

## FINGER FOODS

Sooner or later, often around seven to eight months, your baby will decide that he wants to feed himself. He will subtly indicate this by grabbing for the spoon, hitting the spoon away, or simply refusing to eat. By this time you will probably be more than happy to give him the opportunity to feed himself. Unfortunately, this desire may come before he can handle a spoon well enough to consume an adequate meal. The result can be a hungry, cranky, and frustrated baby and a mess of splattered purées for you to clean up.

One way to handle this difficult stage is to serve your baby a well-balanced selection of "finger foods" that he can pick up, chew easily, and swallow without choking. Don't worry about discouraging his willingness to eat with a spoon. You can always give him a spoon and serve a thick purée. (See *Self-Feeding* section in chapter 3.) He is more likely to become discouraged if he becomes frustrated in trying to get enough to eat. He may then give up entirely and you will end up feeding him for much longer than is necessary. Instead, as your baby picks up his finger foods, he will be gaining valuable eye, hand, and muscular co-ordination; and will also be eating the foods that are so necessary for his growth. This stage can be a happy and healthy one for both of you!

## SOME GENERAL SUGGESTIONS

► For your own convenience, serve finger foods that fit in with the meals you are preparing for the rest of your family.

► Just as you planned to keep on hand a store of purées,

plan to have a ready supply of finger foods, frozen, canned, or fresh.

▶ For specific nutritional, buying, storage, and preparation information, look up any food in the recipe chapters.

▶ The consistency of any finger food should be firm enough for your baby to pick up, yet tender enough for him to chew and swallow easily. A cooked food is the proper consistency as soon as you are able to pierce it easily with a fork.

▶ Avoid small pieces of firm food such as raw peas or hard vegetables that may cause choking.

▶ If your baby is swallowing food whole and it is not being digested, it will show up whole in his bowel movements. In that case, you should cut the food into smaller pieces and make sure it is very tender.

▶ There is one thing that you should buy which will save you considerable clean-up time. It is a plastic "catchall" bib and it means just that. The bottom of the bib is folded up to form a pocket so that the pieces of food that do not make it to your baby's mouth, or that he decides to reject, drop into the pocket instead of on the floor.

You can easily make this bib by folding up the bottom of any plastic or cloth bib about 2 inches, then sewing or stapling the edges. You can also fasten the edges with paper clips, which can then be removed for easy cleaning. Remember, when you fasten the edges, you must allow the pocket to buckle out so that the food will be caught.

▶ One additional word of warning. Your baby may discover that it is fun to drop these finger foods from his high chair and watch them land on the floor. This may be educational, but it is also a nuisance for you to clean up. So watch out for this game and discourage it immediately. Since your baby will usually do this when he is no longer hungry, the simplest thing is to just take him out of his chair and declare the meal finished.

The following section lists some easy and nutritious finger foods according to their basic food group—*Cereal Grains, Fruit, Vegetables,* and *Protein Foods.*

## CEREAL GRAINS

The cereal-grain foods are economical sources of incomplete protein, carbohydrates, minerals, and the B vitamins.

**Dry, Ready-To-Eat Cereals:** These are some of the easiest finger foods, and, since you are faced with an overwhelming selection, here are some general rules:

▶ Do not buy the sugar-frosted, honey-coated, or chocolate-flavor cereals.

▶ Do not buy the flaked cereals—your baby could choke on them.

▶ Buy those cereals with a definite shape that your baby can easily pick up.

▶ There is some controversy over the nutritional value of some of these ready-to-eat cereals. You should read the labels carefully and buy only those that are "enriched."

▶ When you first introduce these cereals, soften them with a little milk, a few at a time. They will be easier to swallow.

**Pasta:** You can now buy spaghetti and macaroni in many different shapes which your baby can easily pick up. Even if he swallows them whole, they will be well digested.

▶ Always buy brands that are "enriched."

▶ Some good shapes are shells, wheels, twists, and small elbow macaroni. The long, thin spaghetti and noodles are very difficult to manage.

▶ You can serve these pastas plain, with a little butter, tomato sauce, or melted cheese as in *Macaroni and Cheese.*

▶ You can take advantage of the prepared spaghetti and macaroni dishes, either frozen or canned. Again, read the labels and buy the brand that is enriched and contains the fewest additives and fillers.

**Baked Goods:** The first breads your baby can eat are either very moist, soft breads, or hard baked goods that he can teethe on.

If a bread or a cracker has a medium, crumbly consistency, he may choke on it.

▶ Always buy crackers, cookies, and breads that are baked with enriched, unbleached, or whole-grain flour. (See *Cereal Grains* in chapter 7.)

▶ You can harden almost any bread by baking it in a very low (150°–200° F.) oven for 15–20 minutes. Your baby will enjoy teething on a variety of hard breads, and they are less expensive and messy than the teething sticks sold for babies.

▶ Stale bagels are also an excellent teething food.

Here are some easy and nutritious recipes for both moist and hard breads. You will be able to serve them to your baby and the rest of your family.

## BANANA BREAD STICKS

¼ cup brown sugar
½ cup vegetable oil (safflower, corn)
2 eggs
1 cup banana, mashed
1¾ cups flour (whole wheat, unbleached, enriched)
2 teaspoons baking powder
½ teaspoon baking soda

1. Preheat oven to 350° F.
2. Beat sugar, eggs, and oil together.
3. Stir in bananas.
4. Mix dry ingredients together—flour, baking powder, baking soda.
5. Add dry mixture to banana mixture, stirring only until smooth.
6. Pour into greased loaf pan.
7. Bake for about 1 hour or until firmly set. Reduce oven to 150° F.

8. Cool, remove from pan. Cut into sticks.

9. Spread out on cookie sheet or foil and bake until the sticks are hard and crunchy. Or, serve as a moist bread.

YIELD: About 2 dozen, depending on size of sticks. Store sticks in tightly covered container in a dry place.

VARIATION:

### Date Bread Sticks

Add ½ cup of finely chopped or puréed dates (good for iron).

### Nut Bread Sticks

Add ½ cup finely chopped nuts.

### Fruit Bread Sticks

Substitute other fruit purées such as apricot, peach, etc., for the banana.

### Carrot Bread Sticks

Substitute ¾ cup finely grated raw carrots for the banana.

## DATE-OATMEAL BREAD

This is a moist bread that is highly nutritious. If you have a blender you can easily mix all the wet ingredients and chop the dates.

1½ cups flour (enriched or unbleached)
½ teaspoon baking powder
1 teaspoon baking soda
¾ cup quick-cooking oatmeal
1 egg
1 cup sour cream
½ cup brown sugar
½ cup dark molasses
⅔ cup chopped dates

1. Preheat oven to 350° F.
2. Grease a loaf pan.
3. Combine flour, baking powder, soda, salt, and oatmeal in mixing bowl.
4. Blend together the egg, sour cream, sugar, and molasses. (If you are using a blender, add dates while blender is on.)
5. Mix in the chopped dates.
6. Pour mixture over dry ingredients and mix well.
7. Turn into the loaf pan and bake 45–55 minutes.


# PEANUT BUTTER COOKIES

This is a healthy cereal/protein snack.

1 cup shortening (melted butter or vegetable oil)
1 cup peanut butter (preferably homemade)
1 cup brown sugar
2 eggs
1 teaspoon vanilla
½ cup non-fat dry milk
2½ cups flour (whole wheat, unbleached, or enriched)
¾ teaspoon baking soda
½ teaspoon baking powder

Preheat oven to 375° F.
1. Beat shortening and peanut butter until creamy. It will be easier if the peanut butter is at room temperature.
2. Gradually add the sugar, beating until mixed.
3. Beat in the eggs and vanilla.
4. Blend in the remaining ingredients.
5. Shape into balls about 1 inch in diameter.
6. Place about 2 inches apart on an ungreased baking sheet.
7. Flatten each cookie.
8. Bake 10–15 minutes. Turn oven off and leave door slightly open. Allow cookies to cool in oven until quite hard.
9. Store in a tightly covered container in a dry place.
YIELD: 4 dozen cookies.

# OATMEAL COOKIES

These old favorites count as a healthy cereal serving; good for an easy snack.

> 1 cup flour (whole wheat, unbleached, or enriched)
> 1¼ teaspoons baking powder
> ½ teaspoon baking soda
> ½ cup melted butter or vegetable oil
> ½ cup brown sugar, packed
> ½ teaspoon coffee cake spice (optional)
> 1 egg
> ¾ teaspoon vanilla
> 1½ cups quick-cooking rolled oats
> ¼ cup wheat germ (optional)

1. Preheat oven to 350° F.
2. Mix together flour, baking powder, soda.
3. Beat butter or oil with sugar until creamy.
4. Beat in egg and vanilla.
5. Blend in flour mixture, oats, and wheat germ.
6. Chill.
7. Shape dough into balls about 1″ in diameter.
8. Place 2 inches apart on an ungreased baking sheet.
9. Bake for 10–15 minutes. Turn off oven, leaving oven door slightly open and allow cookies to cool. They should be quite hard.
10. Store in a tightly covered container in a dry place.

YIELD: 3–4 dozen cookies.

# FRUITS

Fruits are some of the easiest and most nutritious finger foods that you can serve your baby. You can look up the specific fruit in chapter 8 for detailed information; however, here are some general suggestions.

▶ To prepare *fresh fruit*, remove skin, seeds, and cut into small pieces, or long thin sticks. To conserve nutrients, prepare fruits just before serving.

▶ To remove skins, dip fruit in boiling water, then rub off skin under cold water. Or use a paring knife.

▶ Apples are an exception, since they are hard enough for your baby to choke on. Instead, remove the skin of a small apple, and let him gnaw on the whole apple. Even if your baby only has a few teeth, he will be able to scrape away most of the apple. This is also an excellent food with which to keep his teeth clean.

▶ When your baby is one year old, you can serve, unpeeled, such fruits as pears, nectarines, and plums. Remember that the skins contain nutrients.

▶ Frozen sticks of bananas are also a good finger and teething food. They are not as messy when eaten frozen, and the cold will be very soothing to his gums.

▶ *Frozen and canned fruits* can also be served. Try to buy those brands that are packed in their own juice instead of sugar syrup. You should also buy the *Grade A* fruits for use as finger foods, since they will have better shape and are usually more tender.

▶ *Dried fruits,* such as pitted prunes, apricots, apples, peaches, and dates are excellent finger foods and good sources of iron. Either buy the moist variety, or soak them in water overnight to soften them. Stewed dried fruit that is sold in jars is very convenient to use; however, it is heavily sweetened and should not be served too often.

The following fruits are convenient to serve as finger foods. Unless noted, they should be introduced peeled and cut into small pieces.

*Apples**  
*Apricots*  
*Avocados*  
*Bananas*  
*Berries†*  
*Cherries†*  
*Oranges, Grapefruit* (sections)  
*Grapes†*  
*Cantaloupes*

*Nectarines*  
*Peaches*  
*Pears*  
*Plums, Prunes*  
*Mangoes*  
*Papayas*

# VEGETABLES

Vegetables are essential in your baby's diet and you can use many as convenient finger foods. For more detailed information, look up the specific vegetable in chapter 9. Here are some general suggestions:

► You will have to cook most vegetables. Whenever possible, cook them in their skins and in large pieces or whole. You will conserve nutrients and it will be easier to peel and cut the vegetables after they are cooked.

► The best way to cook most vegetables is to steam them only until they are tender and can be pierced with a fork.

► Cooked vegetables can be served cut in small pieces, long thin strips, or whole.

► Tomatoes are the only raw vegetables that a young baby can eat as a finger food. Dip them in boiling water to remove the skins easily and spoon out the seeds.

* Serve whole to prevent possible choking.
† Do not serve until your baby is able to digest the skins, at around one year.

▶ Raw vegetables are not suitable for finger food because most are quite hard. If your baby has even a few teeth, he might bite off a piece of the vegetable and choke on it.

▶ While your baby is teething, but does not yet have teeth, you can give him thick sticks of cold, raw vegetables to chew on. Some good ones are: *carrots, celery, kohlrabi,* and *turnips.* You can prepare a few sticks at a time and keep them crisp and handy in a glass of water in your refrigerator.

▶ You might also try giving your baby raw leafy greens or lettuce, when he is at the stage of chewing paper. He may even obtain some vitamins!

▶ *Frozen vegetables* can be treated like fresh vegetables. You will save money and time if you buy the large bags of cut vegetables and use only a few pieces for each meal. The *Grade A* will be the most tender.

▶ *Canned vegetables* are very convenient to use as finger foods, since they do not require cooking and can be served directly from the can. *Grade A* vegetables will be the most tender and juicy.

The following vegetables, either canned, frozen, or fresh are good to serve as finger foods:

> *Asparagus*
> *Beans, Green* or *Yellow*
> *Beans, Baked*
> *Broccoli* (flowerets)
> *Carrots*
> *Cauliflower* (flowerets)
> *Corn-on-Cob* (make a slice down the middle of each row of kernels, so your baby will not eat the skins)
> *Leafy Greens*
> *Lima Beans*
> *Peas* (young, small ones with tender skins)
> *Soybeans* (cook until they are very soft)
> *Summer Squash*
> *Tomatoes*

## PROTEIN FOODS

Your baby will require two daily servings of high-quality protein food for good growth and energy. Yet, many protein foods are difficult for a baby to chew and swallow. Your baby may reject, at first, even the tenderest pieces of meat or poultry. However, there are finger foods with which you can satisfy your baby's need for protein. Here are some suggestions for foods that are both nutritious and convenient to prepare. For specific buying and storing information, look up the food in chapter 10.

**Eggs.** Eggs are almost a complete food—high in iron, protein, vitamins, and fat. They are your best protein finger food, since they are inexpensive, you can prepare them easily and quickly, and even a toothless baby will be able to swallow them. Eggs can be served as often as once a day. You can also combine eggs with other foods, that cannot easily be prepared as finger foods. Here is the basic recipe for preparing eggs, along with some variations.

## ALL-PURPOSE OMELET

1 egg or 2 egg yolks (the size egg depends on how much your baby will eat)
1 tablespoon liquid (milk, fruit, or vegetable juice)

1. Lightly grease a small frying pan, using vegetable oil, butter, or margarine. Heat the pan over low heat.
2. Beat the egg and liquid together.
3. Pour the egg mixture into the pan. Allow it to sit for about a minute, or until the bottom has set.
4. Fold the omelet in half, then in half again. You want the

pieces of omelet to be thick enough for your baby to easily pick up.

5. Allow it to cook another minute or until it is firm. Do not overcook, because the omelet will become dry and hard.

6. Cut it into small pieces and serve.

7. Leftover omelet can be wrapped and stored in the refrigerator for 1 day. Do not freeze cooked omelets.

VARIATIONS:

You can add almost any food to an omelet, either finely chopped or puréed. You can make all-in-one meals by combining a vegetable, rice or cereal, and the egg. As you can see, it is a good way to use leftovers from family meals. Whatever combination of food that you use in your omelet, you must add enough egg for a firm consistency. Usually 1 egg for each added ¼ cup of food will be enough. The Mini-Blend jar is very convenient for blending these omelets. Here are some suggestions:

### Wheat-Germ Omelet

Beat 1 tablespoon wheat germ with the egg and liquid. Allow it to sit for 5 minutes before cooking. This is a cereal/protein serving. (You can also use cooked cereal or rice.)

### Meat, Poultry, Fish Omelet

Place 2 tablespoons cooked meat in blender with egg and liquid. *Purée*. If you do not have a blender, use very finely chopped meats, poultry or fish. This is really a double protein serving.

### Fruit/Vegetable Omelet

Beat in ¼ cup of any fruit or vegetable purée with the egg. Or use a blender to *purée* everything together. This is especially good for serving your baby leafy greens.

**Meats and Poultry.** These are the most difficult foods for your baby to chew and swallow, no matter how tender they are. The best way to initially feed your baby beef, veal, pork, lamb, chicken, or turkey is to first cook and *purée* the meat, then prepare it either in *all-purpose croquettes* or as *meat balls*. An older baby will enjoy spareribs or drumsticks.

## ALL-PURPOSE CROQUETTES

This is a good finger food that can be made from leftovers, and frozen for future use.

> 3 cups cooked vegetables, fish, meat, rice, etc. (try and use equal amounts)
> 2 teaspoons lemon juice (optional)
> 1 cup White Sauce or 1 cup milk with a beaten egg
> 2 slightly beaten eggs
> 1 cup wheat germ or whole-wheat bread crumbs

1. Chop all cooked ingredients to desired texture, or *purée* in blender adding White Sauce or milk and egg. It should have a stiff consistency.

2. Shape into small balls or sticks, using about 2 tablespoons for each. You should have about 20 pieces.

3. Dip in beaten egg and then roll in wheat germ.

4. Sauté in butter until brown. You can also bake them at 375° F. for 10–15 minutes.

5. Spread out on a flat sheet and freeze at once. Store in freezer in meal-sized servings for 2–4 months.

YIELD: About 20 servings.

*Note:* You can also use your family's favorite croquette recipe—just make smaller pieces.

## MEAT BALLS

This is a good finger food that you can feed your baby in place of the controversial frankfurter or hot dog. You can use various ground meats or poultry.

> 2 pounds ground meat
> 2 eggs, beaten
> ¼ cup rolled oats
> ½ cup wheat germ

1. Mix all ingredients together.
2. Shape into balls or sticks, each the size of one serving.
3. Brown in lightly greased pan.
4. Add about ½ inch of water or vegetable juice. Cover the pan tightly and simmer over low heat for 30 minutes. You can also place the covered pan in a 350° F. oven.
5. Drain and cool.

YIELD: about 20 servings or meat balls. You can freeze them for 3–4 months.

**VARIATION:**

Instead of the oatmeal and wheat germ, use bread crumbs, mashed potatoes, rice, or cooked cereal.

## SPARERIBS

This is a good teething and finger food. As soon as your baby has even a few teeth, he will be able to gnaw the bone clean. You can use either pork spareribs, or breast of lamb which is very inexpensive. You can cook them either by roasting or braising. Pork must be *thoroughly* cooked.

### Roasted Spareribs

1. Preheat oven to 325° F.

2. Place spareribs in shallow pan, cover with foil, and roast for ½ hour. Pour off fat. You may also precook the ribs by simmering them, in water to cover, for ½ hour. The object is to remove most of the fat.

3. Increase the oven heat to 400° F., and roast the ribs uncovered for 1 hour or until fork tender. You can baste them with a little honey or molasses if desired.

### Braised Spareribs

1. Cut into single ribs.

2. Brown the ribs in hot butter or oil in a frying pan.

3. Add enough water, tomato, or apple juice to almost cover the ribs.

4. Cover the pan and simmer over low heat about 1½ hours. Add more liquid as necessary.

Store the cooked spareribs in the refrigerator for up to three days, or freeze in individual servings for up to two months.

## STEAMED DRUMSTICKS

Your baby may be able to eat steamed chicken legs or drumsticks as soon as he has teeth. You can begin by cutting most of the flesh away and letting him chew on the meat next to the bone.

1. Preheat oven to 350° F.

2. Wrap each drumstick in aluminum foil, or place in baking dish with a little water and cover tightly.

3. *Bake* in oven for 30 minutes or *steam* the drumsticks in a steamer for 30 minutes or until tender.

4. Store them in the refrigerator for 2–3 days, or freeze them separately for up to four months. You can then reheat in the foil.

## LIVER

Liver is one highly nutritious meat that most babies can chew as finger food. You can use either beef, calf, or chicken liver. It is very easy to prepare.

1. Place the whole pieces of liver in a pot with a small amount of boiling water, or use your steamer.

2. Cover and simmer over low heat for 5–10 minutes. Do not overcook the liver because it will become tough. You can even serve it slightly pink.

3. Cut out any veins or outside membrane and slice into very thin pieces.

4. Do not freeze cooked liver because it will become tough when reheated. If you are buying liver only for your baby, you can cut the raw liver into single servings and freeze it for three months.

**Bacon** may be served as a finger food. However, you must remember that it is mostly fat, with very little meat, so, you should not count it as a serving of a protein food. It is also a highly salted food and should not be served too often.

**Delicatessen meats,** such as boiled or baked ham and roast beef, can be served as *"instant"* finger foods, if they are sliced very thin. They are expensive, but very convenient, and your baby really eats very little. Do not use luncheon meats, salami, or bologna, except as a last resort. They contain many additives and artificial flavorings and color. Besides, they are an even more expensive source of protein than plain ham or roast beef.

**Hamburgers,** medium broiled, can be cut in small pieces. Be careful how you buy ground meat. (See *Meats,* chapter 10.)

**Frankfurters** also can be used as finger foods, but, please, only as a last resort. The controversy over this old stand-by food concerns the many chemical additives, artificial flavorings and colors that are used, and also the low percentage of meat or protein. The current Department of Agriculture "recipe" for frankfurters includes 30 per cent fat, 15 per cent poultry, 10 per cent water, 2 per cent corn syrup, and 3.5 per cent cereals and non-fat dry milk. "*All meat*" frankfurters do not contain any poultry products, and the "*all beef*" only contain beef as their meat ingredient. However, both of these higher-priced types of frankfurters can contain non-fat dry milk, cereals, and starch. You are paying a high price for these ingredients and, actually, the lower-priced frankfurters can be just as nutritious. If you do serve them to your baby, read the list of ingredients and buy the brand with the fewest number of additives and fillers. To prepare, cook them and remove the skins.

**Fish.** Fish is a good protein finger food that is soft enough for your baby to chew and swallow. Read the *Fish* section in chapter 10 for details on the types of fish and ways of preparing. You can serve your baby small flakes of the cooked fish or use the following recipe for fish sticks. If your family eats fish, separate a few flakes for your baby. Do not freeze the cooked fish flakes because they will become tough. When your baby is one year old, you can try serving him the canned tuna and salmon flakes.

## STEAMED FISH STICKS

This is a good protein food that your baby can feed himself. You will find they make a delicious hors d'oeuvre served with horseradish.

3 pounds whitefish, pike, etc. (frozen fillets are easy to use)
2 small onions
2 eggs, beaten
3 tablespoons cracker meal or wheat germ
½ cup water or vegetable liquid

1. Finely chop or grind the raw fish fillets.

2. Chop the onions.

3. Mix the fish, onions, eggs, and cracker meal until well blended, adding a small amount of water.

4. Form the chopped fish mixture into sticks about the size of a short frankfurter. You may also shape into balls. You should have about 30 pieces.

5. In the bottom of your steamer basket, or any pot you use for steaming, place a few slices of carrot, onion, and celery. This is used to raise the fish above the water and add a mild flavor, but the vegetables are not really necessary if you have a steamer.

6. Place the fish sticks on top of the vegetables, cover tightly, and steam over a low heat for 2 hours. Add water as necessary.

7. Cool, arrange the sticks on a flat sheet, and freeze. You can store them in meal-sized servings for up to two months. They will also keep in the refrigerator for 3–4 days.

YIELD: About 30 pieces.

**Cheese.** Cheese is a protein food that contains the same nutrients as milk. It is not a source of iron, as are the other protein foods. However it is a convenient finger food that is readily available. Your baby will enjoy chewing the sliced semihard cheeses such as American, Swiss, Meunster, and Cheddar.

When buying cheese, read the labels carefully to avoid those types which contain additives, artificial flavor and color, or fillers. Remember that the words "imitation," "flavored," "cheese food" indicate that the product is not pure cheese.

# APPENDIX A

# NUTRITIVE VALUES OF FOODS

The following table is compiled from:
United States Department of Agriculture
Home and Garden Bulletin No. 72,
*The Nutritive Values of Foods*
Agriculture Handbook No. 8,
*Composition of Foods.*

I have found that knowing the nutritional composition of foods is very useful for understanding their nutritional cost. These values are a basis for comparing the kinds and amounts of nutrients in different foods or different forms of the same food. For example, lamb liver is as high, if not higher, in the important nutrients as steak; however, it is considerably less expensive. Just look through and check the foods that you usually serve, then pick out the ones that are economical.

You do not need to use these values in planning your baby's daily diet. Although, you might want to compare the nutrients he consumes in a typical day with the advisable daily intakes that are described in chapter 1.

The values for calories and nutrients are the amounts present in the edible part of the item, unless noted otherwise. For many of the prepared items, values have been calculated from the ingredients in typical recipes. If a food is fortified with one or more nutrients, the information is on the label. The values shown in this table are based on products from several manufacturers and may differ slightly from those in a specific product.

# NUTRITIVE VALUE OF FOODS

(A dash in the columns for nutrients shows that no suitable value could be found although there is reason to believe that a measurable amount of the nutrient may be present)

| Food, approximate measure, and weight (in grams) | Water | Food energy | Protein | Fat | Fatty acids Saturated (total) | Fatty acids Unsaturated linoleic | Carbohydrate | Calcium | Iron | Vitamin A value | Thiamin | Riboflavin | Niacin | Ascorbic acid |
|---|---|---|---|---|---|---|---|---|---|---|---|---|---|---|
| | Per-cent | Calo-ries | Grams | Grams | Grams | Grams | Grams | Milli-grams | Milli-grams | Inter-national units | Milli-grams | Milli-grams | Milli-grams | Milli-grams |
| **MILK, CHEESE, CREAM, IMITATION CREAM; RELATED PRODUCTS** | | | | | | | | | | | | | | |
| Milk: | | | | | | | | | | | | | | |
| Fluid: | | | | | | | | | | | | | | |
| Whole, 3.5% fat....1 cup ........ 244 | 87 | 160 | 9 | 9 | 5 | Trace | 12 | 288 | .1 | 350 | .07 | .41 | .2 | 2 |
| Nonfat (skim) ....1 cup ........ 245 | 90 | 90 | 9 | Trace | — | — | 12 | 296 | .1 | 10 | .09 | .44 | .2 | 2 |
| Partly skimmed, 2% nonfat milk solids added ....1 cup ........ 246 | 87 | 145 | 10 | 5 | 3 | Trace | 15 | 352 | .1 | 200 | .10 | .52 | .2 | 2 |
| Canned, concentrated, undiluted: | | | | | | | | | | | | | | |
| Evaporated, unsweetened ...1 cup ........ 252 | 74 | 345 | 18 | 20 | 11 | 1 | 24 | 635 | .3 | 810 | .10 | .86 | .5 | 3 |
| Condensed, sweetened ....1 cup ........ 306 | 27 | 980 | 25 | 27 | 15 | 1 | 166 | 802 | .3 | 1,100 | .24 | 1.16 | .6 | 3 |
| Dry, nonfat instant: | | | | | | | | | | | | | | |
| Low-density (1⅓ cups needed for reconstitution to 1 quart) ....1 cup ........ 68 | 4 | 245 | 24 | Trace | — | — | 35 | 879 | .4 | 20 | .24 | 1.21 | .6 | 5 |
| High-density (⅞ cup needed for reconstitution to 1 quart) ....1 cup ........ 104 | 4 | 375 | 37 | 1 | — | — | 54 | 1,345 | .6 | 30 | .36 | 1.85 | .9 | 7 |
| Buttermilk: | | | | | | | | | | | | | | |
| Fluid, cultured, made from skim milk ....1 cup ........ 245 | 90 | 90 | 9 | Trace | — | — | 12 | 296 | .1 | 10 | .10 | .44 | .2 | 2 |

| | | | | | | | | | | | | | | | |
|---|---|---|---|---|---|---|---|---|---|---|---|---|---|---|---|
| **Cheese:** | | | | | | | | | | | | | | | |
| Cheddar ..........1 ounce ..... | 28 | 37 | 115 | 7 | 9 | 5 | Trace | 1 | 213 | .3 | 370 | .01 | .13 | Trace | 0 |
| Cottage, large or small curd: | | | | | | | | | | | | | | | |
| Creamed .........1 cup ....... | 245 | 78 | 260 | 33 | 10 | 6 | Trace | 7 | 230 | .7 | 420 | .07 | .61 | .2 | 0 |
| Uncreamed .......1 cup ...... | 200 | 79 | 170 | 34 | 1 | Trace | Trace | 5 | 180 | .8 | 20 | .06 | .56 | .2 | 0 |
| Cream .............1 ounce .... | 28 | 51 | 107 | 2 | 11 | 6 | Trace | 1 | 18 | Trace | 440 | Trace | .07 | Trace | 0 |
| Parmesan, grated ....1 tablespoon .. | 5 | 17 | 25 | 2 | 2 | 1 | Trace | Trace | 68 | Trace | 60 | Trace | .04 | Trace | 0 |
| 1 ounce ..... | 28 | 17 | 130 | 12 | 9 | 5 | Trace | 1 | 383 | .1 | 360 | .01 | .25 | .1 | 0 |
| Swiss ............1 ounce ..... | 28 | 39 | 105 | 8 | 8 | 4 | Trace | 1 | 262 | .3 | 320 | Trace | .11 | Trace | 0 |
| Pasteurized processed cheese: | | | | | | | | | | | | | | | |
| American .......1 ounce ..... | 28 | 40 | 105 | 7 | 9 | 5 | Trace | 1 | 198 | .3 | 350 | .01 | .12 | Trace | 0 |
| Swiss ...........1 ounce ..... | 28 | 40 | 100 | 8 | 8 | 4 | Trace | 1 | 251 | .3 | 310 | Trace | .11 | Trace | 0 |
| Pasteurized process cheese food, | | | | | | | | | | | | | | | |
| American .......1 tablespoon . | 14 | 43 | 45 | 3 | 3 | 2 | Trace | 1 | 80 | .1 | 140 | Trace | .08 | Trace | 0 |
| 1 ounce ..... | 28 | 49 | 80 | 5 | 6 | 3 | Trace | 2 | 160 | .2 | 250 | Trace | .15 | Trace | 0 |
| **Cream:** | | | | | | | | | | | | | | | |
| Half-and-half (cream and milk) .......1 tablespoon . | 15 | 80 | 20 | 1 | 2 | 1 | Trace | 1 | 16 | Trace | 70 | Trace | .02 | Trace | Trace |
| Light, coffee or table..1 tablespoon . | 15 | 72 | 30 | 1 | 3 | 2 | Trace | 1 | 15 | Trace | 130 | Trace | .02 | Trace | Trace |
| Sour ..............1 tablespoon . | 12 | 72 | 25 | Trace | 2 | 1 | Trace | 1 | 12 | Trace | 100 | Trace | .02 | Trace | Trace |
| Imitation cream products (made with vegetable fat): | | | | | | | | | | | | | | | |
| Creamers: | | | | | | | | | | | | | | | |
| Powdered ........1 teaspoon ... | 2 | 2 | 10 | Trace | 1 | 1 | 0 | 1 | 1 | Trace | ²Trace | — | — | — | — |
| Liquid (frozen) ....1 tablespoon . | 15 | 77 | 20 | Trace | 2 | 1 | 0 | 2 | 2 | — | ²10 | 0 | 0 | — | — |
| Malted milk: | | | | | | | | | | | | | | | |
| Dry powder, approx. 3 heaping teaspoons per ounce .......1 ounce ..... | 28 | 3 | 115 | 4 | 2 | — | — | 20 | 82 | .6 | 290 | .09 | .15 | .1 | 0 |
| Milk desserts: | | | | | | | | | | | | | | | |
| Custard, baked ......1 cup ....... | 265 | 77 | 305 | 14 | 15 | 7 | 1 | 29 | 297 | 1.1 | 930 | .11 | .50 | .3 | 1 |
| Ice cream: | | | | | | | | | | | | | | | |
| Regular (approx. 10% fat) .......1 cup ....... | 133 | 63 | 255 | 6 | 14 | 8 | Trace | 28 | 194 | .1 | 590 | .05 | .28 | .1 | 1 |
| Rich (approx.16% fat) .....1 cup ....... | 148 | 63 | 330 | 4 | 24 | 13 | 1 | 27 | 115 | Trace | 980 | .03 | .16 | .1 | 1 |
| Ice milk ..........1 cup ....... | 131 | 67 | 200 | 6 | 7 | 4 | Trace | 29 | 204 | .1 | 280 | .07 | .29 | .1 | 1 |

| Food, approximate measure, and weight (in grams) | Grams | Water | Food energy | Protein | Fat | Fatty acids | | Carbohydrate | Calcium | Iron | Vitamin A value | Thiamin | Riboflavin | Niacin | Ascorbic acid |
| --- | --- | --- | --- | --- | --- | --- | --- | --- | --- | --- | --- | --- | --- | --- | --- |
| | | | | | | Saturated (total) | Unsaturated linoleic | | | | | | | | |
| | | Percent | Calories | Grams | Grams | Grams | Grams | Grams | Milligrams | Milligrams | International units | Milligrams | Milligrams | Milligrams | Milligrams |
| **Yoghurt:** | | | | | | | | | | | | | | | |
| Made from partially skimmed milk .....1 cup ........ | 245 | 89 | 125 | 8 | 4 | 2 | Trace | 13 | 294 | .1 | 170 | .10 | .44 | .2 | 2 |
| Made from whole milk. 1 cup ........ | 245 | 88 | 150 | 7 | 8 | 5 | Trace | 12 | 272 | .1 | 340 | .07 | .39 | .2 | 2 |
| **EGGS** | | | | | | | | | | | | | | | |
| Eggs, large, 24 ounces per dozen: | | | | | | | | | | | | | | | |
| Raw or cooked in shell or with nothing added: | | | | | | | | | | | | | | | |
| Whole, without shell. 1 egg ....... | 50 | 74 | 80 | 6 | 6 | 2 | Trace | Trace | 27 | 1.1 | 590 | .05 | .15 | Trace | 0 |
| White of egg .....1 white ...... | 33 | 88 | 15 | 4 | Trace | — | — | Trace | 3 | Trace | 0 | Trace | .09 | Trace | 0 |
| Yolk of egg ......1 yolk ...... | 17 | 51 | 60 | 3 | 5 | 2 | Trace | Trace | 24 | .9 | 580 | .04 | .07 | Trace | 0 |
| Scrambled with milk and fat ..........1 egg ...... | 64 | 72 | 110 | 7 | 8 | 3 | Trace | 1 | 51 | 1.1 | 690 | .05 | .18 | Trace | 0 |
| **MEAT, POULTRY; RELATED PRODUCTS** | | | | | | | | | | | | | | | |
| Bacon (20 slices per lb, raw), broiled or fried, crisp ..............2 slices ...... | 15 | 8 | 90 | 5 | 8 | 3 | 1 | 1 | 2 | .5 | 0 | .08 | .05 | .8 | — |
| Beef,[3] cooked: | | | | | | | | | | | | | | | |
| Cuts braised, slimmered, or pot-roasted .....3 ounces .... | 85 | 53 | 245 | 23 | 16 | 8 | Trace | 0 | 10 | 2.9 | 30 | .04 | .18 | 3.5 | — |
| Hamburger (ground beef), broiled: | | | | | | | | | | | | | | | |
| Lean ..........3 ounces .... | 85 | 60 | 185 | 23 | 10 | 5 | Trace | 0 | 10 | 3.0 | 20 | .08 | .20 | 5.1 | — |
| Regular ..........3 ounces .... | 85 | 54 | 245 | 21 | 17 | 8 | Trace | 0 | 9 | 2.7 | 30 | .07 | .18 | 4.6 | — |
| Roast, oven-cooked, no liquid added: | | | | | | | | | | | | | | | |
| Relatively fat, such as rib ..........3 ounces ..... | 85 | 40 | 375 | 17 | 34 | 16 | 1 | 0 | 8. | 2.2 | 70 | .05 | .13 | 3.1 | — |

| Food (measure) | Grams | Water (%) | Food energy (calories) | Protein (g) | Fat (g) | Saturated (g) | Oleic (g) | Linoleic (g) | Carbohydrate (g) | Calcium (mg) | Iron (mg) | Vitamin A (I.U.) | Thiamin (mg) | Riboflavin (mg) | Niacin (mg) | Ascorbic acid (mg) |
|---|---|---|---|---|---|---|---|---|---|---|---|---|---|---|---|---|
| Relatively lean, such as heel or round..3 ounces | 85 | 62 | 165 | 25 | 7 | 3 | 3 | Trace | 0 | 11 | 3.2 | 10 | .06 | .19 | 4.5 | — |
| **Steak, broiled:** Relatively fat, such as sirloin......3 ounces | 85 | 44 | 330 | 20 | 27 | 13 | 12 | 1 | 0 | 9 | 2.5 | 50 | .05 | .16 | 4.0 | — |
| Relatively lean, such as round......3 ounces | 85 | 55 | 220 | 24 | 13 | 6 | 6 | Trace | 0 | 10 | 3.0 | 20 | .07 | .19 | 4.8 | — |
| **Beef, canned:** Corned beef......3 ounces | 85 | 59 | 185 | 22 | 10 | 5 | 4 | Trace | 0 | 17 | 3.7 | 20 | .01 | .20 | 2.9 | — |
| Corned beef hash......3 ounces | 85 | 67 | 155 | 7 | 10 | 5 | 4 | Trace | 9 | 11 | 1.7 | — | .01 | .08 | 1.8 | — |
| Beef, dried or chipped....2 ounces | 57 | 48 | 115 | 19 | 4 | 2 | 2 | Trace | 0 | 11 | 2.9 | — | .04 | .18 | 2.2 | — |
| Beef potpie, baked, 4¼-inch diam., weight before baking about 8 ounces......1 pie | 227 | 55 | 560 | 23 | 33 | 9 | 20 | 2 | 43 | 32 | 4.1 | 1,860 | .25 | .27 | 4.5 | 7 |
| **Chicken, cooked:** Flesh only, broiled....3 ounces | 85 | 71 | 115 | 20 | 3 | 1 | 1 | 1 | 0 | 8 | 1.4 | 80 | .05 | .16 | 7.4 | — |
| Chicken, canned, boneless......3 ounces | 85 | 65 | 170 | 18 | 10 | 3 | 4 | 2 | 0 | 18 | 1.3 | 200 | .03 | .11 | 3.7 | 3 |
| Chicken potpie, baked 4¼-inch diam., weight before baking about 8 ounces......1 pie | 227 | 57 | 535 | 23 | 31 | 10 | 15 | 3 | 42 | 68 | 3.0 | 3,020 | .25 | .26 | 4.1 | 5 |
| Heart, beef, lean, braised.3 ounces | 85 | 61 | 160 | 27 | 5 | — | — | — | 1 | 5 | 5.0 | 20 | .21 | 1.04 | 6.5 | 1 |
| Kidney, braised beef....3.5 ounces | 100 | 53 | 252 | 33 | 12 | — | — | — | .8 | 18 | 13.1 | 1,150 | .51 | 4.82 | 10.7 | — |
| **Lamb, cooked:** Chop, broiled......4 ounces | 112 | 47 | 400 | 25 | 33 | 18 | 12 | 1 | 0 | 10 | 1.5 | — | .14 | .25 | 5.6 | — |
| Leg, roasted......3 ounces | 85 | 54 | 235 | 22 | 16 | 9 | 6 | Trace | 0 | 9 | 1.4 | — | .13 | .23 | 4.7 | — |
| Shoulder, roasted....3 ounces | 85 | 50 | 285 | 18 | 23 | 13 | 9 | 1 | 0 | 9 | 1.0 | — | .11 | .20 | 4.0 | — |
| **Liver:** Beef, sauteed......3.5 ounces | 100 | 56 | 229 | 26 | 11 | — | — | — | 5.3 | 11 | 8.8 | 53,400 | .26 | 4.19 | 16.5 | 27 |
| Calf, sauteed......3.5 ounces | 100 | 51 | 261 | 29 | 13 | — | — | — | 4 | 13 | 14.2 | 32,700 | .24 | 4.17 | 16.5 | 37 |
| Lamb, broiled......3.5 ounces | 100 | 50 | 261 | 32 | 12 | — | — | — | 2.8 | 11 | 17.9 | 74,500 | .40 | 5.11 | 24.9 | 36 |
| Chicken, simmered....3.5 ounces | 100 | 65 | 165 | 20 | 4 | — | — | — | 3.1 | 16 | 8.5 | 12,300 | .17 | 2.69 | 11.7 | 16 |
| **Pork, light cure, cooked:** Ham, light cure, lean and fat, roasted....3 ounces | 85 | 54 | 245 | 18 | 19 | 7 | 8 | 2 | 0 | 8 | 2.2 | 0 | .40 | .16 | 3.1 | — |

| Food, approximate measure, and weight (in grams) | Water | Food energy | Protein | Fat | Fatty acids Saturated (total) | Fatty acids Unsaturated linoleic | Carbohydrate | Calcium | Iron | Vitamin A value | Thiamin | Riboflavin | Niacin | Ascorbic acid |
|---|---|---|---|---|---|---|---|---|---|---|---|---|---|---|
| | Grams Percent | Calories | Grams | Grams | Grams | Grams | Grams | Milligrams | Milligrams | International units | Milligrams | Milligrams | Milligrams | Milligrams |
| **Luncheon meat:** | | | | | | | | | | | | | | |
| Boiled ham, sliced ..2 ounces .... 57 | 59 | 135 | 11 | 10 | 4 | 1 | 0 | 6 | 1.6 | 0 | .25 | .09 | 1.5 | — |
| **Pork, fresh,[3] cooked:** | | | | | | | | | | | | | | |
| Chop, thick, with bone. 1 chop, 3.5 ounces . 98 | 42 | 260 | 16 | 21 | 8 | 2 | 0 | 8 | 2.2 | 0 | .63 | .18 | 3.8 | — |
| Roast, oven-cooked, no liquid added ....3 ounces ... 85 | 46 | 310 | 21 | 24 | 9 | 2 | 0 | 9 | 2.7 | 0 | .78 | .22 | 4.7 | — |
| Cuts, simmered ......3 ounces .... 85 | 46 | 320 | 20 | 26 | 9 | 2 | 0 | 8 | 2.5 | 0 | .46 | .21 | 4.1 | — |
| **Sausage:** | | | | | | | | | | | | | | |
| Bologna, slice, 3-in. diam. x ⅛-inch ....2 slices ..... 26 | 56 | 80 | 3 | 7 | — | — | Trace | 2 | .5 | — | .04 | .06 | .7 | — |
| Braunschweiger, slice 2-in. diam. x ¼ in...2 slices ..... 20 | 53 | 65 | 3 | 5 | — | — | Trace | 2 | 1.2 | 1,310 | .03 | .29 | 1.6 | — |
| Deviled ham, canned ..1 tablespoon 13 | 51 | 45 | 2 | 4 | 2 | Trace | 0 | 1 | .3 | — | .02 | .01 | .2 | — |
| Frankfurter, heated (8 per lb. purchased pkg.) .........1 frank. 56 | 57 | 170 | 7 | 15 | — | — | 1 | 3 | .8 | — | .08 | .11 | 1.4 | — |
| Salami, dry type .....1 ounce ...... 28 | 30 | 130 | 7 | 11 | — | — | Trace | 4 | 1.0 | — | .10 | .07 | 1.5 | — |
| Salami, cooked ......1 ounce ...... 28 | 51 | 90 | 5 | 7 | — | — | Trace | 3 | .7 | — | .07 | .07 | 1.2 | — |
| Turkey, roasted flesh only.3.5 ounces 100 | 62 | 190 | 32 | 6 | — | — | 0 | 8 | 1.8 | — | .05 | .18 | 7.7 | — |
| **Veal, medium fat, cooked, bone removed:** | | | | | | | | | | | | | | |
| Cutlet ............3 ounces .... 85 | 60 | 185 | 23 | 9 | 5 | Trace | — | 9 | 2.7 | — | .06 | .21 | 4.6 | — |
| Roast ............3 ounces .... 85 | 55 | 230 | 23 | 14 | 7 | Trace | 0 | 10 | 2.9 | — | .11 | .26 | 6.6 | — |
| **FISH AND SHELLFISH:** | | | | | | | | | | | | | | |
| Bluefish, baked with table fat .........3 ounces .... 85 | 68 | 135 | 22 | 4 | — | — | 0 | 25 | .6 | 40 | .09 | .08 | 1.6 | — |

| Food, approximate measure | Grams | Water (%) | Food energy (cal) | Protein (g) | Fat (g) | Saturated fatty acids (g) | Oleic (g) | Linoleic (g) | Carbohydrate (g) | Calcium (mg) | Iron (mg) | Vitamin A (I.U.) | Thiamine (mg) | Riboflavin (mg) | Niacin (mg) | Ascorbic acid (mg) |
|---|---|---|---|---|---|---|---|---|---|---|---|---|---|---|---|---|
| Cod, broiled ........3.5 ounces .... | 100 | 65 | 170 | 29 | 5 | — | — | — | 0 | 31 | 1.0 | 180 | .08 | .11 | 3.0 | — |
| Crabmeat, canned ....3 ounces ..... | 85 | 77 | 85 | 15 | 2 | — | — | — | 1 | 38 | .7 | — | .07 | .07 | 1.6 | — |
| Fish sticks, breaded, cooked ..........8 ounce pkg... 10 sticks or | 227 | 66 | 400 | 38 | 20 | 5 | — | 10 | 15 | 25 | 0.9 | — | .09 | .16 | 3.6 | — |
| Flounder, baked ....3.5 ounces ... | 100 | 58 | 202 | 30 | 8 | — | — | — | 0 | 23 | 1.4 | — | .07 | .08 | 2.5 | 0 |
| Haddock, breaded, fried ............3 ounces..... | 85 | 66 | 140 | 17 | 5 | 1 | — | Trace | 5 | 34 | 1.0 | — | .03 | .06 | 2.7 | 2 |
| Halibut, broiled ......3.5 ounces ... | 100 | 67 | 171 | 25 | 7 | — | — | — | 0 | 16 | .8 | 680 | .05 | .07 | 8.3 | — |
| Ocean perch, breaded, fried ............3 ounces .... | 85 | 59 | 195 | 16 | 11 | — | — | — | 6 | 28 | 1.1 | — | .08 | .09 | 1.5 | — |
| Salmon, pink, canned ..3 ounces .... | 85 | 71 | 120 | 17 | 5 | 1 | — | Trace | 0 | ¹167 | .7 | 60 | .03 | .16 | 6.8 | — |
| Sardines, Atlantic, canned in oil, drained solids .....3 ounces .... | 85 | 62 | 175 | 20 | 9 | — | — | — | 0 | 372 | 2.5 | 190 | .02 | .17 | 4.6 | — |
| Shad, baked with table fat and bacon ......3 ounces .... | 85 | 64 | 170 | 20 | 10 | — | — | — | 0 | 20 | .5 | 20 | .11 | .22 | 7.3 | — |
| Shrimp, canned, meat .3 ounces .... | 85 | 70 | 100 | 21 | 1 | — | — | — | 1 | 98 | 2.6 | 50 | .01 | .03 | 1.5 | — |
| Swordfish, broiled with butter or margarine .3 ounces .... | 85 | 65 | 150 | 24 | 5 | — | — | — | 0 | 23 | 1.1 | 1,750 | .03 | .04 | 9.3 | — |
| Tuna, canned in oil, drained solids .....3 ounces .... | 85 | 61 | 170 | 24 | 7 | 2 | — | 1 | 0 | 7 | 1.6 | 70 | .04 | .10 | 10.1 | — |
| **MATURE DRY BEANS AND PEAS, NUTS, PEANUTS; RELATED PRODUCTS** | | | | | | | | | | | | | | | | |
| Almonds, shelled, whole kernels ............1 cup ....... | 142 | 5 | 850 | 26 | 77 | 6 | — | 15 | 28 | 332 | 6.7 | 0 | .34 | 1.31 | 5.0 | Trace |
| Beans, dry: | | | | | | | | | | | | | | | | |
| Common varieties as Great Northern, navy, and others: | | | | | | | | | | | | | | | | |
| Cooked, drained: | | | | | | | | | | | | | | | | |
| Great Northern ..1 cup ........ | 180 | 69 | 210 | 14 | 1 | — | — | — | 38 | 90 | 4.9 | 0 | .25 | .13 | 1.3 | 0 |
| Navy (pea) .....1 cup ........ | 190 | 69 | 225 | 15 | 1 | — | — | — | 40 | 95 | 5.1 | 0 | .27 | .13 | 1.3 | 0 |
| Canned, solids and liquid: | | | | | | | | | | | | | | | | |
| White with — | | | | | | | | | | | | | | | | |
| Frankfurters (sliced) ....1 cup ....... | 255 | 71 | 365 | 19 | 18 | — | — | — | 32 | 94 | 4.8 | 330 | .18 | .15 | 3.3 | Trace |

| Food, approximate measure, and weight (in grams) | | Water | Food energy | Protein | Fat | Fatty acids Saturated (total) | Unsaturated linoleic | Carbohydrate | Calcium | Iron | Vitamin A value | Thiamin | Riboflavin | Niacin | Ascorbic acid |
|---|---|---|---|---|---|---|---|---|---|---|---|---|---|---|---|
| | Grams | Percent | Calories | Grams | Grams | Grams | Grams | Grams | Milligrams | Milligrams | International units | Milligrams | Milligrams | Milligrams | Milligrams |
| Pork and tomato sauce .......1 cup | 255 | 71 | 310 | 16 | 7 | 2 | 1 | 49 | 138 | 4.6 | 330 | .20 | .08 | 1.5 | 5 |
| Pork and sweet sauce .....1 cup | 255 | 66 | 385 | 16 | 12 | 4 | 1 | 54 | 161 | 5.9 | — | .15 | .10 | 1.3 | — |
| Red kidney......1 cup | 255 | 76 | 230 | 15 | 1 | — | — | 42 | 74 | 4.6 | 10 | .13 | .10 | 1.5 | — |
| Lima, cooked, drained .1 cup | 190 | 64 | 260 | 16 | 1 | 1 | — | 49 | 55 | 5.9 | — | .25 | .11 | 1.3 | — |
| Cashew nuts, roasted ...1 cup | 140 | 5 | 785 | 24 | 64 | 11 | 4 | 41 | 53 | 5.3 | 140 | .60 | .35 | 2.5 | — |
| Coconut, fresh meat only: Shredded or grated, firmly packed ......1 cup | 130 | 51 | 450 | 5 | 46 | 39 | Trace | 12 | 17 | 2.2 | 0 | .07 | .03 | .7 | 4 |
| Cowpeas or blackeye peas, dry, cooked .....1 cup | 248 | 80 | 190 | 13 | 1 | — | — | 34 | 42 | 3.2 | 20 | .41 | .11 | 1.1 | Trace |
| Lentils, cooked .........1 cup | 200 | 72 | 212 | 16 | Trace | — | — | 38 | 50 | 4.2 | 40 | .14 | .12 | 1.2 | 0 |
| Peanuts, roasted, salted, halves .......1 cup | 144 | 2 | 840 | 37 | 72 | 16 | 21 | 27 | 107 | 3.0 | — | .46 | .19 | 24.7 | 0 |
| Peanut butter .........1 tablespoon | 16 | 2 | 95 | 4 | 8 | 2 | 2 | 3 | 9 | .3 | — | .02 | .02 | 2.4 | 0 |
| Peas, split, dry, cooked..1 cup | 250 | 70 | 290 | 20 | 1 | — | — | 52 | 28 | 4.2 | 100 | .37 | .22 | 2.2 | — |
| Pecans, halves ......1 cup | 108 | 3 | 740 | 10 | 77 | 5 | 15 | 16 | 79 | 2.6 | 140 | .93 | .14 | 1.0 | 2 |
| Soybeans, cooked ......1 cup | 200 | 71 | 260 | 22 | 11.4 | — | 7 | 22 | 146 | 5.4 | 60 | .42 | .18 | 1.2 | 0 |
| Walnuts, black or native, chopped ......1 cup | 126 | 3 | 790 | 26 | 75 | 4 | 36 | 19 | Trace | 7.6 | 380 | .28 | .14 | .9 | — |

## VEGETABLES AND VEGETABLE PRODUCTS

| | | | | | | | | | | | | | | | |
|---|---|---|---|---|---|---|---|---|---|---|---|---|---|---|---|
| Asparagus, green: Cooked, drained: Spears, ½-in diam. at base.....4 spears | 60 | 94 | 10 | 1 | Trace | — | — | 2 | 13 | .4 | 540 | .10 | .11 | .8 | 16 |
| Pieces, 1½ to 2-in. lengths ........1 cup | 145 | 94 | 30 | 3 | Trace | — | — | 5 | 30 | .9 | 1,310 | .23 | .26 | 2.0 | 39 |

| Food | Measure | (g) | Water % | Cal. | Protein (g) | Fat (g) | Sat. | Oleic | Linoleic | Carb. (g) | Calcium (mg) | Iron (mg) | Vit. A (IU) | Thiamin (mg) | Riboflavin (mg) | Niacin (mg) | Ascorbic (mg) |
|---|---|---|---|---|---|---|---|---|---|---|---|---|---|---|---|---|---|
| Canned, solids and liquid | 1 cup | 244 | 94 | 45 | 5 | 1 | — | — | — | 7 | 44 | 4.1 | 1,240 | .15 | .22 | 2.0 | 37 |
| Beans: Lima, cooked, drained | 1 cup | 170 | 71 | 190 | 13 | 1 | — | — | — | 34 | 80 | 4.3 | 480 | .31 | .17 | 2.2 | 29 |
| Snap: Green: Cooked, drained | 1 cup | 125 | 92 | 30 | 2 | Trace | — | — | — | 7 | 63 | .8 | 680 | .09 | .11 | .6 | 15 |
| Canned, solids and liquid | 1 cup | 239 | 94 | 45 | 2 | Trace | — | — | — | 10 | 81 | 2.9 | 690 | .07 | .10 | .7 | 10 |
| Yellow or wax: Cooked, drained | 1 cup | 125 | 93 | 30 | 2 | Trace | — | — | — | 6 | 63 | 0.8 | 290 | .09 | .11 | .6 | 16 |
| Canned, solids and liquid | 1 cup | 239 | 94 | 45 | 2 | 1 | — | — | — | 10 | 81 | 2.9 | 140 | .07 | .10 | .7 | 12 |
| Sprouted mung beans, cooked, drained | 1 cup | 125 | 91 | 35 | 4 | Trace | — | — | — | 7 | 21 | 1.1 | 30 | .11 | .13 | .9 | 8 |
| Beets: Cooked, drained, peeled: Diced or sliced | 1 cup | 170 | 91 | 55 | 2 | Trace | — | — | — | 12 | 24 | .9 | 30 | .05 | .07 | .5 | 10 |
| Canned, solids and liquid | 1 cup | 246 | 90 | 85 | 2 | Trace | — | — | — | 19 | 34 | 1.5 | 20 | .02 | .05 | .2 | 7 |
| Beet greens, leaves and stems, cooked, drained | 1 cup | 145 | 94 | 25 | 3 | Trace | — | — | — | 5 | 144 | 2.8 | 7,400 | .10 | .22 | .4 | 22 |
| Blackeye peas. See Cowpeas. | | | | | | | | | | | | | | | | | |
| Broccoli, cooked, drained: Stalks cut into ½-in. pieces | 1 cup | 155 | 91 | 40 | 5 | 1 | — | — | — | 7 | 136 | 1.2 | 3,880 | .14 | .31 | 1.2 | 140 |
| Chopped, yield from 10-oz frozen pkg | 1¾ cups | 250 | 92 | 65 | 7 | 1 | — | — | — | 12 | 135 | 1.8 | 6,500 | .15 | .30 | 1.3 | 143 |
| Brussels sprouts | 1 cup | 155 | 88 | 55 | 7 | 1 | — | — | — | 10 | 50 | 1.7 | 810 | .12 | .22 | 1.2 | 135 |
| Cabbage, common: Raw, finely shredded or chopped | 1 cup | 90 | 92 | 20 | 1 | Trace | — | — | — | 5 | 44 | .4 | 120 | .05 | .05 | .3 | 42 |
| Cooked | 1 cup | 145 | 94 | 30 | 2 | Trace | — | — | — | 6 | 64 | .4 | 190 | .06 | .06 | .4 | 48 |
| Cabbage, celery or Chinese, raw, cut in 1-in. pieces | 1 cup | 75 | 95 | 10 | 1 | Trace | — | — | — | 2 | 32 | .5 | 110 | .04 | .03 | .5 | 19 |

| Food, approximate measure, and weight (in grams) | | Water | Food energy | Protein | Fat | Fatty acids | | Carbohydrate | Calcium | Iron | Vitamin A value | Thiamin | Riboflavin | Niacin | Ascorbic acid |
|---|---|---|---|---|---|---|---|---|---|---|---|---|---|---|---|
| | | | | | | Saturated (total) | Unsaturated linoleic | | | | | | | | |
| | Grams | Per-cent | Calo-ries | Grams | Grams | Grams | Grams | Grams | Milli-grams | Milli-grams | Inter-national units | Milli-grams | Milli-grams | Milli-grams | Milli-grams |
| **Carrots:** | | | | | | | | | | | | | | | |
| Raw: | | | | | | | | | | | | | | | |
| Whole, 5½ x 1 inch..1 carrot | 50 | 88 | 20 | 1 | Trace | — | — | 5 | 18 | .4 | 5,500 | .03 | .03 | .3 | 4 |
| Grated | 110 | 88 | 45 | 1 | Trace | — | — | 11 | 41 | .8 | 12,100 | .06 | .06 | .7 | 9 |
| Cooked, diced | 145 | 91 | 45 | 1 | Trace | — | — | 10 | 48 | .9 | 15,220 | .08 | .07 | .7 | 9 |
| Cauliflower, cooked, flowerbuds 1 cup | 120 | 93 | 25 | 3 | Trace | — | — | 5 | 25 | .8 | 70 | .11 | .10 | .7 | 66 |
| Celery, raw: | | | | | | | | | | | | | | | |
| Stalk, large outer 1 stalk | 40 | 94 | 5 | Trace | — | — | — | 2 | 16 | .1 | 100 | .01 | .01 | .1 | 4 |
| Pieces, diced 1 cup | 100 | 94 | 15 | Trace | Trace | — | — | 4 | 39 | .3 | 240 | .03 | .03 | .3 | 9 |
| Collards, cooked 1 cup | 190 | 91 | 55 | 5 | 1 | — | — | 9 | 289 | 1.1 | 10,260 | .27 | .37 | 2.4 | 87 |
| Corn, sweet: | | | | | | | | | | | | | | | |
| Cooked 1 ear | 140 | 74 | 70 | 3 | 1 | — | — | 16 | 2 | .5 | 310 | .09 | .08 | 1.0 | 7 |
| Canned, solids and liquid 1 cup | 256 | 81 | 170 | 5 | 2 | — | — | 40 | 10 | 1.0 | 690 | .07 | .12 | 2.3 | 13 |
| Cowpeas, cooked, immature seeds 1 cup | 160 | 72 | 175 | 13 | 1 | — | — | 29 | 38 | 3.4 | 560 | .49 | .18 | 2.3 | 28 |
| Cucumbers, 10-ounce: Raw, pared 1 cucumber | 207 | 96 | 30 | 1 | Trace | — | — | 7 | 35 | .6 | Trace | .07 | .09 | .4 | 23 |
| Dandelion greens, cooked 1 cup | 180 | 90 | 60 | 4 | 1 | — | — | 12 | 252 | 3.2 | 21,060 | .24 | .29 | — | 32 |
| Endive, curly (including escarole) 2 ounces | 57 | 93 | 10 | 1 | Trace | — | — | 2 | 46 | 1.0 | 1,870 | .04 | .08 | .3 | 6 |
| Kale, leaves including stems, cooked 1 cup | 110 | 91 | 30 | 4 | 1 | — | — | 4 | 147 | 1.3 | 8,140 | — | — | — | 68 |
| Lettuce, raw: | | | | | | | | | | | | | | | |
| Butterhead, as Boston types; head; head, 4-inch diameter 1 head | 220 | 95 | 30 | 3 | Trace | — | — | 6 | 77 | 4.4 | 2,130 | .14 | .13 | .6 | 18 |
| Crisphead, as Iceberg; head 1 head | 454 | 96 | 60 | 4 | Trace | — | — | 13 | 91 | 2.3 | 1,500 | .29 | .27 | 1.3 | 29 |

| Food, approximate measure | Grams | Water (percent) | Food energy (calories) | Protein (grams) | Fat (grams) | Saturated (grams) | Unsaturated Oleic (grams) | Unsaturated Linoleic (grams) | Carbohydrate (grams) | Calcium (mg) | Iron (mg) | Vitamin A (I.U.) | Thiamine (mg) | Riboflavin (mg) | Niacin (mg) | Ascorbic acid (mg) |
|---|---|---|---|---|---|---|---|---|---|---|---|---|---|---|---|---|
| Looseleaf, or bunching varieties, leaves ... 2 large | 50 | 94 | 10 | 1 | 1 | — | — | — | 2 | 34 | .7 | 950 | .03 | .04 | .2 | 9 |
| Mushrooms, canned, solids and liquid .... 1 cup | 244 | 93 | 40 | 5 | Trace | — | — | — | 6 | 15 | 1.2 | Trace | .04 | .60 | 4.8 | 4 |
| Mustard greens, cooked.. 1 cup | 140 | 93 | 35 | 3 | 1 | — | — | — | 6 | 193 | 2.5 | 8,120 | .11 | .19 | .9 | 68 |
| Okra, cooked ..... 8 pods | 85 | 91 | 25 | 2 | Trace | — | — | — | 5 | 78 | .4 | 420 | .11 | .15 | .8 | 17 |
| Onions: | | | | | | | | | | | | | | | | |
| Cooked ......... 1 cup | 210 | 92 | 60 | 3 | Trace | — | — | — | 14 | 50 | .8 | 80 | .06 | .06 | .4 | 14 |
| Young green, small, without tops ... 6 onions | 50 | 88 | 20 | 1 | Trace | — | — | — | 5 | 20 | .3 | Trace | .02 | .02 | .2 | 12 |
| Parsley, raw, chopped... 1 tablespoon | 4 | 85 | Trace | Trace | Trace | — | — | — | Trace | 8 | .2 | 340 | Trace | .01 | Trace | 7 |
| Parsnips, cooked ....... 1 cup | 155 | 82 | 100 | 2 | 1 | — | — | — | 23 | 70 | .9 | 50 | .11 | .12 | .2 | 16 |
| Peas, green: | | | | | | | | | | | | | | | | |
| Cooked ......... 1 cup | 160 | 82 | 115 | 9 | 1 | — | — | — | 19 | 37 | 2.9 | 860 | .44 | .17 | 3.7 | 33 |
| Canned, solids and liquid ......... 1 cup | 249 | 83 | 165 | 9 | 1 | — | — | — | 31 | 50 | 4.2 | 1,120 | .23 | .13 | 2.2 | 22 |
| Peppers, sweet: Raw, about 5 per pound: | | | | | | | | | | | | | | | | |
| Green pod without stem and seeds... 1 pod | 74 | 93 | 15 | 1 | Trace | — | — | — | 4 | 7 | .5 | 310 | .06 | .06 | .4 | 94 |
| Cooked, boiled, drained ......... 1 pod | 73 | 95 | 15 | 1 | Trace | — | — | — | 3 | 7 | .4 | 310 | .05 | .05 | .4 | 70 |
| Potatoes, medium (about 3 per pound raw): | | | | | | | | | | | | | | | | |
| Baked, peeled after baking ..... 1 potato | 99 | 75 | 90 | 3 | Trace | — | — | — | 21 | 9 | .7 | Trace | .10 | .04 | 1.7 | 20 |
| Boiled, peeled after boiling. ..... 1 potato | 136 | 80 | 105 | 3 | Trace | — | — | — | 23 | 10 | .8 | Trace | .13 | .05 | 2.0 | 22 |
| French-fried, piece 2x½x½ inch: | | | | | | | | | | | | | | | | |
| Cooked in deep fat.. 10 pieces | 57 | 45 | 155 | 2 | 7 | 2 | 2 | 4 | 20 | 9 | .7 | Trace | .07 | .04 | 1.8 | 12 |
| Frozen, heated .... 10 pieces | 57 | 53 | 125 | 2 | 5 | 1 | 1 | 2 | 19 | 5 | 1.0 | Trace | .08 | .01 | 1.5 | 12 |
| Mashed: | | | | | | | | | | | | | | | | |
| Milk added ........ 1 cup | 195 | 83 | 125 | 4 | 1 | — | — | — | 25 | 47 | .8 | 50 | .16 | .10 | 2.0 | 19 |
| Pumpkin, canned...... 1 cup | 228 | 90 | 75 | 2 | 1 | — | — | — | 18 | 57 | .9 | 14,590 | .07 | .12 | 1.3 | 12 |
| Spinach: | | | | | | | | | | | | | | | | |
| Cooked ......... 1 cup | 180 | 92 | 40 | 5 | 1 | — | — | — | 6 | 167 | 4.0 | 14,580 | .13 | .25 | 1.0 | 50 |
| Canned, drained solids ......... 1 cup | 180 | 91 | 45 | 5 | 1 | — | — | — | 6 | 212 | 4.7 | 14,400 | .03 | .21 | .6 | 24 |

| Food, approximate measure, and weight (in grams) | | Water | Food energy | Protein | Fat | Saturated (total) | Unsaturated linoleic | Carbohydrate | Calcium | Iron | Vitamin A value | Thiamin | Riboflavin | Niacin | Ascorbic acid |
|---|---|---|---|---|---|---|---|---|---|---|---|---|---|---|---|
| | Grams | Percent | Calories | Grams | Grams | Grams | Grams | Grams | Milligrams | Milligrams | International units | Milligrams | Milligrams | Milligrams | Milligrams |
| Squash: | | | | | | | | | | | | | | | |
| Cooked: | | | | | | | | | | | | | | | |
| Summer, diced .....1 cup ........ | 210 | 96 | 30 | 2 | Trace | — | — | 7 | 52 | .8 | 820 | .10 | .16 | 1.6 | 21 |
| Winter, baked, mashed ........1 cup ........ | 205 | 81 | 130 | 4 | 1 | — | — | 32 | 57 | 1.6 | 8,610 | .10 | .27 | 1.4 | 27 |
| Sweet potatoes: | | | | | | | | | | | | | | | |
| Cooked, medium, 5x2 inches: | | | | | | | | | | | | | | | |
| Baked, peeled after baking ........1 sweet potato. | 110 | 64 | 155 | 2 | 1 | — | — | 36 | 44 | 1.0 | 8,910 | .10 | .07 | .7 | 24 |
| Boiled, peeled after boiling .........1 sweet potato. | 147 | 71 | 170 | 2 | 1 | — | — | 39 | 47 | 1.0 | 11,610 | .13 | .09 | .9 | 25 |
| Candied, 3½x2¼ inches ........1 sweet potato. | 175 | 60 | 295 | 2 | 6 | 2 | 1 | 60 | 65 | 1.6 | 11,030 | .10 | .08 | .8 | 17 |
| Canned, vacuum or solid pack .......1 cup ........ | 218 | 72 | 235 | 4 | Trace | — | — | 54 | 54 | 1.7 | 17,000 | .10 | .10 | 1.4 | 30 |
| Tomatoes: | | | | | | | | | | | | | | | |
| Raw, approx. 3-in. diam., 2⅛ in.high...1 tomato .... | 200 | 94 | 40 | 2 | Trace | — | — | 9 | 24 | .9 | 1,640 | .11 | .07 | 1.3 | [7]42 |
| Canned, solids and liquid ........1 cup ........ | 241 | 94 | 50 | 2 | 1 | — | — | 10 | 14 | 1.2 | 2,170 | .12 | .07 | 1.7 | 41 |
| Tomato catsup: Tablespoon ........1 tablespoon . | 15 | 69 | 15 | Trace | Trace | — | — | 4 | 3 | .1 | 210 | .01 | .01 | .2 | 2 |
| Tomato juice, canned: | | | | | | | | | | | | | | | |
| Cup .............1 cup ........ | 243 | 94 | 45 | 2 | Trace | — | — | 10 | 17 | 2.2 | 1,940 | .12 | .07 | 1.9 | 39 |
| Turnips, cooked, diced...1 cup ........ | 155 | 94 | 35 | 1 | Trace | — | — | 8 | 54 | .6 | Trace | .06 | .08 | .5 | 34 |
| Turnip greens, cooked...1 cup ........ | 145 | 94 | 30 | 3 | Trace | — | — | 5 | 252 | 1.5 | 8,270 | .15 | .33 | .7 | 68 |
| FRUITS AND FRUIT PRODUCTS | | | | | | | | | | | | | | | |
| Apples, raw (about 3 per lb.)5 ...........1 apple ..... | 150 | 85 | 70 | Trace | Trace | — | — | 18 | 8 | .4 | 50 | .04 | .02 | .1 | 3 |

| Food, approximate measure | Grams | Water (%) | Food energy (cal.) | Protein (g) | Fat (g) | Satur- ated fatty acids (total) (g) | Unsatur- ated fatty acids (g) | Carbo- hydrate (g) | Calcium (mg) | Iron (mg) | Vitamin A (I.U.) | Thia- mine (mg) | Ribo- flavin (mg) | Niacin (mg) | Ascorbic acid (mg) |
|---|---|---|---|---|---|---|---|---|---|---|---|---|---|---|---|
| Apple juice, bottled or canned ....... 1 cup | 248 | 88 | 120 | Trace | Trace | — | — | 30 | 15 | 1.5 | — | .02 | .05 | .2 | 2 |
| Applesauce, canned: Sweetened ....... 1 cup | 255 | 76 | 230 | 1 | Trace | — | — | 61 | 10 | 1.3 | 100 | .05 | .03 | .1 | [8]3 |
| Unsweetened or artificially sweetened ... 1 cup | 244 | 88 | 100 | 1 | Trace | — | — | 26 | 10 | 1.2 | 100 | .05 | .02 | .1 | [8]2 |
| Apricots: Raw (about 12 per lb.)[5] 3 apricots | 114 | 85 | 55 | 1 | Trace | — | — | 14 | 18 | .5 | 2,890 | .03 | .04 | .7 | 10 |
| Canned in heavy sirup. 1 cup | 259 | 77 | 220 | 2 | Trace | — | — | 57 | 28 | .8 | 4,510 | .05 | .06 | .9 | 10 |
| Dried, uncooked (40 halves per cup) .... 1 cup | 150 | 25 | 390 | 8 | 1 | — | — | 100 | 100 | 8.2 | 16,350 | .02 | .23 | 4.9 | 19 |
| Cooked, unsweetened, fruit and liquid ... 1 cup | 285 | 76 | 240 | 5 | 1 | — | — | 62 | 63 | 5.1 | 8,550 | .01 | .13 | 2.8 | 8 |
| Apricot nectar, canned...1 cup | 251 | 85 | 140 | 1 | Trace | — | — | 37 | 23 | .5 | 2,380 | .03 | .03 | .5 | [8]8 |
| Avocados, whole fruit, raw:[5] | | | | | | | | | | | | | | | |
| California (mid- and late-winter) ...1 avocado | 284 | 74 | 370 | 5 | 37 | 7 | 5 | 13 | 22 | 1.3 | 630 | .24 | .43 | 3.5 | 30 |
| Florida (late summer, fall) ....1 avocado | 454 | 78 | 390 | 4 | 33 | 7 | 4 | 27 | 30 | 1.8 | 880 | .33 | .61 | 4.9 | 43 |
| Bananas, raw, medium size[5] ....1 banana | 175 | 76 | 100 | 1 | Trace | — | — | 26 | 10 | .8 | 230 | .06 | .07 | .8 | 12 |
| Banana flakes ....1 cup | 100 | 3 | 340 | 4 | 1 | — | — | 89 | 32 | 2.8 | 760 | .18 | .24 | 2.8 | 7 |
| Blackberries, raw ....1 cup | 144 | 84 | 85 | 2 | 1 | — | — | 19 | 46 | 1.3 | 290 | .05 | .06 | .5 | 30 |
| Blueberries, raw ....1 cup | 140 | 83 | 85 | 1 | 1 | — | — | 21 | 21 | 1.4 | 140 | .04 | .08 | .6 | 20 |
| Cantaloups, raw, medium, 5-inch diameter[5] ...½ melon | 385 | 91 | 60 | 1 | Trace | — | — | 14 | 27 | .8 | [6]6,540 | .08 | .06 | 1.2 | 63 |
| Cherries, canned, red, sour, pitted, water pack ......1 cup | 244 | 88 | 105 | 2 | Trace | — | — | 26 | 37 | .7 | 1,660 | .07 | .05 | .5 | 12 |
| Cranberry-juice cocktail, canned ......1 cup | 250 | 83 | 165 | Trace | Trace | — | — | 42 | 13 | .8 | Trace | .03 | .03 | .1 | [10]40 |
| Cranberry sauce, sweetened, canned, strained ......1 cup | 277 | 62 | 405 | Trace | 1 | — | — | 104 | 17 | .6 | 60 | .03 | .03 | .1 | 6 |
| Dates, pitted, cut ......1 cup | 178 | 22 | 490 | 4 | 1 | — | — | 130 | 105 | 5.3 | 90 | .16 | .17 | 3.9 | 0 |
| Figs, dried, large ......1 fig | 21 | 23 | 60 | 1 | Trace | — | — | 15 | 26 | .6 | 20 | .02 | .02 | .1 | 0 |

| Food, approximate measure, and weight (in grams) | Water | Food energy | Protein | Fat | Fatty acids Saturated (total) | Fatty acids Unsaturated linoleic | Carbohydrate | Calcium | Iron | Vitamin A value | Thiamin | Riboflavin | Niacin | Ascorbic acid |
|---|---|---|---|---|---|---|---|---|---|---|---|---|---|---|
| | Percent | Calories | Grams | Grams | Grams | Grams | Grams | Milligrams | Milligrams | International units | Milligrams | Milligrams | Milligrams | Milligrams |
| Fruit cocktail, canned, in heavy sirup ........1 cup ........ 256 | 80 | 195 | 1 | Trace | — | — | 50 | 23 | 1.0 | 360 | .05 | .03 | 1.3 | 5 |
| Grapefruit: | | | | | | | | | | | | | | |
| Raw, medium, 3¾-in. diam.[5] | | | | | | | | | | | | | | |
| White ..........½ grapefruit.. 241 | 89 | 45 | 1 | Trace | — | — | 12 | 19 | .5 | 10 | .05 | .02 | .2 | 44 |
| Pink or red .......½ grapefruit.. 241 | 89 | 50 | 1 | Trace | — | — | 13 | 20 | .5 | 540 | .05 | .02 | .2 | 44 |
| Canned, sirup pack ....1 cup.. 254 | 81 | 180 | 2 | Trace | — | — | 45 | 33 | .8 | 30 | .08 | .05 | .5 | 76 |
| Grapefruit juice: | | | | | | | | | | | | | | |
| Fresh ...........1 cup ........ 246 | 90 | 95 | 1 | Trace | — | — | 23 | 22 | .5 | (¹) | .09 | .04 | .4 | 92 |
| Canned, white: | | | | | | | | | | | | | | |
| Unsweetened ......1 cup ....... 247 | 89 | 100 | 1 | Trace | — | — | 24 | 20 | 1.0 | 20 | .07 | .04 | .4 | 84 |
| Sweetened ......1 cup ....... 250 | 86 | 130 | 1 | Trace | — | — | 32 | 20 | 1.0 | 20 | .07 | .04 | .4 | 78 |
| Frozen, concentrate, unsweetened: | | | | | | | | | | | | | | |
| Diluted with 3 parts water, by volume..1 cup ....... 247 | 89 | 100 | 1 | Trace | — | — | 24 | 25 | .2 | 20 | .10 | .04 | .5 | 96 |
| Dehydrated crystals prepared with water 1 cup ....... 247 | 90 | 100 | 1 | Trace | — | — | 24 | 22 | .2 | 20 | .10 | .05 | .5 | 91 |
| Grapes, raw[5] ........1 cup ....... 153 | 82 | 65 | 1 | 1 | — | — | 15 | 15 | .4 | 100 | .05 | .03 | .2 | 3 |
| Grape juice: | | | | | | | | | | | | | | |
| Canned or bottled ....1 cup ........ 253 | 83 | 165 | 1 | Trace | — | — | 42 | 28 | .8 | — | .10 | .05 | .5 | Trace |
| Frozen concentrate, sweetened: | | | | | | | | | | | | | | |
| Diluted with 3 parts water, by volume.1 cup ....... 250 | 86 | 135 | 1 | Trace | — | — | 33 | 8 | .3 | 10 | .05 | .08 | .5 | (²) |
| Grape juice drink, canned.1 cup ....... 250 | 86 | 135 | Trace | Trace | — | — | 35 | 8 | .3 | — | .03 | .03 | .3 | (²) |
| Lemon juice, raw ......1 cup ....... 244 | 91 | 60 | 1 | Trace | — | — | 20 | 17 | .5 | 50 | .07 | .02 | .2 | 112 |
| Lemonade concentrate: | | | | | | | | | | | | | | |
| Diluted with 4⅓ parts water, by volume...1 cup ....... 248 | 88 | 110 | Trace | Trace | — | — | 28 | 2 | Trace | Trace | Trace | .02 | .2 | 17 |
| Lime juice: | | | | | | | | | | | | | | |

| Food | grams | Water (%) | Food energy (cal.) | Protein (g) | Fat (g) | | | Carbohydrate (g) | Calcium (mg) | Iron (mg) | Vitamin A (I.U.) | Thiamine (mg) | Riboflavin (mg) | Niacin (mg) | Ascorbic acid (mg) |
|---|---|---|---|---|---|---|---|---|---|---|---|---|---|---|---|
| Fresh .........1 cup | 246 | 90 | 65 | 1 | Trace | — | — | 22 | 22 | .5 | 20 | .05 | .02 | .2 | 79 |
| Canned, unsweetened . 1 cup | 246 | 90 | 65 | 1 | Trace | — | — | 22 | 22 | .5 | 20 | .05 | .02 | .2 | 52 |
| Limeade concentrate, frozen: Diluted with 4⅓ parts water, by volume...1 cup | 247 | 90 | 100 | Trace | Trace | — | — | 27 | 2 | Trace | Trace | Trace | Trace | Trace | 5 |
| Oranges, raw, 2⅝-in. diam., all commercial varieties[5] .....1 orange | 180 | 86 | 65 | 1 | Trace | — | — | 16 | 54 | .5 | 260 | .13 | .05 | .5 | 66 |
| Orange juice, fresh, all varieties ..........1 cup | 248 | 88 | 110 | 2 | 1 | — | — | 26 | 27 | .5 | 500 | .22 | .07 | 1.0 | 124 |
| Canned, unsweetened .1 cup | 249 | 87 | 120 | 2 | Trace | — | — | 28 | 25 | 1.0 | 500 | .17 | .05 | .7 | 100 |
| Frozen concentrate: Diluted with 3 parts water, by volume. 1 cup | 249 | 87 | 120 | 2 | Trace | — | — | 29 | 25 | .2 | 550 | .22 | .02 | 1.0 | 120 |
| Dehydrated crystals, prepared with water.1 cup | 248 | 88 | 115 | 2 | 1 | — | — | 27 | 25 | .5 | 500 | .20 | .07 | 1.0 | 109 |
| Orange-apricot juice drink ..........1 cup | 249 | 87 | 125 | 1 | Trace | — | — | 32 | 12 | .2 | 1,440 | .05 | .02 | .5 | [10]40 |
| Orange and grapefruit juice: Frozen concentrate: Diluted with 3 parts water, by volume ..........1 cup | 248 | 88 | 110 | 1 | Trace | — | — | 26 | 20 | .2 | 270 | .16 | .02 | .2 | 102 |
| Papayas, raw, ½-inch cubes.......1 cup | 182 | 88 | 70 | 1 | Trace | — | — | 18 | 36 | .5 | 3,190 | .07 | .08 | .5 | 102 |
| Peaches: Raw: Whole, medium, 2-inch diameter..1 peach | 114 | 89 | 35 | 1 | Trace | — | — | 10 | 9 | .5 | [11]1,320 | .02 | .05 | 1.0 | 7 |
| Sliced ...........1 cup | 168 | 89 | 65 | 1 | Trace | — | — | 16 | 15 | .8 | [12]2,230 | .03 | .08 | 1.6 | 12 |
| Canned, yellow-fleshed, solids and liquids: Sirup pack, heavy: Halves or slices..1 cup | 257 | 79 | 200 | 1 | Trace | — | — | 52 | 10 | .8 | 1,100 | .02 | .06 | 1.4 | 7 |
| Water pack ......1 cup | 245 | 91 | 75 | 1 | Trace | — | — | 20 | 10 | .7 | 1,100 | .02 | .06 | 1.4 | 7 |
| Dried, uncooked ...1 cup | 160 | 25 | 420 | 5 | 1 | — | — | 109 | 77 | 9.6 | 6,240 | .02 | .31 | 8.5 | 28 |
| Cooked, unsweetened, 10-12 halves and juice .......1 cup | 270 | 77 | 220 | 3 | 1 | — | — | 58 | 41 | 5.1 | 3,290 | .01 | .15 | 4.2 | 6 |

| Food, approximate measure, and weight (in grams) | Water | Food energy | Protein | Fat | Fatty acids Saturated (total) | Fatty acids Unsaturated linoleic | Carbohydrate | Calcium | Iron | Vitamin A value | Thiamin | Riboflavin | Niacin | Ascorbic acid |
|---|---|---|---|---|---|---|---|---|---|---|---|---|---|---|
| | Percent | Calories | Grams | Grams | Grams | Grams | Grams | Milligrams | Milligrams | International units | Milligrams | Milligrams | Milligrams | Milligrams |
| Frozen: | | | | | | | | | | | | | | |
| Carton, 12 ounces, not thawed ..... 1 carton ..... 340 | 76 | 300 | 1 | Trace | — | — | 77 | 14 | 1.7 | 2,210 | .03 | .14 | 2.4 | [14]135 |
| Pears: | | | | | | | | | | | | | | |
| Raw, 3x2½-inch diameter[5] ..... 1 pear ..... 182 | 83 | 100 | 1 | 1 | — | — | 25 | 13 | .5 | 30 | .04 | .07 | .2 | 7 |
| Canned, solids and liquid: | | | | | | | | | | | | | | |
| Sirup pack, heavy: | | | | | | | | | | | | | | |
| Halves or slices .. 1 cup ..... 255 | 80 | 195 | 1 | 1 | — | — | 50 | 13 | .5 | Trace | .03 | .05 | .3 | 4 |
| Pineapple: | | | | | | | | | | | | | | |
| Raw, diced ..... 1 cup ..... 140 | 85 | 75 | 1 | Trace | — | — | 19 | 24 | .7 | 100 | .12 | .04 | .3 | 24 |
| Canned, heavy sirup pack, solids and liquid: | | | | | | | | | | | | | | |
| Crushed ..... 1 cup ..... 260 | 80 | 195 | 1 | Trace | — | — | 50 | 29 | .8 | 120 | .20 | .06 | .5 | 17 |
| Sliced, slices and juice ..... 2 small or 1 large ..... 122 | 80 | 90 | Trace | Trace | — | — | 24 | 13 | .4 | 50 | .09 | .03 | .2 | 8 |
| Pineapple juice, canned.. 1 cup ..... 249 | 86 | 135 | 1 | Trace | — | — | 34 | 37 | .7 | 120 | .12 | .04 | .5 | [8]22 |
| Plums, all except prunes: | | | | | | | | | | | | | | |
| Raw, 2-inch diameter, about 2 ounces[5] ... 1 plum ..... 60 | 87 | 25 | Trace | Trace | — | — | 7 | 7 | .3 | 140 | .02 | .02 | .3 | 3 |
| Canned, sirup pack (Italian prunes): | | | | | | | | | | | | | | |
| Plums (with pits) and juice[5] ..... 1 cup ..... 256 | 77 | 205 | 1 | Trace | — | — | 53 | 22 | 2.2 | 2,970 | .05 | .05 | .9 | 4 |
| Prunes, dried, "softenized," medium: | | | | | | | | | | | | | | |
| Uncooked[5] ..... 4 prunes ..... 32 | 28 | 70 | Trace | Trace | — | — | 18 | 14 | 1.1 | 440 | .02 | .04 | .4 | 1 |
| Cooked, unsweetened . 1 cup ..... 270 | 66 | 295 | 2 | 1 | — | — | 78 | 60 | 4.5 | 1,860 | .08 | .18 | 1.7 | 2 |
| Prune juice, canned or bottled ..... 1 cup ..... 256 | 80 | 200 | 1 | Trace | — | — | 49 | 36 | 10.5 | — | .03 | .03 | 1.0 | [8]5 |
| Raisins, seedless, 1 cup ..... 165 | 18 | 480 | 4 | Trace | — | — | 128 | 102 | 5.8 | 30 | .18 | .13 | .8 | 2 |

Raspberries, red:

| Food | Grams | Water (%) | Food energy (cal) | Protein (g) | Fat (g) | Saturated fatty acids (g) | Oleic (g) | Linoleic (g) | Carbohydrate (g) | Calcium (mg) | Iron (mg) | Vitamin A (I.U.) | Thiamin (mg) | Riboflavin (mg) | Niacin (mg) | Ascorbic acid (mg) |
|---|---|---|---|---|---|---|---|---|---|---|---|---|---|---|---|---|
| Raw .......... 1 cup ........ | 123 | 84 | 70 | 1 | 1 | — | — | — | 17 | 27 | 1.1 | 160 | .04 | .11 | 1.1 | 31 |
| Frozen, 10-ounce carton, not thawed .. 1 carton ..... | 284 | 74 | 275 | 2 | 1 | — | — | — | 70 | 37 | 1.7 | 200 | .06 | .17 | 1.7 | 59 |
| Rhubarb, cooked, sugar added ........ 1 cup ........ | 272 | 63 | 385 | 1 | Trace | — | — | — | 98 | 212 | 1.6 | 220 | .06 | .15 | .7 | 17 |
| **Strawberries:** | | | | | | | | | | | | | | | | |
| Raw .......... 1 cup ........ | 149 | 90 | 55 | 1 | 1 | — | — | — | 13 | 31 | 1.5 | 90 | .04 | .10 | 1.0 | 88 |
| Frozen, 10-ounce carton, not thawed .. 1 carton .. | 284 | 71 | 310 | 1 | 1 | — | — | — | 79 | 40 | 2.0 | 90 | .06 | .17 | 1.5 | 150 |
| Tangerines, raw, medium .. 1 tangerine .. | 116 | 87 | 40 | 1 | Trace | — | — | — | 10 | 34 | .3 | 360 | .05 | .02 | .1 | 27 |
| Tangerine juice, canned, sweetened ........ 1 cup ........ | 249 | 87 | 125 | 1 | 1 | — | — | — | 30 | 45 | .5 | 1,050 | .15 | .05 | .2 | 55 |
| Watermelon, raw, wedge . 1 wedge ...... | 925 | 93 | 115 | 2 | 1 | — | — | — | 27 | 30 | 2.1 | 2,510 | .13 | .13 | .7 | 30 |

## GRAIN PRODUCTS

| Food | Grams | Water (%) | Food energy (cal) | Protein (g) | Fat (g) | Saturated fatty acids (g) | Oleic (g) | Linoleic (g) | Carbohydrate (g) | Calcium (mg) | Iron (mg) | Vitamin A (I.U.) | Thiamin (mg) | Riboflavin (mg) | Niacin (mg) | Ascorbic acid (mg) |
|---|---|---|---|---|---|---|---|---|---|---|---|---|---|---|---|---|
| Bagel, 3-in. diam. ...... 1 bagel ...... | 55 | 29 | 165 | 6 | 2 | — | 1 | — | 30 | 8 | 1.2 | 0 | .15 | .11 | 1.4 | 0 |
| Barley, pearled, light, uncooked ........ 1 cup ........ | 200 | 11 | 700 | 16 | 2 | Trace | 1 | — | 158 | 32 | 4.0 | 0 | .24 | .10 | 6.2 | 0 |
| Biscuits, baking powder, from home recipe with enriched flour, 2-in. diam. ........ 1 biscuit ..... | 28 | 27 | 105 | 2 | 5 | 1 | 2 | 1 | 13 | 34 | .4 | Trace | .06 | .06 | .1 | Trace |
| Biscuits, baking powder, from mix, 2-in. diam. .. 1 biscuit ..... | 28 | 28 | 90 | 2 | 3 | 1 | 1 | 1 | 15 | 19 | .6 | Trace | .08 | .07 | .6 | Trace |
| Bran flakes (40% bran), added thiamin and iron . 1 cup ........ | 35 | 3 | 105 | 4 | 1 | — | — | — | 28 | 25 | 12.3 | 0 | .14 | .06 | 2.2 | 0 |
| Bran flakes with raisins, added thiamin and iron . 1 cup ........ | 50 | 7 | 145 | 4 | 1 | — | — | — | 40 | 28 | 13.5 | Trace | .16 | .07 | 2.7 | 0 |
| **Breads:** | | | | | | | | | | | | | | | | |
| Boston brown bread, slice 3x3/4 in. ...... 1 slice ........ | 48 | 45 | 100 | 3 | 1 | — | — | — | 22 | 43 | .9 | 0 | .05 | .03 | .6 | 0 |
| Cracked-wheat bread: Slice ........ 1 slice ...... | 25 | 35 | 65 | 2 | 1 | — | — | — | 13 | 22 | .3 | Trace | .03 | .02 | .3 | Trace |
| French or vienna bread: Enriched, 1 lb. loaf .. 1 loaf ........ | 454 | 31 | 1,315 | 41 | 14 | 3 | 8 | 2 | 251 | 195 | 10.0 | Trace | 1.27 | 1.00 | 11.3 | Trace |

| Food, approximate measure, and weight (in grams) | Water | Food energy | Protein | Fat | Fatty acids | | Carbohydrate | Calcium | Iron | Vitamin A value | Thiamin | Riboflavin | Niacin | Ascorbic acid |
| | | | | | Saturated (total) | Unsaturated linoleic | | | | | | | | |
| *Grams* | *Percent* | *Calories* | *Grams* | *Grams* | *Grams* | *Grams* | *Grams* | *Milligrams* | *Milligrams* | *International units* | *Milligrams* | *Milligrams* | *Milligrams* | *Milligrams* |
|---|---|---|---|---|---|---|---|---|---|---|---|---|---|---|
| Italian bread: | | | | | | | | | | | | | | |
| Enriched, 1 lb. loaf..1 loaf ....... 454 | 32 | 1,250 | 41 | 4 | Trace | 2 | 256 | 77 | 10.0 | 0 | 1.32 | .91 | 11.8 | 0 |
| Raisin bread: | | | | | | | | | | | | | | |
| Slice ..........1 slice ...... 25 | 35 | 65 | 2 | 1 | — | — | 13 | 18 | .3 | Trace | .01 | .02 | .2 | Trace |
| Rye bread: | | | | | | | | | | | | | | |
| American, light (⅓ rye, ⅔ wheat): | | | | | | | | | | | | | | |
| Slice .........1 slice ...... 25 | 36 | 60 | 2 | Trace | — | — | 13 | 19 | .4 | 0 | .05 | .02 | .4 | 0 |
| Pumpernickel, loaf, | | | | | | | | | | | | | | |
| 1 lb. .........1 loaf ....... 454 | 34 | 1,115 | 41 | 5 | — | — | 241 | 381 | 10.9 | 0 | 1.04 | .64 | 5.4 | 0 |
| White bread, enriched: | | | | | | | | | | | | | | |
| Slice .......1 slice ...... 25 | 36 | 70 | 2 | 1 | — | — | 13 | 21 | .6 | Trace | .06 | .05 | .6 | Trace |
| Slice, toasted .....1 slice ...... 22 | 25 | 70 | 2 | 1 | — | — | 13 | 21 | .6 | Trace | .06 | .05 | .6 | Trace |
| Whole-wheat bread: | | | | | | | | | | | | | | |
| Slice .......1 slice ...... 28 | 36 | 65 | 3 | 1 | — | — | 14 | 24 | .8 | Trace | .09 | .03 | .8 | Trace |
| Slice, toasted .....1 slice ...... 24 | 24 | 65 | 3 | 1 | — | 1 | 14 | 24 | .8 | Trace | .09 | .03 | .8 | Trace |
| Breadcrumbs, dry, grated.1 cup ....... 100 | 6 | 390 | 13 | 5 | 1 | 1 | 73 | 122 | 3.6 | Trace | .22 | .30 | 3.5 | Trace |
| Buckwheat flour, light, | | | | | | | | | | | | | | |
| sifted .........1 cup ....... 98 | 12 | 340 | 6 | 1 | — | — | 78 | 11 | 1.0 | 0 | .08 | .04 | .4 | 0 |
| Bulgur, canned, seasoned.1 cup ....... 135 | 56 | 245 | 8 | 4 | — | — | 44 | 27 | 1.9 | 0 | .08 | .05 | 4.1 | 0 |
| Cookies: | | | | | | | | | | | | | | |
| Brownies with nuts: | | | | | | | | | | | | | | |
| Made from home | | | | | | | | | | | | | | |
| recipe with | | | | | | | | | | | | | | |
| enriched flour ...1 brownie.... 20 | 10 | 95 | 1 | 6 | 1 | 1 | 10 | 8 | .4 | 40 | .04 | .02 | .1 | Trace |
| Made from mix ....1 brownie.... 20 | 11 | 85 | 1 | 4 | 1 | 1 | 13 | 9 | .4 | 20 | .03 | .02 | .1 | Trace |
| Chocolate chip: | | | | | | | | | | | | | | |
| Made from home | | | | | | | | | | | | | | |
| recipe with | | | | | | | | | | | | | | |
| enriched flour ....1 cookie ...... 10 | 3 | 50 | 1 | 3 | 1 | 1 | 6 | 4 | .2 | 10 | .01 | .01 | .1 | Trace |

| Food (approximate measure) | Grams | Water (%) | Food energy (cal.) | Protein (g) | Fat (g) | Saturated (g) | Unsat. oleic (g) | Carbohydrate (g) | Calcium (mg) | Iron (mg) | Vitamin A (I.U.) | Thiamine (mg) | Riboflavin (mg) | Niacin (mg) | Ascorbic acid (mg) |
|---|---|---|---|---|---|---|---|---|---|---|---|---|---|---|---|
| Commercial ......1 cookie | 10 | 3 | 50 | 1 | 2 | 1 | 1 | 7 | 4 | .2 | 10 | Trace | Trace | Trace | Trace |
| Fig bars, commercial ..1 cookie | 14 | 14 | 50 | 1 | 1 | — | — | 11 | 11 | .2 | 20 | Trace | 0.1 | .1 | Trace |
| Corn flakes, added nutrients: | | | | | | | | | | | | | | | |
| Plain ............1 cup | 25 | 4 | 100 | 2 | Trace | — | — | 21 | 4 | .4 | 0 | .11 | .02 | .5 | 0 |
| Corn (hominy) grits, degermed, cooked: | | | | | | | | | | | | | | | |
| Enriched .........1 cup | 245 | 87 | 125 | 3 | Trace | — | — | 27 | 2 | .7 | [15]150 | .10 | .07 | 1.0 | 0 |
| Cornmeal: | | | | | | | | | | | | | | | |
| Whole-ground, unbolted, dry.....1 cup | 122 | 12 | 435 | 11 | 5 | 1 | 2 | 90 | 24 | 2.9 | [15]620 | .46 | .13 | 2.4 | 0 |
| Degermed, enriched: | | | | | | | | | | | | | | | |
| Dry form .........1 cup | 138 | 12 | 500 | 11 | 2 | — | — | 108 | 8 | 4.0 | [15]610 | .61 | .36 | 4.8 | 0 |
| Cooked ...........1 cup | 240 | 88 | 120 | 3 | 1 | — | — | 26 | 2 | 1.0 | [15]140 | .14 | .10 | 1.2 | 0 |
| Corn muffins, made with enriched degermed cornmeal and enriched flour; muffin 2⅜-in diam. ......1 muffin | 40 | 33 | 125 | 3 | 4 | 2 | Trace | 19 | 42 | .7 | [15]120 | .08 | .09 | .6 | Trace |
| Crackers: | | | | | | | | | | | | | | | |
| Graham, 2½-in. square .4 crackers | 28 | 6 | 110 | 2 | 3 | — | — | 21 | 11 | .4 | 0 | .01 | .06 | .4 | 0 |
| Saltines ...........4 crackers | 11 | 4 | 50 | 1 | 1 | — | — | 8 | 2 | .1 | 0 | Trace | Trace | .1 | 0 |
| Doughnuts, cake type ...1 doughnut | 32 | 24 | 125 | 1 | 6 | 1 | 1 | 16 | 13 | [16].4 | 30 | [16].05 | [16].05 | [16].4 | Trace |
| Farina, quick-cooking, enriched, cooked.....1 cup | 245 | 89 | 105 | 3 | Trace | — | — | 22 | 147 | [17].7 | 0 | [17].12 | [17].07 | [17]1.0 | 0 |
| Macaroni, cooked: | | | | | | | | | | | | | | | |
| Enriched: Cooked, until tender.1 cup | 140 | 72 | 155 | 5 | 1 | — | — | 32 | 8 | [17]1.3 | 0 | [17].20 | [17].11 | [17]1.5 | 0 |
| Unenriched: Cooked, until tender.1 cup | 140 | 72 | 155 | 5 | 1 | — | — | 32 | 11 | .6 | 0 | .01 | .01 | .4 | 0 |
| Macaroni (enriched) and cheese, baked ...1 cup | 200 | 58 | 430 | 17 | 22 | 10 | 2 | 40 | 362 | 1.8 | 860 | .20 | .40 | 1.8 | Trace |
| Canned ..............1 cup | 240 | 80 | 230 | 9 | 10 | 4 | 1 | 26 | 199 | 1.0 | 260 | .12 | .24 | 1.0 | Trace |
| Muffins, with enriched white flour; muffin, 3-inch diam. ....1 muffin | 40 | 38 | 120 | 3 | 4 | 1 | 1 | 17 | 42 | .6 | 40 | .07 | .09 | .6 | Trace |
| Noodles (egg noodles), cooked: | | | | | | | | | | | | | | | |
| Enriched .........1 cup | 160 | 70 | 200 | 7 | 2 | 1 | Trace | 37 | 16 | [17]1.4 | 110 | [17].22 | [17].13 | [17]1.9 | 0 |
| Unenriched .......1 cup | 160 | 70 | 200 | 7 | 2 | 1 | Trace | 37 | 16 | 1.0 | 110 | .05 | .03 | .6 | 0 |

| Food, approximate measure, and weight (in grams) | | Water | Food energy | Protein | Fat | Fatty acids | | Carbohydrate | Calcium | Iron | Vitamin A value | Thiamin | Riboflavin | Niacin | Ascorbic acid |
|---|---|---|---|---|---|---|---|---|---|---|---|---|---|---|---|
| | | | | | | Saturated (total) | Unsaturated linoleic | | | | | | | | |
| | Grams | Percent | Calories | Grams | Grams | Grams | Grams | Grams | Milligrams | Milligrams | International units | Milligrams | Milligrams | Milligrams | Milligrams |
| Oatmeal or rolled oats, cooked .......... 1 cup ........ | 240 | 87 | 130 | 5 | 2 | — | 1 | 23 | 22 | 1.4 | 0 | .19 | .05 | .2 | 0 |
| Pancakes, 4-inch diam.: | | | | | | | | | | | | | | | |
| Wheat, enriched flour (home recipe) ...... 1 cake ....... | 27 | 50 | 60 | 2 | 2 | Trace | Trace | 9 | 27 | .4 | 30 | .05 | .06 | .4 | Trace |
| Buckwheat (made from mix with egg and milk) ............. 1 cake ....... | 27 | 58 | 55 | 2 | 2 | 1 | Trace | 6 | 59 | .4 | 60 | .03 | .04 | .2 | Trace |
| Plain or buttermilk (made from mix with egg and milk) ...... 1 cake ....... | 27 | 51 | 60 | 2 | 2 | 1 | Trace | 9 | 58 | .3 | 70 | .04 | .06 | .2 | Trace |
| Pizza (cheese) 5½-in. sector; ⅛ of 14-in. diam. pie .......... 1 sector ...... | 75 | 45 | 185 | 7 | 6 | 2 | Trace | 27 | 107 | .7 | 290 | .04 | .12 | .7 | 4 |
| Popcorn, popped, plain ... 1 cup ......... | 6 | 4 | 25 | 1 | Trace | — | — | 5 | 1 | .2 | 0 | — | .01 | .1 | 0 |
| Pretzels: | | | | | | | | | | | | | | | |
| Dutch, twisted ........ 1 pretzel ..... | 16 | 5 | 60 | 2 | 1 | — | — | 12 | 4 | .2 | 0 | Trace | Trace | .1 | 0 |
| Thin, twisted .......... 1 pretzel ..... | 6 | 5 | 25 | 1 | Trace | — | — | 5 | 1 | .1 | 0 | Trace | Trace | Trace | 0 |
| Stick, regular, 3⅛ inches .......... 5 sticks ...... | 3 | 5 | 10 | Trace | Trace | — | — | 2 | 1 | Trace | 0 | Trace | Trace | Trace | 0 |
| Rice, brown ........... 1 cup ......... | 205 | 70 | 238 | 5 | 1 | — | — | 51 | 24 | 1.0 | 0 | .18 | .04 | 2.8 | 0 |
| Rice, white: | | | | | | | | | | | | | | | |
| Enriched: | | | | | | | | | | | | | | | |
| Raw .............. 1 cup ......... | 185 | 12 | 670 | 12 | 1 | — | — | 149 | 44 | [18]5.4 | 0 | [18].81 | [18].06 | [18]6.5 | 0 |
| Cooked ........... 1 cup ......... | 205 | 73 | 225 | 4 | Trace | — | — | 50 | 21 | [18]1.8 | 0 | [18].23 | [18].02 | [18]2.1 | 0 |
| Instant, ready-to-serve ........ 1 cup ......... | 165 | 73 | 180 | 4 | Trace | — | — | 40 | 5 | [18]1.3 | 0 | [18].21 | [18]— | [18]1.7 | 0 |
| Unenriched, cooked .. 1 cup ......... | 205 | 73 | 225 | 4 | Trace | — | — | 50 | 21 | .4 | 0 | .04 | .02 | .8 | 0 |
| Parboiled, cooked .... 1 cup ......... | 175 | 73 | 185 | 4 | Trace | — | — | 41 | 33 | [18]1.4 | 0 | [18].19 | [18]— | [18]2.1 | 0 |

| | Grams | | | | | | | | | | | | | | |
|---|---|---|---|---|---|---|---|---|---|---|---|---|---|---|---|---|
| Rice, puffed, added nutrients .........1 cup | 15 | 4 | 60 | 1 | Trace | — | — | — | 13 | 3 | .3 | 0 | .07 | .01 | .7 | 0 |
| Rolls, enriched: Cloverleaf or pan: | | | | | | | | | | | | | | | | |
| Home recipe .......1 roll | 35 | 26 | 120 | 3 | 3 | 1 | 1 | 1 | 20 | 16 | .7 | 30 | .09 | .09 | .8 | Trace |
| Commercial .......1 roll | 28 | 31 | 85 | 2 | 2 | Trace | Trace | Trace | 15 | 21 | .5 | Trace | .08 | .05 | .6 | Trace |
| Frankfurter or hamburger .......1 roll | 40 | 31 | 120 | 3 | 2 | 1 | 1 | 1 | 21 | 30 | .8 | Trace | .11 | .07 | .9 | Trace |
| Rye wafers, whole-grain, 1⅞x3½ inches .....2 wafers | 13 | 6 | 45 | 2 | Trace | — | — | — | 10 | 7 | .5 | 0 | .04 | .03 | .2 | 0 |
| Spaghetti, cooked, tender stage, enriched ......1 cup | 140 | 72 | 155 | 5 | 1 | — | — | — | 32 | 11 | [17]1.3 | 0 | [17].20 | [17].11 | [17]1.5 | 0 |
| Spaghetti with meat balls and tomato sauce: | | | | | | | | | | | | | | | | |
| Home recipe ........1 cup | 248 | 70 | 330 | 19 | 12 | 4 | 4 | 1 | 39 | 124 | 3.7 | 1,590 | .25 | .30 | 4.0 | 22 |
| Canned ..........1 cup | 250 | 78 | 260 | 12 | 10 | 2 | 2 | 4 | 28 | 53 | 3.3 | 1,000 | .15 | .18 | 2.3 | 5 |
| Waffles, with enriched flour, 7-in. diam. .....1 waffle | 75 | 41 | 210 | 7 | 7 | 2 | 2 | 1 | 28 | 85 | 1.3 | 250 | .13 | .19 | 1.0 | Trace |
| Waffles, made from mix, enriched, egg and milk added, 7-in. diam. .....1 waffle | 75 | 42 | 205 | 7 | 8 | 3 | 3 | 1 | 27 | 179 | 1.0 | 170 | .11 | .17 | .7 | Trace |
| Wheat, puffed, added nutrients ........1 cup | 15 | 3 | 55 | 2 | Trace | — | — | — | 12 | 4 | .6 | 0 | .08 | .03 | 1.2 | 0 |
| Wheat, shredded, plain ...1 biscuit | 25 | 7 | 90 | 2 | 1 | — | — | — | 20 | 11 | .9 | 0 | .06 | .03 | 1.1 | 0 |
| Wheat flakes, added nutrients ........1 cup | 30 | 4 | 105 | 3 | Trace | — | — | — | 24 | 12 | 1.3 | 0 | .19 | .04 | 1.5 | 0 |
| Wheat flours: | | | | | | | | | | | | | | | | |
| Whole-wheat, from hard wheats, stirred.1 cup | 120 | 12 | 400 | 16 | 2 | Trace | 1 | 1 | 85 | 49 | 4.0 | 0 | .66 | .14 | 5.2 | 0 |
| All-purpose or family flour, enriched: | | | | | | | | | | | | | | | | |
| Sifted .........1 cup | 115 | 12 | 420 | 12 | 1 | — | — | — | 88 | 18 | [17]3.3 | 0 | [17].51 | [17].30 | [17]4.0 | 0 |
| Unsifted ........1 cup | 125 | 12 | 455 | 13 | 1 | — | — | — | 95 | 20 | [17]3.6 | 0 | [17].55 | [17].33 | [17]4.4 | 0 |
| Self-rising, enriched ..1 cup | 125 | 12 | 440 | 12 | 1 | — | — | — | 93 | 331 | [17]3.6 | 0 | [17].55 | [17].33 | [17]4.4 | 0 |
| Cake or pastry flour, sifted ....1 cup | 96 | 12 | 350 | 7 | 1 | — | — | — | 76 | 16 | .5 | 0 | .03 | .03 | .7 | 0 |
| Wheat germ, toasted ....1 cup | 65 | 3 | 260 | 20 | 8 | 3 | 3 | 3 | 33 | 31 | 6 | 74 | 1.1 | .66 | 3.5 | 6.6 |

# FATS, OILS

| Food, approximate measure, and weight (in grams) | Water | Food energy | Protein | Fat | Fatty acids | | Carbohydrate | Calcium | Iron | Vitamin A value | Thiamin | Riboflavin | Niacin | Ascorbic acid |
|---|---|---|---|---|---|---|---|---|---|---|---|---|---|---|
| | | | | | Saturated (total) | Unsaturated linoleic | | | | | | | | |
| | Grams | Per-cent | Calories | Grams | Grams | Grams | Grams | Grams | Milli-grams | Milli-grams | International units | Milli-grams | Milli-grams | Milli-grams | Milli-grams |
| **Butter:** | | | | | | | | | | | | | | |
| Regular ........1 tablespoon . 14 | 16 | 100 | Trace | 12 | 6 | Trace | Trace | 3 | 0 | 470[19] | — | — | — | 0 |
| Whipped, 6 sticks or 2,8-oz. containers per pound ........1 tablespoon . 9 | 16 | 65 | Trace | 8 | 4 | Trace | Trace | 2 | 0 | 310[19] | — | — | — | 0 |
| **Fats, cooking:** | | | | | | | | | | | | | | |
| Lard ........1 cup ....... 205 | 0 | 1,850 | 0 | 205 | 78 | 20 | 0 | 0 | 0 | 0 | 0 | 0 | 0 | 0 |
| 1 tablespoon . 13 | 0 | 115 | 0 | 13 | 5 | 1 | 0 | 0 | 0 | 0 | 0 | 0 | 0 | 0 |
| Vegetable fats ........1 cup ....... 200 | 0 | 1,770 | 0 | 200 | 50 | 44 | 0 | 0 | 0 | — | 0 | 0 | 0 | 0 |
| 1 tablespoon . 13 | 0 | 110 | 0 | 13 | 3 | 3 | 0 | 0 | 0 | — | 0 | 0 | 0 | 0 |
| **Margarine:** | | | | | | | | | | | | | | |
| Regular ........1 tablespoon . 14 | 16 | 100 | Trace | 12 | 2 | 3 | Trace | 3 | 0 | 470[20] | — | — | — | 0 |
| Soft, 2,8-oz. tubs per pound ........1 tablespoon . 14 | 16 | 100 | Trace | 11 | 2 | 4 | Trace | 3 | 0 | 470[20] | — | — | — | 0 |
| Mayonnaise ........1 tablespoon . 14 | 15 | 100 | Trace | 11 | 2 | 6 | Trace | 3 | .1 | 40 | Trace | .01 | Trace | — |
| **Oils, salad or cooking:** | | | | | | | | | | | | | | |
| Corn ........1 tablespoon . 14 | 0 | 125 | 0 | 14 | 1 | 7 | 0 | 0 | 0 | — | 0 | 0 | 0 | 0 |
| Cottonseed ........1 tablespoon . 14 | 0 | 125 | 0 | 14 | 4 | 7 | 0 | 0 | 0 | — | 0 | 0 | 0 | 0 |
| Olive ........1 tablespoon . 14 | 0 | 125 | 0 | 14 | 2 | 1 | 0 | 0 | 0 | — | 0 | 0 | 0 | 0 |
| Peanut ........1 tablespoon . 14 | 0 | 125 | 0 | 14 | 3 | 4 | 0 | 0 | 0 | — | 0 | 0 | 0 | 0 |
| Safflower ........1 tablespoon . 14 | 0 | 125 | 0 | 14 | 1 | 10 | 0 | 0 | 0 | — | 0 | 0 | 0 | 0 |
| Soybean ........1 tablespoon . 14 | 0 | 125 | 0 | 14 | 2 | 7 | 0 | 0 | 0 | — | 0 | 0 | 0 | 0 |

# SUGARS, SWEETS

| Food, approximate measure, and weight (in grams) | Water | Food energy | Protein | Fat | Saturated (total) | Unsaturated linoleic | Carbohydrate | Calcium | Iron | Vitamin A value | Thiamin | Riboflavin | Niacin | Ascorbic acid |
|---|---|---|---|---|---|---|---|---|---|---|---|---|---|---|
| Honey, strained or extracted ........1 tablespoon . 21 | 17 | 65 | Trace | 0 | — | — | 17 | 1 | .1 | 0 | Trace | .01 | .1 | Trace |
| Jams and preserves ........1 tablespoon . 20 | 29 | 55 | Trace | Trace | — | — | 14 | 4 | .2 | Trace | Trace | .01 | Trace | Trace |
| Jellies ........1 tablespoon . 18 | 29 | 50 | Trace | Trace | — | — | 13 | 4 | .3 | Trace | Trace | .01 | Trace | 1 |

| Food, approximate measure | | | | | | | | | | | | | | | |
|---|---|---|---|---|---|---|---|---|---|---|---|---|---|---|---|
| **Molasses, cane:** | | | | | | | | | | | | | | | |
| Light (first extraction). 1 tablespoon | 20 | 24 | 50 | — | — | — | — | 13 | 33 | .9 | — | .01 | .01 | Trace | — |
| Blackstrap (third extraction) ......1 tablespoon | 20 | 24 | 45 | — | — | — | — | 11 | 137 | 3.2 | — | .02 | .04 | .4 | — |
| **Sirups:** | | | | | | | | | | | | | | | |
| Sorghum .........1 tablespoon | 21 | 23 | 55 | — | — | — | — | 14 | 35 | 2.6 | — | — | .02 | Trace | — |
| Table blends, chiefly corn, light and dark. 1 tablespoon | 21 | 24 | 60 | 0 | 0 | — | — | 15 | 9 | .8 | 0 | 0 | 0 | 0 | 0 |
| **Sugars:** | | | | | | | | | | | | | | | |
| Brown, firm packed...1 cup | 220 | 2 | 820 | 0 | 0 | — | — | 212 | 187 | 7.5 | 0 | .02 | .07 | .4 | 0 |
| **White:** | | | | | | | | | | | | | | | |
| Granulated .......1 cup | 200 | Trace | 770 | 0 | 0 | — | — | 199 | 0 | .2 | 0 | 0 | 0 | 0 | 0 |
| Granulated 1 tablespoon | 11 | Trace | 40 | 0 | 0 | — | — | 11 | 0 | Trace | 0 | 0 | 0 | 0 | 0 |
| Powdered, stirred before measuring.1 cup | 120 | Trace | 460 | 0 | 0 | — | — | 119 | 0 | .1 | 0 | 0 | 0 | 0 | 0 |

## MISCELLANEOUS ITEMS

| Food, approximate measure | | | | | | | | | | | | | | | |
|---|---|---|---|---|---|---|---|---|---|---|---|---|---|---|---|
| Bouillon cubes, approx. ½ in. | 4 | 4 | 5 | 1 | Trace | — | Trace | Trace | — | — | — | — | — | — | — |
| **Gelatin:** | | | | | | | | | | | | | | | |
| Plain, dry powder in envelope ......1 envelope | 7 | 13 | 25 | 6 | Trace | — | — | 0 | — | — | — | — | — | — | — |
| Dessert powder, 3-oz. package ...1 package | 85 | 2 | 315 | 8 | 0 | — | — | 75 | — | — | — | — | — | — | — |
| Gelatin dessert, prepared with water .........1 cup | 240 | 84 | 140 | 4 | 0 | — | — | 34 | — | — | — | — | — | — | — |
| **Olives, pickled:** | | | | | | | | | | | | | | | |
| Green .........4 medium or 3 extra large or 2 giant | 16 | 78 | 15 | Trace | 2 | Trace | Trace | Trace | 8 | .2 | 40 | Trace | — | — | — |
| Ripe: Mission .......3 small or 2 large | 10 | 73 | 15 | Trace | 2 | Trace | Trace | Trace | 9 | .1 | 10 | Trace | Trace | — | — |
| **Pickles, cucumber:** | | | | | | | | | | | | | | | |
| Dill, medium, whole, 3¾ in. long, 1¼ in. diam. .........1 pickle | 65 | 93 | 10 | 1 | Trace | — | — | 1 | 17 | .7 | 70 | Trace | .01 | Trace | 4 |

| Food, approximate measure, and weight (in grams) | Water | Food energy | Protein | Fat | Fatty acids Saturated (total) | Fatty acids Unsaturated linoleic | Carbohydrate | Calcium | Iron | Vitamin A value | Thiamin | Riboflavin | Niacin | Ascorbic acid |
|---|---|---|---|---|---|---|---|---|---|---|---|---|---|---|
| | Grams | Percent | Calories | Grams | Grams | Grams | Grams | Grams | Milligrams | Milligrams | International units | Milligrams | Milligrams | Milligrams | Milligrams |
| Fresh, sliced, 1½ in. diam., ¼ in. thick...2 slices | 15 | 79 | 10 | Trace | Trace | — | — | 3 | 5 | .3 | 20 | Trace | Trace | Trace | 1 |
| Sweet, gherkin, small, whole, approx.2¼ in. long, ¾ in. diam....1 pickle | 15 | 61 | 20 | Trace | Trace | — | — | 6 | 2 | .2 | 10 | Trace | Trace | Trace | 1 |
| Popcorn. See Grain Products. | | | | | | | | | | | | | | | |
| Pudding, home recipe with starch base: | | | | | | | | | | | | | | | |
| Vanilla (blanc mange).1 cup | 255 | 76 | 285 | 9 | 10 | 5 | Trace | 41 | 298 | Trace | 410 | .08 | .41 | .3 | 2 |
| Pudding mix, dry form, | | | | | | | | | | | | | | | |
| 4-oz. package ....1 package | 113 | 2 | 410 | 3 | 2 | 1 | Trace | 103 | 23 | 1.8 | Trace | .02 | .08 | .5 | 0 |
| Sherbet.1 cup | 193 | 67 | 260 | 2 | 2 | — | — | 59 | 31 | Trace | 120 | .02 | .06 | Trace | 4 |
| Soups: | | | | | | | | | | | | | | | |
| Canned, condensed, ready-to-serve: | | | | | | | | | | | | | | | |
| Prepared with an equal volume of milk: | | | | | | | | | | | | | | | |
| Cream of chicken. 1 cup | 245 | 85 | 180 | 7 | 10 | 3 | 3 | 15 | 172 | .5 | 610 | .05 | .27 | .7 | 2 |
| Cream of mushroom. 1 cup | 245 | 83 | 215 | 7 | 14 | 4 | 5 | 16 | 191 | .5 | 250 | .05 | .34 | .7 | 1 |
| Tomato. 1 cup | 250 | 84 | 175 | 7 | 7 | 3 | 1 | 23 | 168 | .8 | 1,200 | .10 | .25 | 1.3 | 15 |
| Prepared with an equal volume of water: | | | | | | | | | | | | | | | |
| Bean with pork. 1 cup | 250 | 84 | 170 | 8 | 6 | 1 | 2 | 22 | 63 | 2.3 | 650 | .13 | .08 | 1.0 | 3 |
| Beef broth, bouillon consommé. 1 cup | 240 | 96 | 30 | 5 | 0 | — | — | 3 | Trace | .5 | Trace | Trace | .02 | 1.2 | — |
| Beef noodle. 1 cup | 240 | 93 | 70 | 4 | 3 | 1 | 1 | 7 | 7 | 1.0 | 50 | .05 | .07 | 1.0 | Trace |
| Cream of chicken. 1 cup | 240 | 92 | 95 | 3 | 6 | 1 | 3 | 8 | 24 | .5 | 410 | .02 | .05 | .5 | Trace |
| Cream of mushroom. 1 cup | 240 | 90 | 135 | 2 | 10 | 1 | 5 | 10 | 41 | .5 | 70 | .02 | .12 | .7 | Trace |
| Minestrone. 1 cup | 245 | 90 | 105 | 5 | 3 | — | — | 14 | 37 | 1.0 | 2,350 | .07 | .05 | 1.0 | — |
| Split pea. 1 cup | 245 | 85 | 145 | 9 | 3 | 1 | Trace | 21 | 29 | 1.5 | 440 | .25 | .15 | 1.5 | 1 |
| Tomato. 1 cup | 245 | 90 | 90 | 2 | 3 | Trace | 1 | 16 | 15 | .7 | 1,000 | .05 | .05 | 1.2 | 12 |

| Food, approximate measure, and weight (in grams) | Water (%) | Food energy (cal.) | Protein (g) | Fat (g) | Saturated (g) | Oleic (g) | Linoleic (g) | Carbohydrate (g) | Calcium (mg) | Iron (mg) | Vitamin A (I.U.) | Thiamin (mg) | Riboflavin (mg) | Niacin (mg) | Ascorbic acid (mg) |
|---|---|---|---|---|---|---|---|---|---|---|---|---|---|---|---|
| Vegetable beef ..1 cup ....... 245 | 92 | 80 | 5 | 2 | — | — | — | 10 | 12 | .7 | 2,700 | .05 | .05 | 1.0 | — |
| Vegetarian ......1 cup ....... 245 | 92 | 80 | 2 | 2 | — | — | — | 13 | 20 | 1.0 | 2,940 | .05 | .05 | 1.0 | — |
| **Dehydrated, dry form:** | | | | | | | | | | | | | | | |
| Chicken noodle (2-oz. package) ..1 package ... 57 | 6 | 220 | 8 | 6 | 2 | 2 | 1 | 33 | 34 | 1.4 | 190 | .30 | .15 | 2.4 | 3 |
| Onion mix (1½-oz. package) .......1 package ... 43 | 3 | 150 | 6 | 5 | 1 | 2 | 1 | 23 | 42 | .6 | 30 | .05 | .03 | .3 | 6 |
| Tomato-vegetable with noodles (2½-oz. package).1 package ... 71 | 4 | 245 | 6 | 6 | 2 | 2 | 1 | 45 | 33 | 1.4 | 1,700 | .21 | .13 | 1.8 | 18 |
| **Frozen, condensed:** | | | | | | | | | | | | | | | |
| **Cream of potato:** | | | | | | | | | | | | | | | |
| Prepared with equal volume of milk ......1 cup ...... 245 | 83 | 185 | 8 | 10 | 5 | 3 | Trace | 18 | 208 | 1.0 | 590 | .10 | .27 | .5 | Trace |
| Prepared with equal volume of water .....1 cup ...... 240 | 90 | 105 | 3 | 5 | 3 | — | — | 12 | 58 | 1.0 | 410 | .05 | .05 | .5 | — |
| **Cream of shrimp:** | | | | | | | | | | | | | | | |
| Prepared with equal volume of milk ......1 cup ...... 245 | 82 | 245 | 9 | 16 | — | — | — | 15 | 189 | .5 | 290 | .07 | .27 | .5 | Trace |
| Prepared with equal volume of water .....1 cup ...... 240 | 88 | 160 | 5 | 12 | — | — | — | 8 | 38 | .5 | 120 | .05 | .05 | .5 | — |
| Tapioca, dry, quick-cooking ...........1 cup ... 152 | 13 | 535 | 1 | Trace | — | — | — | 131 | 15 | .6 | 0 | 0 | 0 | 0 | 0 |
| Tapioca cream pudding.1 cup ...... 165 | 72 | 220 | 8 | 8 | 4 | 2 | Trace | 28 | 173 | .7 | 480 | .07 | .30 | .2 | 2 |
| White sauce, medium...1 cup ........ 250 | 73 | 405 | 10 | 31 | 16 | 10 | 1 | 22 | 288 | .5 | 1,150 | .10 | .43 | .5 | 2 |
| **Yeast:** | | | | | | | | | | | | | | | |
| Brewer's, dry ......1 tablespoon . 8 | 5 | 25 | 3 | Trace | — | — | — | 3 | 17 | 1.4 | Trace | 1.25 | .34 | 3.0 | Trace |

Yoghurt. See Milk, Cheese, Cream, Imitation Cream.

[1]Value applies to unfortified product value for fortified low-density product would be 1,500 I.U., and the fortified high-density product would be 2,290 I.U.

[2]Contributed largely from beta-carotene used for coloring.

[3]Outer layer of fat on the cut was removed to within approximately ½-inch of the lean. Deposits of fat within the cut were not removed.

[4]If bones are discarded, value will be greatly reduced.

[5]Measure and weight apply to entire vegetable or fruit including parts not usually eaten.

[6]Based on yellow varieties; white varieties contain only a trace of cryptoxanthin and carotenes, the pigments in corn that have biological activity.

[7]Year-round average. Samples marketed from November through May, average 29 milligrams per 200-gram tomato; from June through October, around 52 milligrams.

[8]This is the amount from the fruit. Additional ascorbic acid may be added by the manufacturer. Refer to the label for this information.

[9]Value for varieties with orange-colored flesh; value for varieties with green flesh would be about 540 I.U.

[10]Value listed is based on products with label stating 30 milligrams per 6 fl. oz. serving.

[11]For white-fleshed varieties value is about 20 I.U. per cup; for red-fleshed varieties, 1,080 I.U. per cup.

[12]Present only if added by the manufacturer. Refer to the label for this information.

[13]Based on yellow-fleshed varieties; for white-fleshed varieties value is about 50 I.U. per 114-gram peach and 80 I.U. per cup of sliced peaches.

[14]This value includes ascorbic acid added by manufacturer.

[15]This value is based on product made from yellow varieties of corn; white varieties contain only a trace.

[16]Based on product made with enriched flour. With unenriched flour, approximate values per doughnut are: iron, 0.2 milligram; thiamin, 0.01 milligram; riboflavin, 0.03 milligram; niacin, 0.2 milligram.

[17]Iron, thiamin, riboflavin, and niacin are based on the minimum levels of enrichment specified in standards of Identity promulgated under the Federal Food, Drug, and Cosmetic Act.

[18]Iron, thiamin, and niacin are based on the minimum levels of enrichment specified in standards of Identity promulgated under the Federal Food, Drug, and Cosmetic Act. Riboflavin is based on unenriched rice. When the minimum level of enrichment for riboflavin specified in the standards of Identity becomes effective the value will be 0.12 milligram per cup of parbolled rice and white rice.

[19]Year-round average.

[20]Based on the average vitamin A content of fortified margarine. Federal specifications for fortified margarine require a minimum of 15,000 I.U. of vitamin A per pound.

# APPENDIX B

# PERSONAL FEEDING CHART

Please use the following pages to note the foods you introduce and your baby's reaction to them. In case of allergic reactions, this record will be very useful to your doctor, to baby sitters, and for your own quick reference in selecting foods.

# PERSONAL FEEDING CHART

| DATE | AGE GIVEN | BEVERAGES | CEREAL | FRUIT | VEGETABLE | DAIRY | PROTEIN | LIKE | DISLIKE | ALLERGY | COMMENTS |
|------|-----------|-----------|--------|-------|-----------|-------|---------|------|---------|---------|----------|
| | | | | | | | | | | | |
| | | | | | | | | | | | |
| | | | | | | | | | | | |
| | | | | | | | | | | | |
| | | | | | | | | | | | |

REACTION

# PERSONAL FEEDING CHART

| DATE | AGE GIVEN | BEVERAGES | CEREAL | FRUIT | VEGETABLE | DAIRY | PROTEIN | REACTION | | | COMMENTS |
|---|---|---|---|---|---|---|---|---|---|---|---|
| | | | | | | | | LIKE | DISLIKE | ALLERGY | |
| | | | | | | | | | | | |
| | | | | | | | | | | | |
| | | | | | | | | | | | |
| | | | | | | | | | | | |
| | | | | | | | | | | | |
| | | | | | | | | | | | |

# BIBLIOGRAPHY

Here is a list of books and pamphlets, published by the U. S. Government, that I have found very informative and useful. They can be ordered from the Superintendent of Documents at little or no cost ($.05–$.20). You can also find them in the reference section of your library. Many states and counties also publish nutritional and buying information. Write to:

Superintendent of Documents
U. S. Government Printing Office
Washington, D.C. 20402

U. S. Department of Health, Education, and Welfare Bulletins

*Infant Care,* Children's Bureau Publication #8 ($.20)

*Nutrition and Healthy Growth,* Children's
  Bureau Publication #352 ($.20)

*Read the Label;* Miscellaneous Publication #3

*What Consumers Should Know About Food Additives,*
  Leaflet #10


U. S. Department of Agriculture Bulletins

  #1 *Family Fare: Food Management and Recipes* ($.45)
  #8 *Home Canning of Fruits and Vegetables* ($.20)
  #10 *Home Freezing of Fruits and Vegetables*
  #40 *Freezing Combination Main Dishes*
  #43 *Money-Saving Main Dishes*
  #58 *Shopper's Guide to U. S. Grades for Food*
  #69 *Home Care of Purchased Frozen Foods*
  #70 *Home Freezing of Poultry*
  #72 *Nutritive Value of Foods*
  #78 *Storing Perishable Foods in the Home*

�ежо *Conserving the Nutritive Values in Foods* ($.10)
✖93 *Freezing Meat and Fish in the Home*
✖94 *Family Food Budgeting for Good Meals and Good Nutrition*
✖103 *Eggs in Family Meals* ($.15)
✖105 *Vegetables in Family Meals* ($.15)
✖106 *Home Care of Meat and Poultry*
✖110 *Poultry in Family Meals* ($.15)
✖112 *Cheese in Family Meals* ($.15)
✖118 *Beef and Veal in Family Meals* ($.15)
✖124 *Lamb in Family Meals* ($.15)
✖125 *Fruits in Family Meals* ($.15)
✖127 *Milk in Family Meals* ($.15)
✖129 *Making Cottage Cheese at Home* ($.05)
✖147 *Baking for People with Food Allergies* ($.10)
✖150 *Cereals and Pastas in Family Meals*
✖162 *Keeping Food Safe to Eat* ($.10)

Foods Your Children Need ($.10)

*FOOD FOR US ALL: The Yearbook of Agriculture*, 1969 ($3.25)

*COMPOSITION OF FOODS: Raw, Processed, Prepared*, 1963 ($2.00)

NUTRITIVE VALUE OF FOODS ($.30)

The following organizations also publish useful booklets and newsletters:

LA LECHE LEAGUE, 9616 Minneapolis Avenue, Franklin Park, Illinois 60131

CONSUMER ACTION NOW, Inc., Park Avenue, New York, N.Y. 10021

THE FEDERATION OF HOMEMAKERS, 922 N. Stuart Street, Arlington, Virginia 22203

*Consumer Reports*, CONSUMERS UNION (at newsstands)

# INDEX

*(Asterisks preceding entries refer to recipes suitable for use by entire family)*

Additives, xv–xvi, xvii, 23, 26–29
Allergies (allergic reactions), 51–52, 98
All-purpose croquettes, 267–68
All-purpose fruit juice, 244
All-purpose meat stew, 197
All-purpose omelet, 265–67
All-purpose raw-vegetable juice, 245–46
Alpha-tocopherol (vitamin E), 13–14
American cheese, 222, 223, 275
Amino acids, 3–4, 30
Antioxidants, 28
Anything custard, 218–19
Apple/grapefruit, raw, 131
Apple juice, xviii, 285
Apples, 5, 118–21, 249, 284–85
  applesauce, 119–20, 250, 285
  baked, 250
  baked sweet potatoes and, 182
  and carrot purée, raw, 119–20
  grapefruit/raw, 131
  raw purée of carrots and, 119–20
  stewed dried, 120–21
  stewed potatoes and, 178
Applesauce, 119, 120, 250, 285
Apricot(s), 121–23, 249, 250, 285
  baked, 122
  nectar, 240, 287
  purée, 121
  stewed, 122
  whip, 230
Ascorbic acid (vitamin C), 11–12, 25, 41
  food sources, 11–12, 274ff.
  juices and, 239–40, 241
Asparagus, 12, 149–50, 186, 264, 280–81
Avocados, 123–24, 249, 285

"Baby Familia" (cereal), 101
Baby-food system, essentials of, 85–97
  cooking methods and time, 92–93
  how to purée, 88–91
    *See also* Purées (puréeing)
  how to use and modify recipes, 92–97
  leftovers, use of, 86–88
  meal-in-one leftover purée, 87–88
  planning, 85–86
  saving time, 86–87
Bacon, 194, 270, 276
Bacterial growth, food care and storage
    and prevention of, 68–69, 70, 71, 73,
    77, 82, 84

Bagels, 258, 289
Baked apples, 250
  and sweet potatoes, 182
Baked apricots, 122
Baked bananas, 125–26
Baked beans, 251
Baked custard, basic, 217–18
  variations, 218–19
Baked fish, 209
Baked goods, 103–6
  as finger food, 257–61
  introducing, 103
  *See also* specific kinds, recipes, uses
Baked sweet potatoes and apples, 182
Baking method for vegetables, 146
Banana(s), xix, 5, 124–26, 131, 249, 285
  baked, 125–26
  *bread sticks, 258–59
  broiled or sautéed, 126
  raw grapefruit and, 131
  raw orange and, 131
*Banana bread sticks, 258–59
Barley, 98, 101, 102, 289
Basic baked custard, 217–18
  variations, 218–19
Basic food groups, balanced menu plan-
    ning and, 39–41
Basic rice purée, 110–11
Beans (legumes), 4, 5, 19, 166–68, 279, 280,
    281
  baked, 251, 264
  cooked, 167, 168
  *See also* specific kinds, recipes, uses
Beans, green or wax. *See* Green beans;
    Wax beans
Beef, 191–98
  cooking, 195–96
  nutritive value, 191, 276–77
  storing, 194–95
  timetable for braising, 196
  *See also* specific kinds, recipes, uses
Beet greens, 163, 281
Beets, 5, 152, 163, 281
Berries, 126–28, 285
  raw, 126–27
  stewed, 127
  *See also* specific kinds, recipes
Beverages, 232–47
  fruit and vegetable juices, 232, 239–47